The Law and the Citizen-Student in Wisconsin

The Law and the Citizen-Student in Wisconsin

A Handbook for Secondary Students

James W. Stewart
University of Wisconsin-River Falls
River Falls, Wisconsin

David R. Zitlow
Whitefish Bay High School
Whitefish Bay, Wisconsin

WEST PUBLISHING COMPANY
St. Paul • New York • Los Angeles • San Francisco

Copy Editor: Rosalie Koskenmaki
Line Art: Tony Bredahl
Photo Research: David Sommer
Composition: P & H Photo Composition
Cover Design: Jack Deskin

Photo credits. Page numbers in bold precede credit lines. **2** James L. Shaffer; **5** David S. Stickler; **6** Dal Bayles; **10** William Lizdas; **12** Wide World Photos; **18** Norris J. Klesman; **23** Bob Rashid; **30** Dal Bayles; **32** Norris J. Klesman; **44** Brent Nicastro; **46** West Publishing Co.; **52** David S. Stickler; **55** David S. Stickler; **59** Bob Combs; **60** James R. Koepnick; **70** James R. Koepnick; **75** Bob Combs; **78** Bob Combs; **82** Dal Bayles; **92** Bob Combs; **94** Bob Combs; **95** James L. Shaffer; **98** Bob Combs; **104** Dal Bayles; **106** Rick Smolan; **107** Dal Bayles; **110** David S. Stickler; **111** Bob Combs; **118** Bob Combs; **123** Dick Steffens; **126** Dal Bayles; **130** Tony Freeman; **134** Wisconsin Department of Natural Resources; **144** Brent Nicastro; **147** Bob Rashid; **153** William Lizdas; **176** Rick Smolan; **180** Brent Nicastro; **186** Brent Nicastro; **195** Bob Combs; **202** Bob Combs; **204** David S. Stickler; **207** Dal Bayles; **214** Dal Bayles; **220** Bob Combs; **224** Bob Combs; **229** Dal Baylis; **233** Dal Bayles.

50 West Kellogg Boulevard
P.O. Box 3526
St. Paul, Minnesota 55165

Printed in the United States of America

Library of Congress Cataloging in Publication Data

Stewart, James W. (James Wade), 1939-
The law and the citizen student in Wisconsin.

Bibliography: p.
Includes index.
1. Law—Wisconsin. 2. Students—legal status, laws, etc.—Wisconsin. I. Zitlow, David R.
II. Title
KFW2481.S83 349.775′088055 81-13052
ISBN 0-314-63146-1 347.750088055 AACR2

The Law and the Citizen Student in Wisconsin
is dedicated to
Richard J. Delorit and Oran W. Palmer, Jr.

Contents

Forward

The argument is made, that we are a nation of law, not of men. The meaning of this statement, of course, is that we do not have to put up with the arbitrary and capricious nature of a ruler or ruling group. We are, instead, "ruled" by law ... under which all citizens, including the "rulers", are equal. This condition of equality under law is a reality, however, only to the degree that citizens know and understand the law. That is, we need to be literate relative to how the law works and doesn't work, and the role of law in a democratic republic.

Being a citizen in a republic carries with it the responsibility of a particular state of mind. It means having an attitude that holds fast to the understanding that it is a privilege to be a citizen of this state and nation. Further, it means that individuals accept the personal responsibility for the task of government. This responsibility starts, perhaps, with a commitment to learn about the law. This learning is the most basic of all education for democracy. As Jefferson said, "the qualifications for self-government are not innate. They are the result of habit and long training."

The habits and training for citizenship in Wisconsin can be advanced through using, *The Law and the Citizen Student in Wisconsin.* This volume makes a significant contribution to the knowledge base needed for responsible citizenship, and the authors are commended for bringing this knowledge to the students of Wisconsin.

H. Michael Hartoonian, Ph.D.
Supervisor of Social Studies Education
Department of Public Instruction
Madison, Wisconsin

Preface

FOR THE PARENTS This text is designed for your son and daughter as citizens and students. We hope you will become involved in their study of the different law-related education concepts, knowledge and information contained in the book. The education of our youth is difficult but we hope you and they realize that a fundamental understanding of the law is essential in order to guarantee successful citizenship.

FOR SCHOOL BOARD MEMBERS This text is a reflection and presentation of what the law is in Wisconsin. Every effort has been made to provide a realistic approach to the study of law for the citizen/student you are responsible for in our society. Schooling is the basic protection against ignorance and we hope your role will be to encourage active and inquiring participation in their development while they are in your care.

Some sections may seem difficult to you, but the material covered reflects the law and must be taught in an effective and courageous manner.

FOR SCHOOL ADMINISTRATORS We hope that you find in selecting this text that issues and challenges will arise. However, since the school is the most significant effort to educate future citizens, the study of law and the legal system is a basic need for the citizen/student in the school.

In many instances the materials should provide a sound inquiry basis for development of effective citizenship education.

FOR THE TEACHERS Law and the Citizen/Student has been designed for the student. We hope you as their mentor will find the contents, questions, the curriculum and information valuable as a basic reference for a foundation for your instruction and their future.

The book is not designed to seek closure, on the contrary, the book, statutes and case studies are structured to give you the opportunity to use the materials, your creativity and the students' interest to develop a life long commitment toward being a functional, literate and participating citizen.

FOR THE STUDENTS The text is for you to begin to develop skills, knowledge and attitudes that follow you into adult life and citizenship responsibilities. We hope for you to be turned on, not turned off by the legal system, the courts, the lawyers, the law enforcement agencies, the politicians, the pressure groups, big business or the nightly news.

The task is to challenge ignorance and to assist you in becoming an educated citizen in areas which even mystify adults! Take the time to study the chapters, the case studies, the questions, related materials and explore the law so that you realize why the law is there for you, your friends, your parents, and your community.

ACKNOWLEDGEMENTS The authors express their appreciation to the following individuals who provided assistance, guidance, and encouragement during the preparation, editing and development of *The Law and the Citizen Student in Wisconsin:*

Attorneys at Law: Lester C. Gaylord, Stuart J. Krueger, Marvin A. Margolis, and Keith D. Rodli.

Law Enforcement Officers: Leroy Konrath and Carl D. Shrank.

Teachers: Bill Alleva and Barney Slowey.

Manuscript Assistants: James Bartholomew and Susan P. Smith.

AUTHORS' NOTE The laws of the State of Wisconsin are constantly changing through legislative enactments or through interpretation or definition in the court system. Occasionally administrative agencies of government also change their rules, regulations, or procedures which may affect materials that are presented in the book. We suggest that you follow those changes through the media or appropriate state agencies to keep the book up-to-date.

Finally, the interpretation of the laws, statutes and materials presented in the book were developed by the authors and any precise interpretation is subject to review and clarification. If you need advice or assistance, consult a competent lawyer or appropriate legal agency.

August, 1981
J.W.S.
D.R.Z.

The Law and the Citizen-Student in Wisconsin

SECTION I

INTRODUCTION TO THE LAW FOR THE CITIZEN-STUDENT

CONTENTS

1

The Citizen-Student as a Citizen in the Future

The worth of a state, in the long run,
is the worth of the individuals composing it.

John Stuart Mill (1806-1873)

The citizen-student eventually becomes the citizen. Many times you have been reminded that with your eighteenth birthday you will be an adult and free to do as you like within the law and customs of society as long as you accept the responsibility for your actions. *The Law and the Citizen-Student* has been designed to assist you in developing knowledge, skills, and attitudes about what citizenship is in Wisconsin. The reference material, examples, questions, answers, cases, and discussions you will engage in while working and studying will provide only a basic outline of the freedoms, responsibilities, and limitations that citizenship involves.

The key to citizenship rests with the value you place on being a citizen. Your individual participation in the process is essential in order to protect yourself, your friends, your family, your community, and your government.

Every freedom you now enjoy or will exercise in the future depends upon how willing you are to protect and enhance those freedoms for yourself and for others.

No democracy, including ours, has lasted over a long period of time. The collapse of democracy will come when the individual is indifferent to the erosion of freedom and our constitutional principles.

The major problems we now have will continue in the future; our problems will be your problems. They do not disappear easily and have to be contained, resolved, solved, and reviewed constantly. You have a unique contribution to make no matter who you are or where you live.

Our society, our local, state, and federal governments, our laws, and our people are unique and have survived because of a collective willingness to participate in a flexible, resilient, and tolerant form of governance.

Our democratic principles and goals will remain strong as long as individual citizens are active, watchful, and protective.

Democracy is hurt by all types of pressure groups, lobby interests, special interest and single-issue political action committees centered around well-organized and well-financed groups.

The art of survival is that of compromise and balance while ensuring that the basic constitutional freedoms remain intact. So!

Who cares a hundred years from now? Who is going to know the difference?

There might not be anyone around a hundred years from now who cares about you, but the fact that you are here now means that you will be the one making the difference now and in the future.

What are some do's and don'ts of being an effective citizen?

DO'S FOR EFFECTIVE CITIZENSHIP

- Assume responsibility in your family, home, school, and community.
- Become active in civic and political activities as a participant, sponsor, worker, campaigner, or even as a candidate.
- Keep informed about the issues, problems, and concerns in your community, country, state, and federal government. Be able to examine the pro and con arguments of the issues.
- Know and protect your citizenship rights, responsibilities, and obligations under the law.

DON'TS FOR EFFECTIVE CITIZENSHIP

- Develop the attitude that all is hopeless, meaningless, and out of control.
- Develop the attitude that citizenship activities and involvement are for someone else.
- Depend on a single source of information or trust others to make up your mind on critical issues.
- Give up your freedom by neglect and indifference or allow anyone or any group to take away your constitutional freedom by enacting laws that curtail those freedoms.

You are always a citizen regardless of your circumstances, position, job, family, or career choice. Be careful to exercise and protect your rights. If you don't, someone will be willing to deny them to you! You and only you can make the democratic difference as a citizen-student and as a citizen of Wisconsin.

SUGGESTED READING

"Students and the Courts: What Lies Ahead?" *Update,* American Bar Association, Fall, 1977, pp. 46-47.

James E. Schnitz, "Law and the Future: Utopia/Dystopia," *Law in American Society* (Chicago: Law in American Society Foundation, December, 1976), vol. 5, no. 4, pp. 25-31.

"A Future Without Violence," *Crime and Criminals* (Minneapolis, MN: Greenhaven Press, Inc., 1976).

2

Our Legal System

What is law?

Law can be defined as a set of rules or regulations by which a government limits the conduct of people within its society.

What is the authority for law in the United States?

The constitution of the United States is the basis of the authority for law in the United States. It sets forth the form of government, the powers and duties of government officials, and the rights and responsibilities of its people. All laws passed by Congress, the individual states, and local ordinances are subject to the limitations and provisions of the federal constitution. For example, even the rules and regulations of your local board of education are limited by the constitution.

What are the sources of law?

There are four sources of law that serve as the basis of our legal system. They are: common law, statutory law, administrative law, and ordinances.

What is common law?

Common law is unwritten law that has developed over a long period of time and upon which much of our legal system is built. In early English history, judges decided cases based on what they felt were the customs and beliefs of the community. The individual judges kept records of the decisions rendered in these courts, and these rulings were used by other judges trying the same kind of case. Over the years, legal principles came to be built on these earlier cases and became **precedents** or legal foundations in deciding cases.

Even today, whether a judge is making a decision or a lawyer is arguing a case, the decision in an earlier case will often be cited as a precedent and will influence the pending decision.

What is statutory law?

Statutory laws are the written laws that are passed by Congress and by state legislatures. These statutes are recorded in code books of law.

What is administrative law?

Certain departments and agencies of government have the power to make rules and regulations that have the effect of laws. For example, on the federal level, the Federal Communications Commission (FCC) regulates television and radio broadcasting. On the state level, the Department of Natural Resources decides on regulations that affect hunting practices within Wisconsin. On the local level, your school board makes rules and regulations which govern the conduct of your local school system. These bodies of rules and regulations made by governmental agencies are called **administrative law.** Administrative law can only be developed under the authority of statutory law.

What are ordinances?

While laws passed by Congress and state legislatures are called statutes, rules passed by local municipalities—such as town boards, city or county boards or councils—are called **ordinances.** Examples of ordinances are local building codes, curfews, tax rates on property, and zoning laws.

Why do citizen-students need to understand the law?

The law has a great influence on every person living in the United States. Laws govern your personal and economic relationships during your lifetime and the distribution of your property after your death. The law on **contracts** deals with promises people make to each other. The area of **tort law** determines who shall bear the cost of an accident when a person is injured or when property is damaged through the carelessness of another. *Criminal* laws restrain people from unfairly interfering with others and provide for punishment for those who violate them. *Property* laws resolve conflicts about ownership of land and personal property, and conflicts between landlords and tenants. **Constitutional** law insures the continuing character of our democratic society by providing for the rights of its individual citizens and by clearly describing the powers of the government.

The law in American society is more than a series of rights, obligations, and regulations that are to be learned and obeyed by citizens. The law provides American citizens with a means to seek justice, to resolve disputes, and to secure change peaceably within their society. Thus, whether the conflict involves our constitutional rights, our property, or our personal behavior, the law can help provide a satisfactory solution.

The law is also a major element in many of the problems and challenges now facing American society—for example, crime, civil rights, and government power. As crime continues to increase, more and more citizens are becoming concerned about or critical of the law as it relates to their personal safety and the security of their property. In addition, with the powers of the government increasing, the opportunity for the official abuse of power has multiplied. This trend has been accompanied by growing feelings of political helplessness, anonymity, and cynicism among the American people. Studying the law can help counteract these unfortunate reactions by clarifying the potential strength and integrity that law holds for American society.

Learning about the law can help you to think about our society and its values; to encourage you to think critically and rationally about societal problems and conflicts; to expose misconceptions and stereotypes people have about the law and our legal system; and, finally, to encourage you to participate in, and contribute to, your society and its system of law and government.

What is law-related education?

The study of law-related education is based on the theory that all people, whether in a primitive society or in a highly technological society, have basic needs: the need to organize, to perpetuate themselves, to protect, to adjust, to penalize, and to survive. Any society, whether it operates under a group consensus (democracy) or an individual consensus (dictatorship), must organize at some point in order to survive. The study of law-related education in our society is essential in order to perpetuate our unique system of **governance.**

The people in our very complex society are combating internal and external pressures for the basic need for survival. Out of this basic need for survival emerges a need for order. (See figure 2.1 for chart showing the relationship between society's needs and the law.) The need for order has manifested itself in the course of human evolution in many forms; our own constitutional form of government is unique in human history. It is essential that our citizens understand the basic structure, the heritage, the social, cultural, and political philosophies that have allowed us to persist and evolve toward the goal of democratic governance.

Our basic need for survival and the need for order are built upon a constantly evolving **ethical** and **moral** system based on the merging of our many kinds of folkways, traditions, mores, customs, religious heritages, and cultural and societal philosophies. The need for order, based on survival instincts and on the ethical and moral value system, has led us to the underlying agreement for **legitimacy** or constitutional principles, which, in our country, has led to the evolution and emergence of the **rule of law.** The rule of law provides or defines the limits to individual and group behavior within the society.

Our approach to the rule of law makes us unique. As a democracy, the head and the heart of our systems of law and justice are the protection of the individual member of society and the protection of the views of its various minorities.

The rule of law is based on our **pluralistic** background and on our diverse heritage of ethnic, racial, religious, and social groups. The system and principles of law are unique in the development of our democracy. The pre-eminent theme is the constitutional foundation, both state and federal, which, as a manifestation of our legitimacy, creates for our people the source of our authority—federal, state, and local. The constitutional foundation places responsibilities in a **check and balance system** made up of the legislative, administrative, and judicial branches of government. This constitutional foundation defines our concept of governance. The checks and balances are designed to administer and protect the rights and responsibilities of the citizen.

These unique approaches have provided the guidelines for our legal system which defines itself in the body of law which is our particular contribution to the evolution of government. The system is designed to seek and protect truth. We Americans believe that, as a result of the pursuit of truth, justice for the individual, the group, or the people as a whole will be assured. It is this equality of opportunity before the law, the search for truth, and the administration of justice through the **adversary process** that decides and defines what **citizenship** is in our society.

Through the search for truth and justice, we test various value systems, ethics, and morality for their strengths and weaknesses. It is the administration of justice through our court system that insures our rights of property, privacy, and, most important, our freedom.

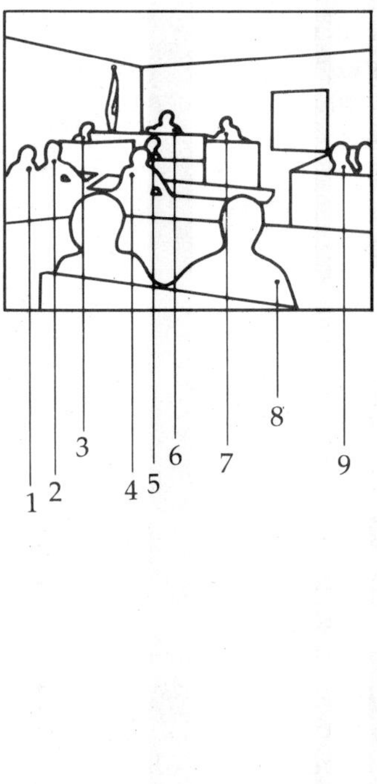

The various participants in this Wisconsin courtroom include: (1) the defendant; (2) the defense attorney; (3) the clerk of the court; (4) the prosecutor; (5) the court reporter; (6) the judge; (7) a witness; (8) some spectators; and (9) the jury.

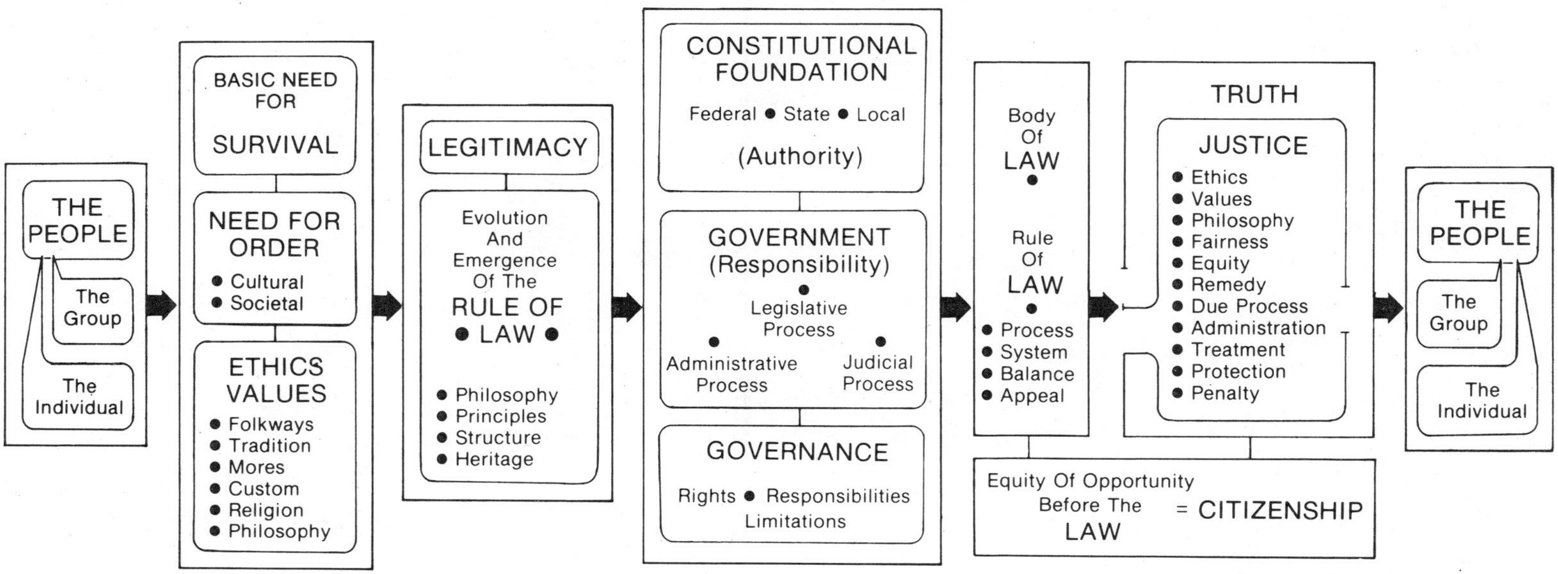

FIGURE 2.1. The interrelationship of law and society.

Figure 2.1, which illustrates the interrelationship of law and society, is a model for law-related education in the United States. The uniqueness of our democracy is that at the head and heart of its development and systems is the protection of the individual and the views of its minorities. The people and their needs give rise to the law and our system of government; both in turn support and protect the people.

The case study which follows, *In re Subpoena to Nixon,* provides an example of how law and society are interrelated. The case also illustrates how an otherwise little-known federal judge, John J. Sirica, was faced with defining what these interrelationships are for the President of the United States.

U.S. District Judge John J. Sirica

CASE STUDY*
In re Subpoena to Nixon

The administration of President Richard Nixon came tumbling down in the early 1970s mainly because of some tape recordings. The recordings were of conversations between Nixon and his top aides, conversations that suggested the President was part of a conspiracy to cover up the Watergate scandal. The series of events now known as the Watergate scandal began on June 17, 1972, when police caught five men breaking into the headquarters of the Democratic National Committee in the Watergate office-hotel complex in Washington, D.C. The five men, it turned out, had connections to the Nixon White House. By the fall of 1972, a full-scale investigation was underway as a federal grand jury tried to find out who had been behind the attempted burglary.

It was more than a year after the break-in, however, before the tapes became a vital element in the ever-widening Watergate investigation. The reason for the delay was that investigators didn't find out about the tapes until July of 1973. The existence of the tapes was revealed by a presidential aide named Alexander Butterfield, who told investigators that Nixon had secretly installed a voice-activated taping system in his White House offices in 1970.

Within days after Butterfield's revelation, Special Watergate Prosecutor Archibald Cox moved to get eight of the tapes by having the grand jury issue a **subpoena** for them. (A subpoena is a legal order requiring someone to bring into court certain documents or other pieces of evidence.) Cox knew the tapes were crucial to the grand jury investigation because they might clear up discrepancies in the previous testimony of several Nixon aides. Those aides had given conflicting accounts of what was said at various meetings with Nixon in 1972 and 1973. The tapes were thus one sure way of finding out who was telling the truth. But when the grand jury issued its subpoena on July 23, 1973, Nixon refused to comply with it. He was not about to give up the tapes without a fight. And so the stage was set for a crucial court test on the powers of the presidency.

The case was argued on August 22, 1973, before U.S. District Judge John J. Sirica, who had already presided over the trials of the men accused of the Watergate break-in. Nixon's attorneys based their case on something called "executive privilege." They told Sirica that under the doctrine of executive privilege, Nixon's communications with his staff were protected from public and court scrutiny. This was necessary, the attorneys said, to insure some measure of confidentiality in the conduct of government affairs. The President's attorneys also argued that only Nixon himself could decide what information was privileged and therefore immune from the grand jury's subpoena powers. Moreover, the attorneys contended that forcing Nixon to turn over the tapes would violate the constitutionally mandated separation of powers between the executive and judicial branches of government.

Cox, of course, offered a far different argument. He said no one was above the law, especially in a criminal case, and that Nixon may have tried to invoke executive privilege "as a cloak for serious criminal wrongdoing."

---

*A summary of the case. For the court's complete opinion, see 360 F.Supp.1 (1973).

A week after the hearing, Sirica handed down a compromise decision in which he sidestepped an immediate ruling on the question of executive privilege. Instead, Sirica said he would decide whether the tapes were privileged only after listening to them in private. "The court has attempted to walk the middle ground between a failure to decide the question of privilege at one extreme, and a wholesale delivery of tapes to the grand jury at the other. The one would be a breach of duty; the other an inexcusable course of conduct," Sirica said. He noted that if the tapes did indeed contain privileged information, that information would not be turned over to the grand jury. However, Sirica said that "if [the tapes] *may* be important in the investigation, if they *may* be safely heard by the grand jury ... would it not be a blot on the page which records the judicial proceedings of this country, if ... the court did not at least call for an inspection of the evidence in chambers?"

In deciding to review the tapes, Sirica had thus rejected Nixon's claim that it is up to the President to determine what information is privileged. That argument, Sirica said, was at odds with previous court rulings that had given the judiciary—not the President—the final say on questions of executive privilege. Sirica also rejected Nixon's arguments about a possible threat to the separation of powers if the subpoena were enforced. The judge pointed out that courts in the past had issued orders to the executive branch and that those orders had been obeyed. Nixon's argument, Sirica said, "tends to set the White House apart as a fourth branch of government." Finally, Sirica said that a grand jury, because its authority comes directly from the people, must be free to find evidence wherever it can in a criminal investigation. "In all candor," Sirica said, "the court fails to perceive any reason for suspending the power of courts to get evidence and rule on questions of privilege in criminal matters simply because it is the President of the United States who holds the evidence."

Nixon quickly appealed Sirica's ruling, but on October 12, 1973, a U.S. Circuit Court of Appeals upheld the decision. Two weeks later, the tapes were turned over to Sirica. In April of 1974 Nixon was forced to turn over another 40 tapes to a U.S. House of Representatives committee considering impeachment proceedings against him. Meanwhile, the scandal over Watergate crept closer and closer to the President's door. On August 9, 1974, with many of his aides in jail or heading there, Nixon became the first president in American history to resign from office.

This Sanders cartoon of 1973 was published during the confrontation between the judicial system and President Richard Nixon. In light of what occurred in those events, do you think:

1. The cartoon expresses the key issues in the contest between the court and the President?

2. The President should be allowed to keep information from the public?

VOCABULARY

Administrative law
Adversary process
Case law
Check and balance system
Citizenship
Common law
Consensus
Constitutional
Contract
Due process
Equity
Ethical
Governance
Legitimacy
Moral
Ordinance
Pluralistic
Precedent
Rule of law
Statutory law
Tort/Tort law

Terms printed in **boldface** in the vocabulary lists in this text are important legal terms or law-related terms that you may wish to study or define. The glossary at the back of this text defines some words in these lists and introduces additional legal or law-related terms not used in this text.

SUGGESTED READING

Lefkowitz, Barry E. "Special Case Study: East Africa Hypothetical," *Individual Rights: A Resource Manual for Teachers*. Pittman, NJ: Institute for Political and Legal Education, 1975, pp. 11-20.

Starr, Isidore. *The Idea of Liberty: First Amendment Freedoms*. St. Paul, MN: West Publishing, 1978.

Starr, Isidore. *Justice: Due Process of Law*. St. Paul, MN: West Publishing, 1981.

"Descriptors for Law-Related Education." Social Studies Curriculum Study Committee, Wisconsin Dept. of Public Instruction, 125 S. Webster Street, Madison, WI 53702.

3

Introduction to the Federal and State Legal System

To the average citizen, and particularly to the citizen-student, our legal system and structure must seem at times very complicated. However, the framers of our federal constitution and later those who developed the separate state constitutions worked very hard to protect the individual in our society.

Society, laws, and our country have all changed greatly since the early 1600s, but the core of the legal system, with a few exceptions, has remained intact for almost two hundred years.

How does the distribution of power affect the structures of government in the United States at the federal and the state level?

Figure 3.1 shows how various government powers are distributed or shared by the federal and state governments.

The tenth amendment clarifies the relationship between the federal system and the rights of the state:

> **Amendment X (1791).** The powers not delegated to the United States by the Constitution, nor prohibited by it to the States, are reserved to the States respectively, or to the people.

When a conflict arises between the two levels of government, the dispute is settled in the court system.

The drafters of the federal constitution built into the constitution a system of checks and balances on which most states have modeled their individual state constitutions. Wisconsin is no exception.

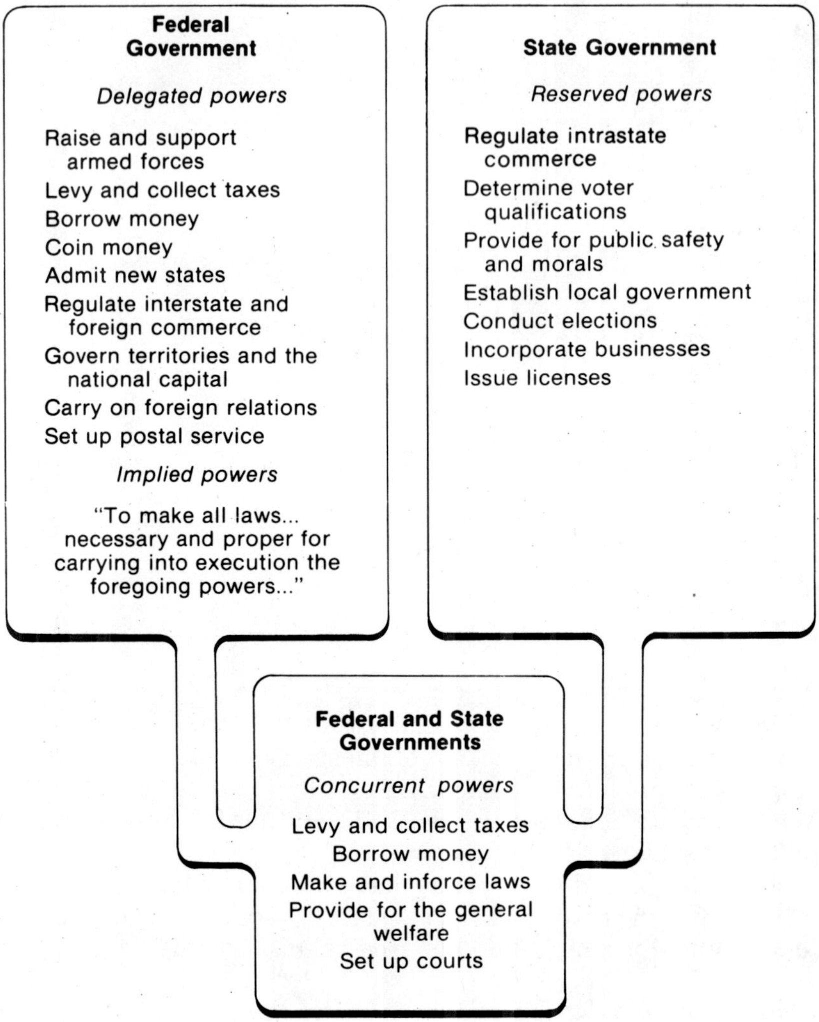

FIGURE 3.1. The distribution of powers in our federal system of government.

How does the federal system provide checks and balances in the legal framework of the constitution?

Figure 3.2 presents the federal system of checks and balances required by the Constitution. Today this check and balance system is our democratic insurance against the abuse of power. Figure 3.3 presents the basic structure of the federal government as of January 1981. You might want to notice how this chart changes under future presidents. The changes made by the presidency and by Congress, and the influence of the courts continually alter the structure of government and reflect, sometimes slowly, their respective views of how the basic government should be organized.

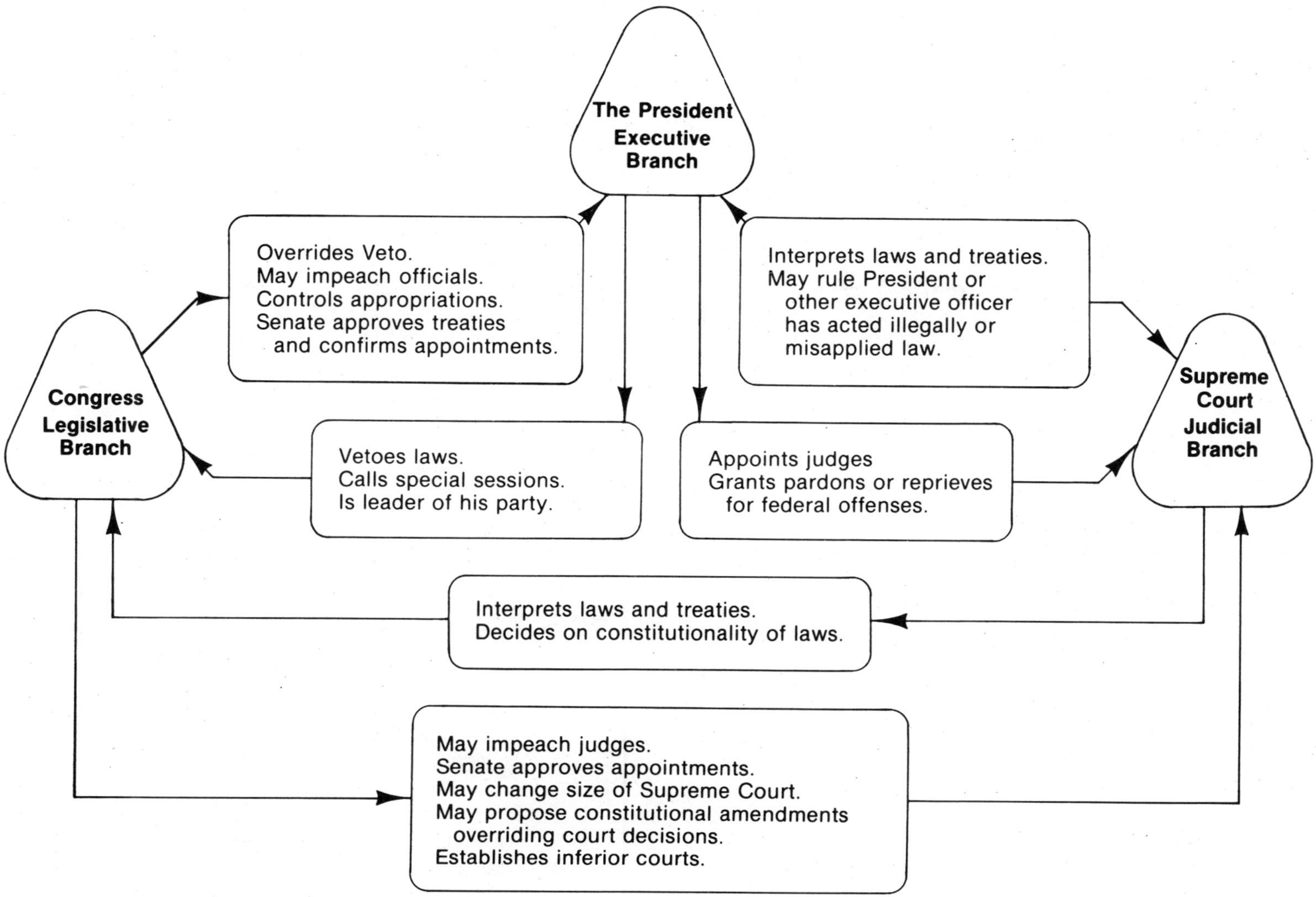

FIGURE 3.2. The federal system of checks and balances.

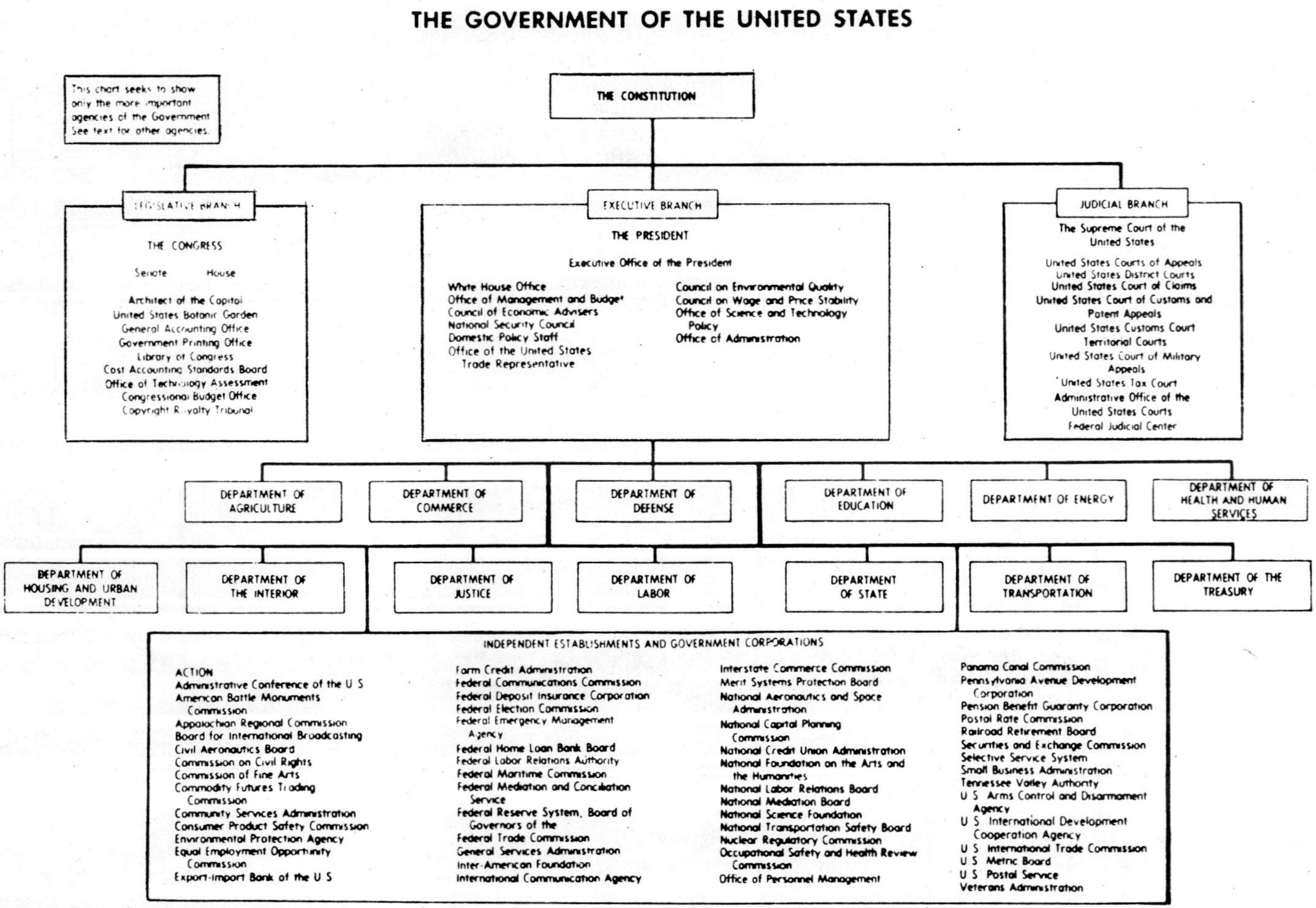

FIGURE 3.3. The principal agencies of the United States government.
Source: *United States Government Manual 1980-1981.* (Washington, DC: Government Printing Office, 1980), p. 32.

and the influence of the courts continually alter the structure of government and reflect, sometimes slowly, their respective views of how the basic government should be organized.

Does federal legislation affect me directly as a citizen-student?

Yes! Listed below are some specific examples of recent major legislation that has been tested in the court system at both the state and federal level.* These examples show that legislation and court decisions affect every citizen.

Two senators confer on the floor of the Wisconsin senate.

Equal Pay Act of 1963

- Requires equal pay for equal work, regardless of sex
- Requires that equal work be determined by equal skill, effort, and responsibility under similar working conditions at the same place of employment
- Requires equal pay when equal work is involved even if different job titles are assigned

(Enforced by the Wage and Hour Division of the U.S. Department of Labor or by private lawsuit)

*Reprinted by permission from *Street Law: A Course in Practical Law,* second edition, by Lee P. Arbetman, Edward T. McMahon, and Edward L. O'Brien (St. Paul, MN: West Publishing Company, 1980). pp. 306-308.

Civil Rights Act of 1964 (amended in 1972)

• Prohibits **discrimination** based on race, color, religion, or national origin in public accommodations (e.g., hotels, restaurants, movie theaters, sports arenas). Does not apply to private clubs not open to the public.

• Prohibits discrimination because of race, color, sex, religion, or national origin by businesses with more than fifteen employees or by labor unions (This section is commonly referred to as Title VII)

• Prohibits discrimination based on race, color, religion, sex, or national origin by state and local governments and public educational institutions

• Prohibits discrimination based on race, color, national origin, or sex in any program or activity receiving federal financial assistance, and authorizes termination of federal funding when this ban is violated

• Permits employment discrimination based on religion, sex, or national origin if it is a necessary qualification of the job

(Enforced by the Equal Employment Opportunity Commission or by private lawsuit)

Voting Rights Act of 1965 (amended in 1970 and 1975)

• Bans literacy and "good character" tests as requirements of voting

• Requires bilingual election materials for most voters who don't speak English

• Reduces residency requirements for voting in federal elections

• Establishes criminal penalties for harassing voters or interfering with voting rights

(Enforced by the U.S. Civil Rights Commission)

Civil Rights Act of 1968

• Prohibits discrimination based on race, color, religion, or national origin in the sale or rental of most housing

(Enforced by the Department of Housing and Urban Development or by lawsuit in a federal court)

Age Discrimination in Employment Act of 1967 (amended in 1978)

• Prohibits arbitrary age discrimination in employment by employers of twenty or more persons, employment agencies, labor organizations with twenty-five or more members, and federal, state, and local governments

• Protects persons between the ages of forty and seventy

• Permits discrimination where age is a necessary qualification for the job

(Enforced by the Equal Employment Opportunity Commission or similar state agency)

Title IX of the Education Act Amendments of 1972

• Prohibits discrimination against students and others on the basis of sex in educational institutions receiving federal funding

• Prohibits sex discrimination in a number of areas, including student and faculty recruitment, admissions, financial aid, facilities, and employment

• Requires that school athletic programs effectively accommodate the interests and abilities of members of both sexes. Equal total expenditure on men's and women's sports is not required

• Does not cover sex-stereotyping in textbooks and other curricular materials

(Enforced by the Department of Education's Office of Civil Rights)

Rehabilitation Act of 1973

• Prohibits private and government employers from discriminating on the basis of physical handicap

• Requires companies that do business with the government to undertake affirmative action to provide jobs for the handicapped

• Prohibits activities and programs receiving federal funds from excluding otherwise qualified handicapped persons from participation or benefits

(Enforced by lawsuit in federal court or, in some cases, state or local human rights or fair employment practices commissions)

How does the organizational structure of the state of Wisconsin compare to the federal organization chart?

Figure 3.4 presents the organization of state government in Wisconsin. Compare this figure with the one on page 22. Then read the profiles of the state executive, legislative, and judicial branches on pages 25-40.

A PROFILE OF THE WISCONSIN EXECUTIVE BRANCH

Although our government today cannot always be neatly and precisely divided into three parts—executive, legislative, judicial—each branch of government does have a definite character and certain unshared

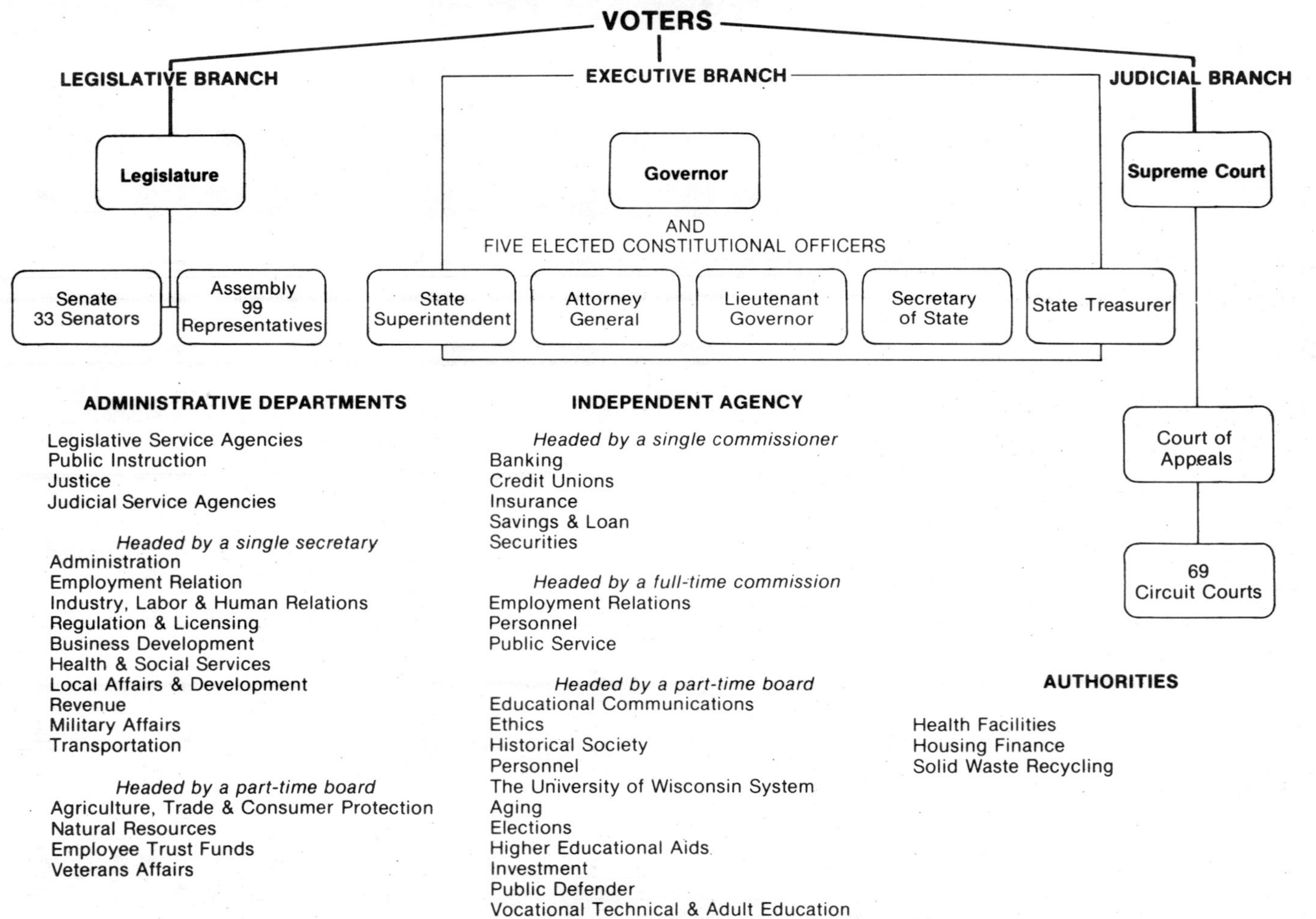

FIGURE 3.4. Organization of the Wisconsin state government as of January 1979. Model based on Wisconsin Legislative Reference Bureau, *The State of Wisconsin 1979-1980 Blue Book* (Madison, WI: Wisconsin Legislative Reference Bureau, 1979), pp. 346-347.

responsibilities. The following material from *Blue Book** briefly explains the structure of Wisconsin's executive branch.

The "republican form of government" guaranteed by the U.S. Constitution contemplates the separation of powers within state government among the **legislative, the executive, and the judicial branches** of government. The legislative branch ... has the broad objective of determining new or changed policies and programs, and of reviewing performance for policies and programs previously authorized; the executive branch carries out these programs and policies; and the judicial branch has responsibility for the adjudication of any conflicts which might arise from the interpretation or application of the laws. It is a traditional concept of American government that the three branches are to function separately, without intermingling of authority, except as specifically provided by law.

"The executive branch carries out these programs and policies"—how neatly this can be stated, and how simple it could be structured when our state's constitution was ratified by the people of Wisconsin in 1848. In their constitution, the people provided for a government elected to represent them at the seat of government and to see that the laws are faithfully executed. They provided for a lieutenant governor to become governor in case there was a vacancy in the governor's office, and made him president of the Senate so that there would be some liaison with the legislative branch. They created an office of state treasurer to handle all the state's fiscal affairs: to collect the tax monies coming in and to pay all the bills arising out of the operation of state government. In deciding to elect a secretary of state, they provided for just about all the "administration" needed in 1848: a small office to carry on the correspondence between the state government in Madison, the citizens back home, the municipalities, and the Federal Government, and to keep the written records of all Wisconsin state government transactions. If the governor or the legislature needed legal advice, an attorney general, elected by the people, would take care of the matter. If the people back home wanted advice on how to run a school system, a state superintendent of public instruction, elected statewide, could provide all the advice necessary.

Perhaps state government never really was as simple as the constitution's basic outline would lead one to believe. Emphatically, it is not that simple today. The Wisconsin Committee on the Reorganization of the Executive Branch, reporting to the 1967 Legislature, came to the conclusion that modern government can no longer be neatly divided into precise "legislative", "executive" and "judicial" domains. In many instances the subjects of legislation had become so complicated and full of technical detail, that the legislature agreed to leave the detailed implementation of a law to the executive branch by granting "rule-making" authority to an administrative agency; at the same time, so as to free the judicial branch from the same staggering load of technical detail, these administrative agencies were given "quasi-judicial" powers. Said the reorganization committee:

*Source: *The Wisconsin Blue Book,* p. 431.

> . . . the complexity of modern life has required the delegation of substantial rule-making and quasi-judicial authority to administrative regulatory agencies of the state government. Some of these regulatory agencies, engaged primarily in the supervision of private business activities, are intended to be relatively independent from executive control.

A PROFILE OF THE WISCONSIN LEGISLATIVE BRANCH

Figure 3.5 shows how the Wisconsin legislature is organized. A description* of the legislature follows.

The legislative branch of Wisconsin state government consists of the *bicameral* Wisconsin Legislature comprising the Senate and Assembly, the staff employed by each house, and the legislative committees and legislative service agencies which the legislature has created. The Wisconsin Legislature makes policy by enactment of laws, while its service agencies carry out research, bill drafting, auditing and housekeeping functions on its behalf.

In the discussion of the framework of Wisconsin government, it was noted that the United States Constitution guarantees each state a republican form of government, that it specifically prohibits a state from doing certain things (such as making treaties, coining money, and imposing import or export duties), and that it gives certain powers exclusively to the Congress of the United States (power to legislate with regard to foreign affairs, interstate and foreign commerce, the postal system, coinage of money, and patents and copyrights).

After prohibiting these powers to the states and delegating specified powers to Congress, the United States Constitution reserves all other powers to the states or to the people.

Under the system of separation of powers in effect in this nation, the power to determine the state's policies and programs lies primarily in the legislative branch of state government. The broad sweep of legislative power to enact laws can be seen from the Wisconsin Constitution's provision, "The legislative power shall be vested in a senate and assembly." There are few limitations on this power. The legislature must provide as uniform a system of town government as practicable, cannot authorize a lottery (with very limited exceptions) or grant a divorce, and cannot enact private or special laws on certain subjects. In addition, no legislation can be enacted that would infringe on the citizen's rights under the Declaration of Rights of the Wisconsin Constitution. Otherwise, except for the framework provided by the constitution, the legislature has wide latitude in the field of legislation.

A different kind of restriction on its powers is provided by the right of the governor to veto legislation, which can then only be enacted by an overriding vote of two-thirds in both houses.

Since its adoption on March 13, 1848, the Wisconsin Constitution has provided that the membership of the Assembly shall be not less

*Source: *The Wisconsin Blue Book,* p. 357.

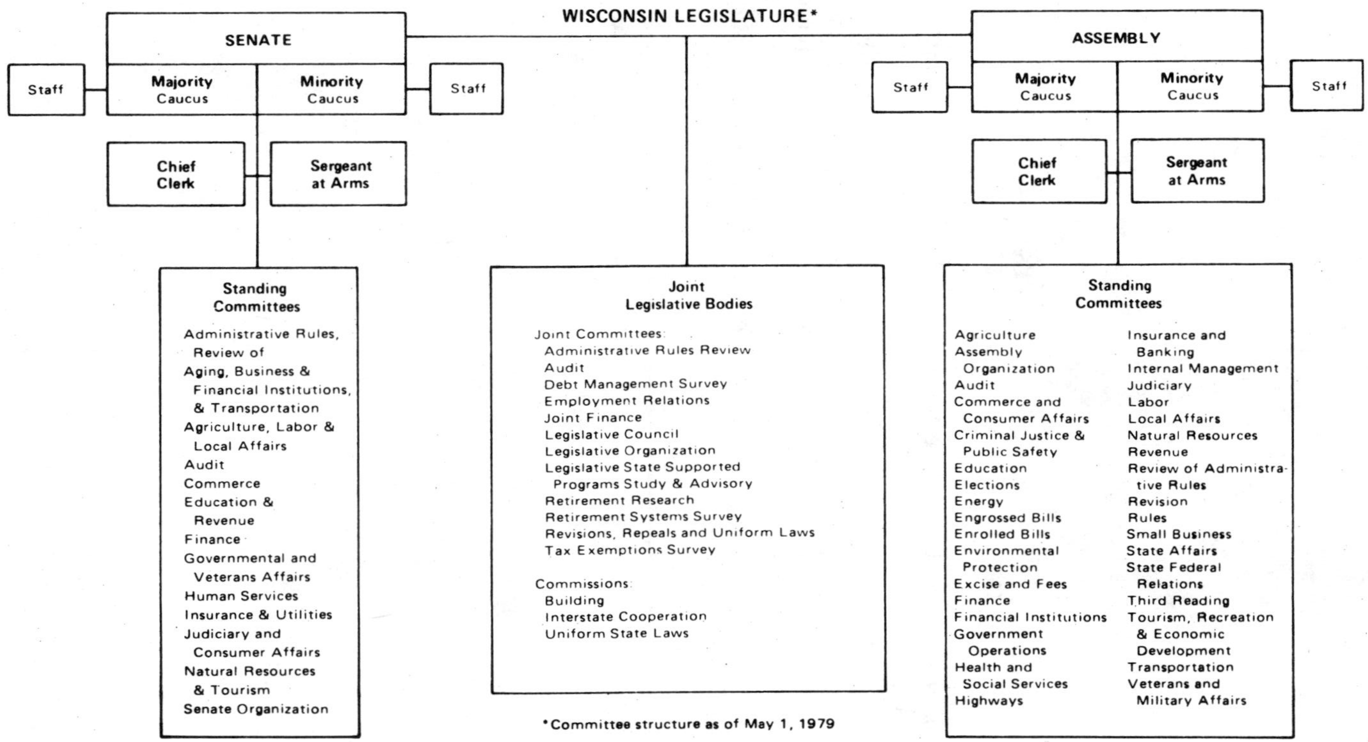

FIGURE 3.5. The organization and committee structure of the Wisconsin legislature as of May 1, 1979. Source: *The Wisconsin Blue Book*, p. 359.

The Capitol building in Madison.

than 54 nor more than 100, while the memberships of the Senate shall consist of not more than one-third nor less than one-fourth of the number of Assembly members. The first legislature numbered 85 members (19 senators and 66 assemblymen). This figure prevailed until 1853, when the membership was increased to 107 (25 senators, 82 assemblymen). Beginning with the 1858 Legislature, 30 senators and 97 assemblymen constituted the 127-member legislature. This lasted until the legislature became a 133-member body in 1862, when the number of senators was increased to 33 and assemblymen to 100. Because of the 1972 reapportionment, the number of representatives was reduced to 99 beginning with the 1973 Legislature. (As a result of a 1969 law, the members of the Assembly are today known as representatives to the Assembly.)

In the beginning, representatives served for terms of a single year's duration, while senators served 2-year terms. By constitutional amendment adopted in 1881, the terms were changed to 2 and 4 years respectively, while the legislature went from annual to biennial sessions at the same time. Under authorization of a constitutional amendment adopted in 1968, the legislature holds continuous sessions under a biennial session schedule (the terms of office remain the same); thus, the 1977 Legislature holds sessions in 1977 and 1978.

A PROFILE OF THE WISCONSIN JUDICIAL BRANCH*

For the average citizen the court system is probably the most remote and least understood branch of government. Though his attention may be drawn to the courts by news accounts of controversial cases and by dramatic portrayals of court proceedings on television, his personal involvement with the courts is likely limited to a traffic violation, a

*Source: *The Wisconsin Blue Book,* p. 657.

divorce proceeding or the settlement of a deceased relative's estate. His experience may lead him to conclude that the judicial system is a complicated maze filled with obscure procedures and language seemingly only half understood by the lawyers and judges themselves.

What may not be readily apparent to him is the tremendous variety and volume of business transacted in our court system. At one time or another almost every aspect of life is touched by the courts. Aside from the duty to try persons accused of criminal violations, the courts must decide civil disputes between private citizens ranging from the routine collection of an overdue charge account to the complex adjudication of an antitrust case involving many millions of dollars and months or even years of costly litigation. The courts also must act as referees between the citizens and their government by deciding what are the permissible limits of governmental power and the extent of an individual's rights and responsibilities.

A judicial system which strives for fairness and justice must be capable of first finding the truth and then deciding disputes under the rule of law. Thus, the courts are the places in which the facts are determined and the rules regulating conduct are interpreted and applied. These rules are derived from a variety of sources including the state and federal constitutions, legislative acts, administrative rules, and custom and experience expressed judicially in the common law. This body of law is constantly changing to meet the needs of our increasingly complex society. However, while these changes are often necessary and desirable, the courts have the added responsibility of ensuring that the fundamental principles of our constitutional system are protected and preserved.

How well the judicial branch performs the tasks we assign it depends a great deal on its organization and structure. In recent years many citizens, lawyers, legislators and judges have complained that the judicial process has become so expensive and time-consuming that justice is denied to many citizens. Consequently, the court system was substantially reorganized, first in 1959, then in 1977-78. Figure 3.6 presents the current organization of the Wisconsin court system.

Municipal Justice Courts

The state constitution was amended in April, 1966, to abolish the constitutional office of justice of the peace. However, the governing bodies of cities, villages, and towns are by statute authorized to establish **municipal justice courts.** The municipal justice is elected for a two-year to four-year term, as determined by the **municipality,** beginning on May 1. The salary is fixed by the local governing body. There is no requirement that the office be filled by a lawyer. Court may be held daily or as provided by ordinance.

These courts have primary **jurisdiction** over offenses against ordinances of the town, village, or city where they are located and where legal relief only is sought. If equity relief is demanded, the action must

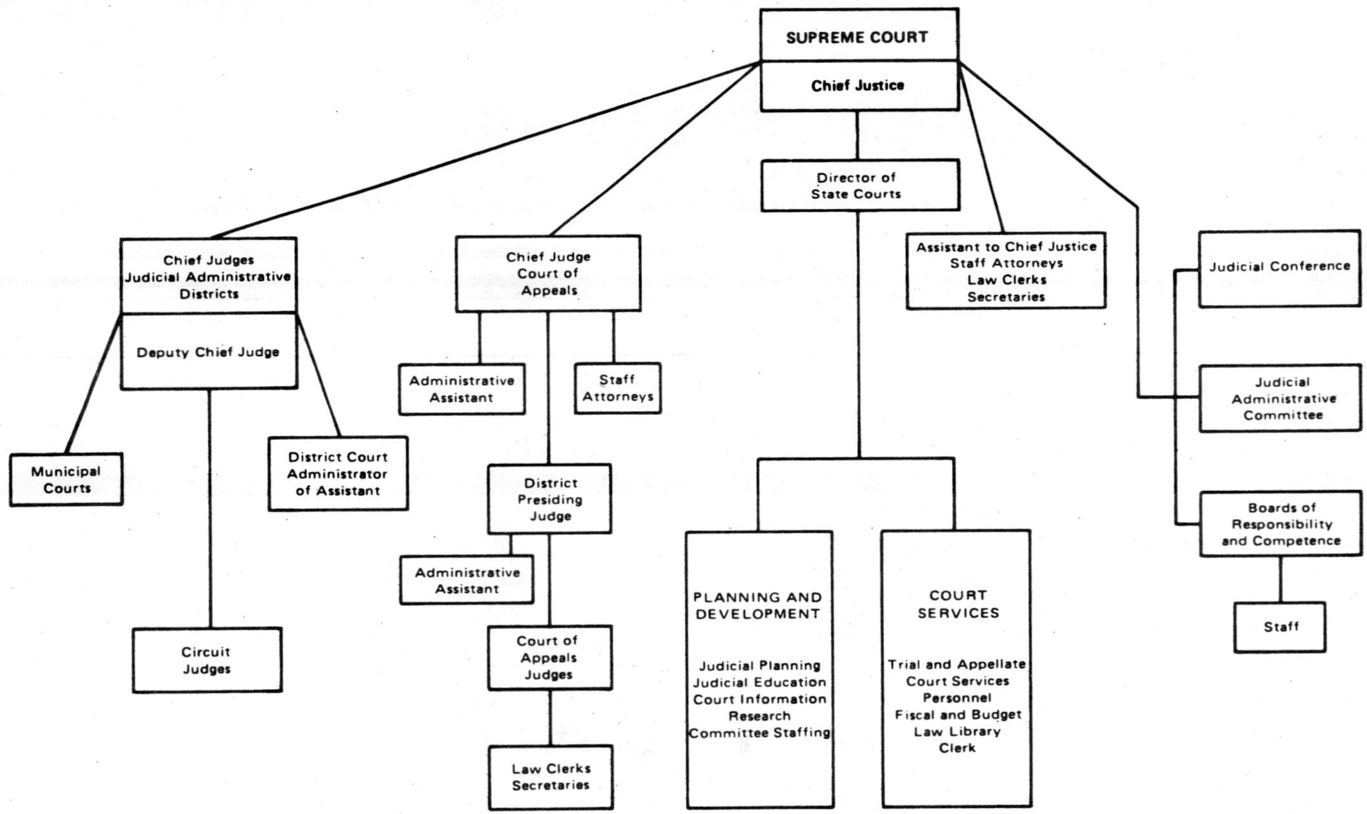

FIGURE 3.6. Organization of the Wisconsin Court System. Source: *The Wisconsin Blue Book,* p. 671.

be brought in a court of record. Jurisdiction is limited to the violations of ordinances enacted by the municipality which creates the municipal justice court. A municipal court may render judgment by ordering paying of a forfeiture plus any costs of prosecution or by imprisonment in default of such payment.

Circuit Courts

In 1978 the Wisconsin Legislature, in special session, passed Senate Bill 1. This bill abolished the two-tier system of trial courts by abolishing county courts and substituting circuit courts.

The **circuit court** is the principal trial court under the State Constitution. The 72 counties of the state are divided into 69 judicial circuits: there is a circuit court for each county, with the exception of several counties with small populations in northern Wisconsin which are part of a single circuit. A single circuit may be divided into several branches with a judge presiding over each.

Circuit judges are elected on a nonpartisan (no political affiliation) basis for a six-year term at the April election and take office on the following August 1. Salaries, which are paid by the state, are fixed by statute and may be changed during the term of office.

The circuit court has both criminal and civil jurisdiction in all actions unless the exclusive jurisdiction is given to some court. **Appeals** from decisions of the circuit court generally go to the court of appeals.

An attorney presents oral arguments to the Wisconsin Supreme Court.

Court of Appeals

The **court of appeals** consists of 12 court of appeals judges who sit both individually and in three-judge panels to decide cases.

Organization. The state is divided into four court of appeals districts with three court of appeals judges elected at-large from each district. The boundaries of the four court of appeals districts follow the boundaries of existing judicial circuits. Each district contains a population of over one million residents. These courts of appeals districts, and the judicial circuits and counties contained therein, are as follows (see also figure 3.7):

District I consists of the 2nd judicial circuit

District II consists of the 1st, 3rd, 4th, 18th, 21st, 22nd, 24th, and 26th judicial circuits

District III consists of the 8th, 10th, 11th, 14th, 15th, 16th, 19th, 20th, and 23rd judicial circuits

District IV consists of the 5th, 6th, 7th, 9th, 12th, 13th, 17th, and 25th judicial circuits.

For each court of appeals district, there are primary or chambers locations where the offices of the appeals judges are located. In addition, other cities are specified where the court shall sit and hear cases for the convenience of the **litigants.** The locations of the four court of appeals districts are:

Appeals District	*Chambers Location*	*Other Locations*
District I	Milwaukee	None
District II	Waukesha	Fond du Lac, Racine
District III	Wausau	Green Bay, Superior, Eau Claire
District IV	Madison	Stevens Point, La Crosse

The Supreme Court is further authorized to designate, by rule, additional locations if the need arises. The chambers and secondary locations specified in Chapter 187, Laws of 1977, are as follows:

> Except for the initial election of the court of appeals in April, 1978, only one court of appeals judge may be elected from each district in any year. Vacancies on the court of appeals are filled in the same manner as vacancies on the Supreme Court, that is, the Governor fills the vacancy by temporary appointment. The person so appointed then serves until a permanent successor is elected to a full six-year term at the first spring election when no other appeals judge is to be elected from the same court of appeals district.

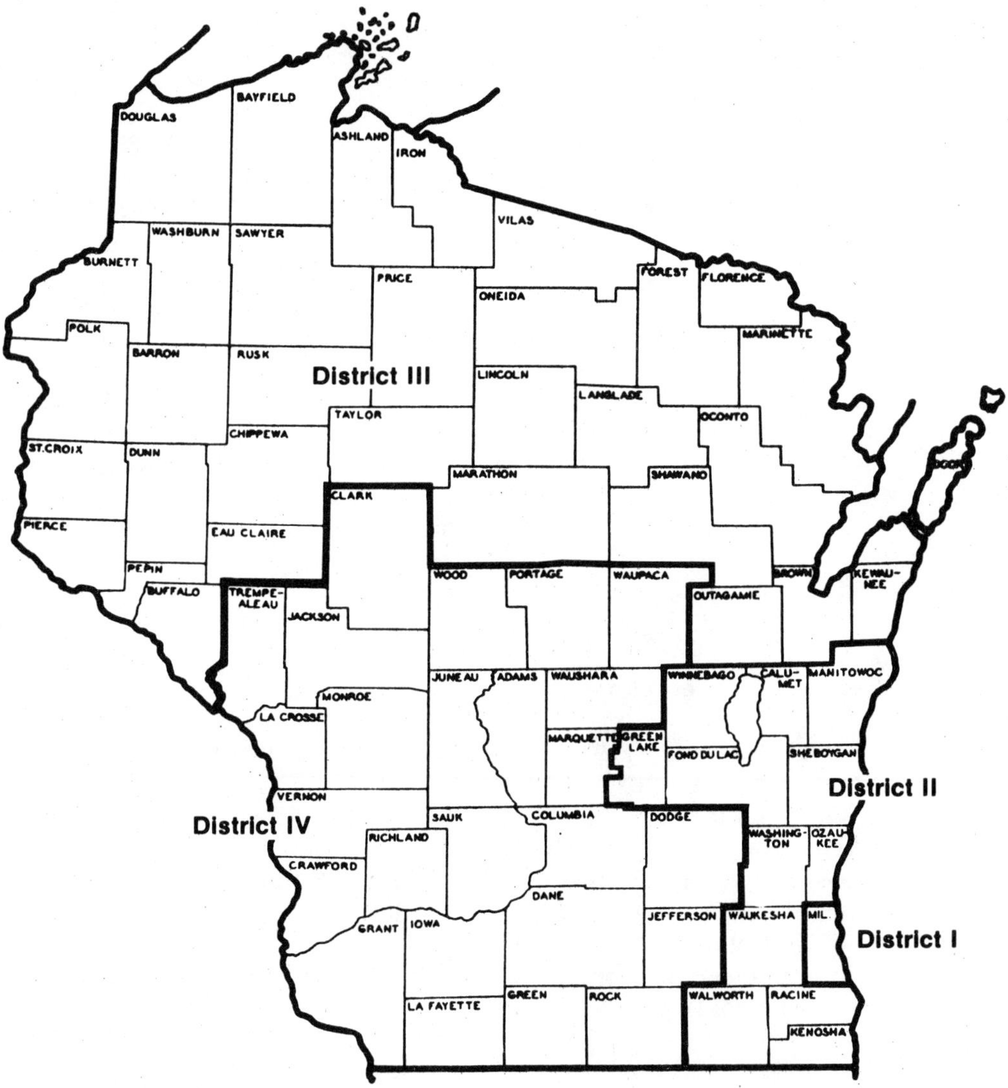

FIGURE 3.7. The four court of appeals districts in Wisconsin. Map also shows the 26 judicial circuits. Source: *Wisconsin Blue Book,* p. 681.

Functions. Appeal means to challenge a decision of a lower court to a higher court. Chapter 187, Laws of 1977, provides that the new court of appeals has **appellate** jurisdiction to hear and decide:

1. All appeals from the trial courts which were formerly appealable directly to the Supreme Court. Such cases are heard by a three-judge panel of the court of appeals; and

2. Lateral appeals formerly appealable from county court to circuit court and cases formerly appealed from county court involving municipal

ordinance violations will be appealed directly to the court of appeals. If a party so requests, such appeals must be heard in the county where the case originated.

Where the state is a party to an appeal, the attorney general is authorized to handle all appeals, civil and criminal, to the court of appeals, except that the district attorney of the county where the case is filed will handle those appeals heard by a single court of appeals judge. Lateral appeals cases are decided by a single court of appeals judge.

In most cases, appeal to the court of appeals must be initiated within 45 days after entry of the judgment or order appealed from, if written notice of such entry is given, or within 90 days if such entry of notice is not provided.

The court of appeals does not have jurisdiction to directly review final decisions and hearing decisions of state administrative agencies. Most of these administrative reviews are heard in the circuit court.

In lieu of an appeal to the court of appeals, the 1977 Act creates three "bypass" procedures whereby a case may receive direct review by the Supreme Court at its discretion.

Wisconsin Supreme Court

Organization. The **Supreme Court** consists of seven justices. Justices are elected for ten-year terms at the nonpartisan April election. Only one justice may be elected at each such election, so that some Supreme Court vacancies are filled by appointment for several years until there is an open April election date at which a full-term successor can be chosen by the people. The term of office begins in August following the April election.

The justice with the greatest seniority on the court serves as chief justice. The courtroom and offices of the court are located in the State Capitol.

The Supreme Court holds one term, beginning in August, and is in session for **oral arguments** each month from September through the following June. The court hears matters during July and August upon the call of the chief justice. The term is dated by the year in which it begins, for example, the 1981-1982 term is called the 1981 term.

The court's staff includes an executive officer who assists the chief justice and the court in their administrative duties; four commissioners who assist the court in its judicial functions; a clerk who keeps the court's records and serves as secretary of the Board of Bar Commissioners; and a marshal. Each justice has a private secretary and a law examiner.

Functions. Under the constitution, the Supreme Court has original jurisdiction in certain cases of statewide concern and appellate juris-

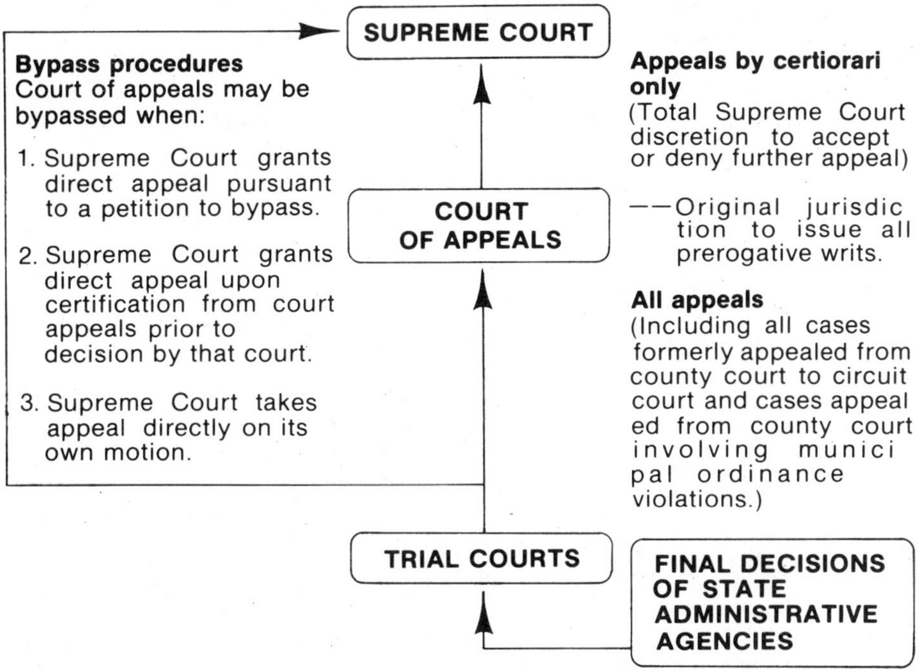

FIGURE 3.8. The Wisconsin Supreme Court hears cases that come to it in one of two ways: from a lower court or through one of the bypass procedures.

diction in all other cases. It is the final authority on the state constitution and the highest judicial **tribunal** for any action begun in the state courts, except that a federal question allows an appeal to the U.S. Supreme Court. The court disposes of cases brought to it on appeal on the record made in trial court, with printed **briefs.** The need for oral arguments by counsel is determined by the court. The court takes up cases in the order briefs are filed. Criminal cases are given preference. All cases are prescreened to determine which ones need oral arguments. Both oral argument cases and briefs-only cases are placed on the court calendar. **Decisions** are in writing and are published in the *Wisconsin Reports* and in the *North Western Reporter.*

The Supreme Court appoints the Board of State Bar Commissioners; licenses attorneys to practice law; and, after a hearing, may reprimand, suspend, or **disbar** attorneys for cause. Since 1929, it has developed rules of **pleading,** practice, and **procedure** for all courts of the state. The justices of the Supreme Court, together with the attorney general, constitute the Board of Trustees of the State Library. The court has also established a Judicial Commission, which is responsible for enforcing the code of judicial ethics adopted by the court.

Figure 3.8 illustrates the appellate jurisdiction of both the state court of appeals and the state Supreme Court under the 1977 Act.

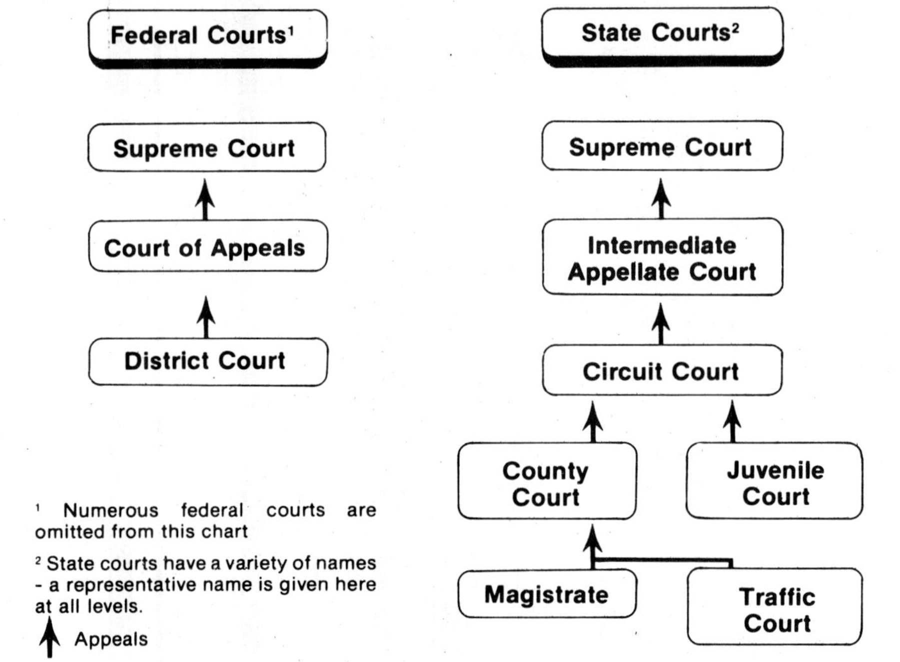

FIGURE 3.9. The organization of federal and state courts.

How does the federal court system compare with the state court system?

Figure 3.9 shows the basic pattern of the state and federal court systems throughout the United States. When conflicts or disputes arise, or a crime is committed, the legal structure, as reflected by the organization of the courts at the state and federal level, ultimately decides the disputes or determines the outcome.

Figure 3.10 shows the federal judicial system. Compare that diagram with the one in Figure 3.6 which shows the Wisconsin judicial system. In what ways is the organization of the Wisconsin judicial system similar to the federal system? In what ways do the two systems differ? How do you account for these differences?

How does Wisconsin fit into the federal court system?

As you can see from Figure 3.11, Wisconsin is part of the Seventh Circuit of the federal Court of Appeals system. The headquarters for this circuit is located in Chicago, Ill.

How does a case originating in Wisconsin get into the federal court system?

Cases originating in Wisconsin may be heard in a federal district court for a variety of reasons. In the federal system, Wisconsin is divided into two district courts, the Eastern District and the Western District. Appeals of cases heard in either of these districts go to the Seventh Circuit court in Chicago. If, on appeal, one of the parties to a case tried by the Seventh Circuit still is not satisfied, then that party may appeal the case to the U.S. Supreme Court in Washington, D.C. (see Figures 3.9 and 3.10). Appeal to the Supreme Court does not automatically mean that the court will try the case. The Supreme Court first has to agree to hear the case that is being appealed. If the court refuses to grant certiorari (agree to hear the case), then the decision of the lower court stands.

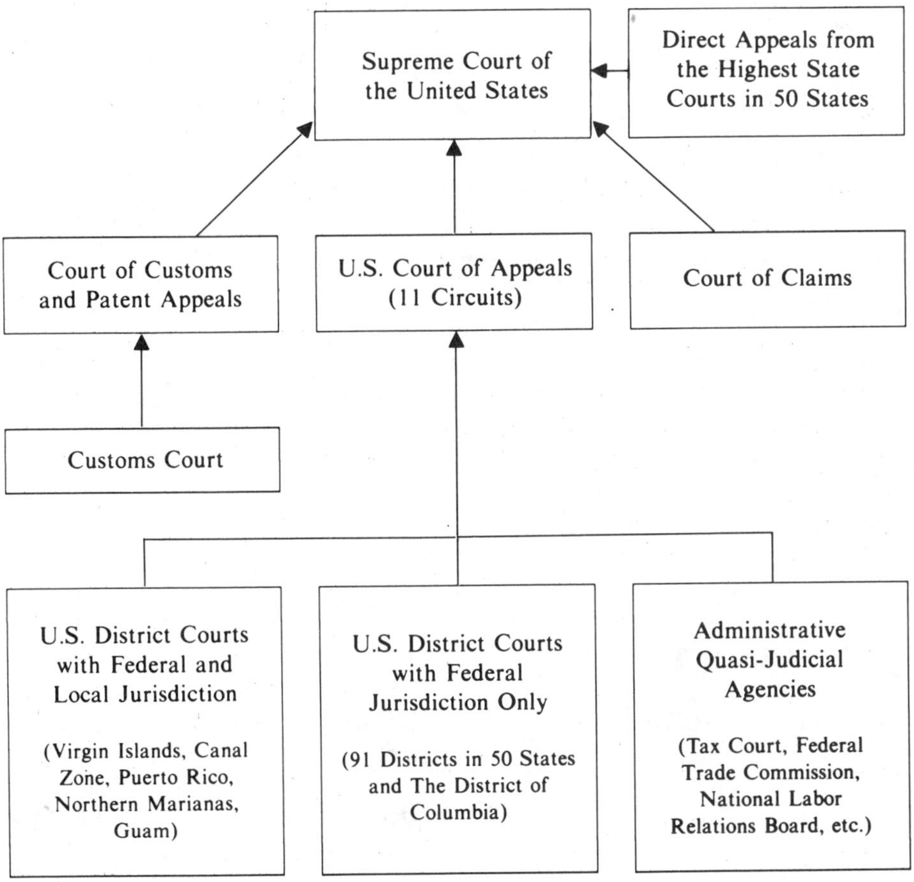

FIGURE 3.10. The federal judicial system. Source: West Publishing Company, St. Paul, MN.

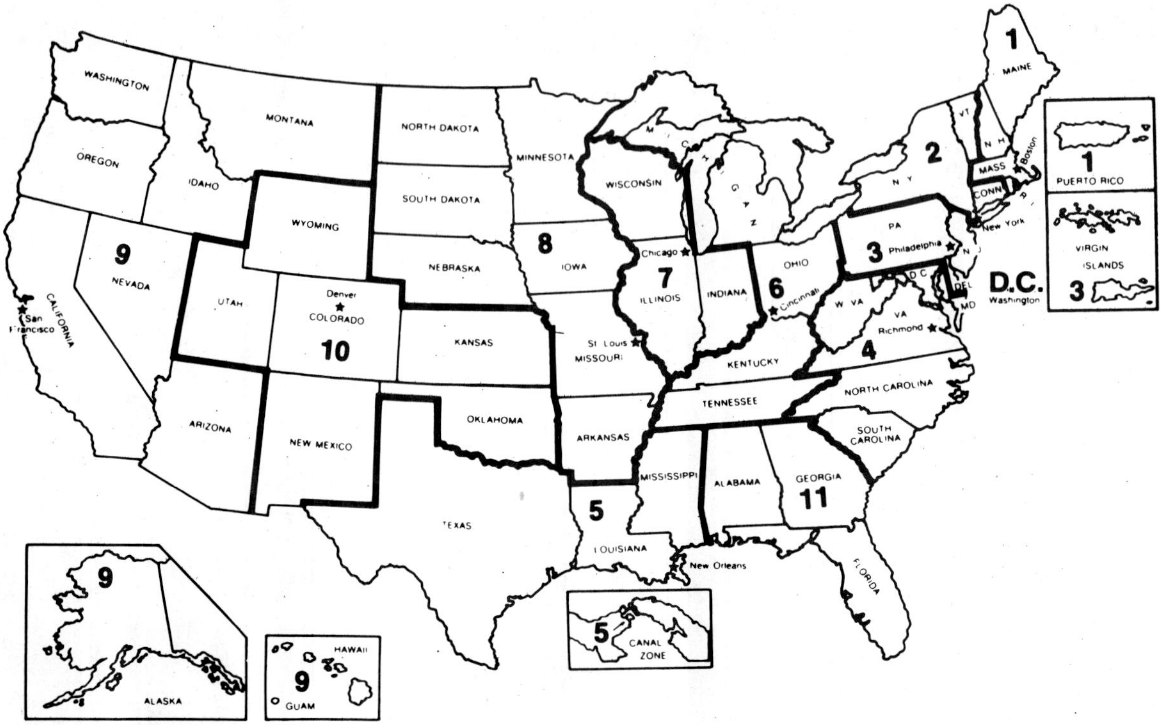

FIGURE 3.11. The eleven federal judicial circuits and the District of Columbia which form the U.S. Court of Appeals system. Source: Reprinted by permission from *1981 Supplement to Federal Jurisdiction and Procedure: Cases and Materials,* third edition, by Ray Forrester and John E. Moye, (St. Paul, MN: West Publishing Company, 1981), p. viii.

SUGGESTED ACTIVITIES

"Appellate Court (Criminal Appeals) Role Play," *Crime and Justice.* Los Angeles: Constitutional Rights Foundation, 1979, pp. 21-24.

Basil Condos, "The Devil and Chief Justice Marshall." Chicago: Law in American Society Foundation, Feb. 1975, vol. 4, no. 2, pp. 31-38.

Shirley Lewis Baugher, "Substance and Procedure: A Simulation Strategy." Chicago: Law in American Society Foundation, Feb. 1975, vol. 4, no. 1, pp. 33-38.

VOCABULARY

Appeal
Appellate
Arguments
Decision
Disbar
Discrimination
Hearing
Jurisdiction
Legislation
Legislature
Municipality
Oral arguments
Pleading
Procedure
Tribunal

REFERENCES

The United States Government Manual available from the U.S. Government Printing Office, Washington, D.C.

The State of Wisconsin 1979-1980 Blue Book compiled by Wisconsin Legislative Reference Bureau available from the Department of Administration, Document Sales and Distribution, 202 South Thornton Avenue, Madison, WI 53702.

SUGGESTED ORGANIZATIONS/AGENCIES

State Agencies

Legislative:

Legislative Reference Bureau
Room 201 North — State Capitol
Madison 53702

Executive:

Office of the Governor
115 East — State Capitol
Madison 53702

Office of the Lieutenant Governor
22 East — State Capitol
Madison 53702

Department of Agriculture, Trade and Consumer Protection
P.O. Box 8911
801 West Badger Road
Madison 53708

Public Service Commission
432 Hill Farms State Office Building
Madison 53702

Department of Regulation and Licensing
Washington Square
1400 East Washington Avenue
Madison 53702

Higher Education Aids Board
150 East Gilman Street
Madison 53704

Department of Public Instruction
General Executive Facility 3
125 South Webster Street
Madison 53702

University of Wisconsin System
1700 Van Hise Hall
Linden Drive
Madison 53706

Board of Vocational, Technical and Adult Education
Seventh Floor
Hill State Farms State Office Building
4802 Sheboygan Avenue
Madison 53702

Department of Natural Resources
P.O. Box 7921
Madison 53702

Department of Transportation
State Patrol Districts

District 1
4845 East Washington Avenue
Madison 53704

District 2
211115 Highway 18
Waukesha 53186

District 3
Route 5, Highways 151-41
Fond du Lac 54935

District 4
Box 843, 2805 Martin Avenue
Wausau 54401

District 5
Route 3, Box 239A
Tomah 54660

District 6
5005 Highway 53 South
Eau Claire 54701

District 8
P.O. Box C
Spooner 54801

Wisconsin State Patrol Academy
Bldg. 1256, Ft. McCoy
Sparta 54656

Department of Health and Social Services
663 W.S. State Office Building
Madison 53702

Division: Community Services — 534 W.S. State Office Building
Correction — 1030 W.S. State Office Building
Health — 434 W.S. State Office Building

Bureau of Alcohol and Other Drug Abuse
Division of Mental Hygiene
One West Wilson Street
Madison 53702

Judicial:

The State Office Public Defender
340 West Washington Avenue
Madison 53702

Trial Division Deputy
Room 500 Century Building
230 West Wells
Milwaukee 53203

Supreme Court
Room 231 East — State Capitol
Madison 53702

Legal Assistance
Wisconsin Judicare
403 Third Street
Wausau, Wisconsin 54401
1-(800) 472-1638
Limited legal assistance to qualified residents in selected Wisconsin counties.

PROFESSIONAL ORGANIZATIONS

Association of Wisconsin School Administrators
1310 Mendota Street
Madison 53714

The Youth Policy and Law Center, Inc.
30 W. Mifflin Street – Suite 904
Madison 53703

Wisconsin Bar Association
402 W. Wilson Street
Madison 53703

Wisconsin Bar Foundation
222 South Hamilton Street
Madison 53703

4

The Citizen-Student and Legal Research

Why should I want to use legal reference materials?

The law changes constantly. What was the law yesterday may not always be the law today or tomorrow. In different situations, the law might have a slightly different twist. In order to keep pace with the changing interpretations and applications of the law, it is important that you be able to update your knowledge.

How are legal cases cited?

When you read a legal case, you will probably see something like this:

Doe v. *Renfrow,* 475 F.Supp. 1012 (1979). This collection of proper names, numbers, abbreviations, and a date is known as a legal **citation,** or a case citation.

A case citation begins with the name of the case: the **plaintiff,** who is the person complaining, followed by a "v.", meaning *versus* or against, and the name of the **defendant,** who is the person being complained against.

The information which follows the name of the case tells in which reference books and on which pages the case can be located.

The first number in each set is the volume number. The abbreviation stands for the name of the series of books which have printed that decision. Each series will generally contain cases which have been decided at the same court level, that is, state, federal district, federal appeals, or supreme court. The number following the abbreviation is the page number of that volume on which the case begins. The sample citation of *Doe* v. *Renfrow* shows that the case can be located on page 1012 of volume 475 of the series abbreviated F.Supp. Each case citation concludes with the (year) in which the case was decided. In the *Doe* case the year of the decision was 1979.

Where can I find legal cases?

If you have the proper citation it is fairly easy to find a particular case. Decisions handed down by the U.S. Supreme Court can be found in the *United States Supreme Court Reports.* A case decided by the U.S. Supreme Court within the last six months can be found in the *United States Law Week.*

The West Publishing Company publishes selected appeals court decisions and all state supreme court decisions in a series of regional reports. These reports include cases from certain geographic areas and are printed in order according to the date of decision. The regional reports and their abbreviations are:

Atlanta (A,A.2d)
Pacific (P.,P.2d)
Southern (So.,So.2d)
South Western (S.W.,S.W.2d)
North Eastern (N.E.,N.E.2d)
North Western (N.W.,N.W.2d)
South Eastern (S.E.,S.E.2d)

Lower federal district court cases are found in a series of reference volumes called *Federal Supplement* (F. Supp.). Decisions of U.S. Federal Courts of Appeal are found in the *Federal Reporter* (F.,F.2d).

Where can I find state and federal laws and local ordinances?

Federal statutes are found in the *United States Code* (U.S.C.). Wisconsin laws are found in the *Wisconsin Statutes.* These volumes can be found in large libraries or on the shelves of law libraries.

Local ordinances of your town, county, village, or city may be found at the office of your local municipality.

What is meant by briefing a case?

In studying law, lawyers examine and organize the information they have on a specific case by **briefing** or outlining it. The purpose of briefing the case is to better understand its content and to identify its central issue.

What does a legal case brief look like?

The form of a legal case brief will generally look like this:

I. *Title of case* (legal citation)
II. *Facts* (a summary of the facts and circumstances which led to the raising of the legal question)
III. *Issues* (the legal questions or problems which result from the factual situation, usually phrased in the form of a question, for example, "whether or not . . .")
IV. *Arguments* (the different arguments or positions presented by both plaintiff and defendant in trying to convince the court to decide the issues in their respective favors)
V. *Reasoning* (considerations that the court based their decision on)
VI. *Decision* (How the court decided the issues; the conclusions they arrived at as a result of the reasoning).

CASE STUDY*
Doe v. Renfrow
(475 F.Supp. 1012 (1979))

Like many schools around the country, the junior-senior high school in Highland, Indiana, had a problem with student drug use. It was a problem that worried parents, teachers, and many of the 2,780 students in the two schools. Those worries deepened in the 1978-79 school year as drug use showed signs of increasing. So severe was the problem that during one three-week period in February and March of 1979, thirteen Highland students were dismissed from school for drug offenses—mainly possession of marijuana or alcohol.

Faced with a situation that seemed to be getting out of hand, the school board decided to take some drastic measures. After a series of meetings, the board, on March 14, 1979, approved a plan to bring specially trained dogs into the junior-senior high school to detect marijuana.

The plan was put into effect on March 23. That morning, as students arrived at school, they were told to stay in their first-period classrooms, for an inspection by one of six teams that had been brought into the building. Each team consisted of a dog, its handler, a teacher, and a uniformed police officer. When a team visited a classroom, students were instructed to sit at their desks while the dog, led by its handler, went up and down the aisles. If the dog detected the odor of marijuana on a student, it would give an alert to its handler. The student involved was then asked to empty his or her pockets or purse. If the dog still continued to give an alert even though no marijuana had been found in the student's pockets or purse, the student was subjected to a body search.

Although police officers were on the scene, school officials had decided before conducting the inspection that no criminal action would be taken against students found with drugs. Instead, the seventeen students who were found to have drugs or drug paraphernalia in their possession either left school voluntarily or were expelled.

But the drug inspection, as it turned out, had one other result: a federal court lawsuit filed by a junior-high student who claimed her constitutional rights had been violated during the inspection. The student, Diane Doe, was one of four students subjected to nude body searches as part of the inspection. In Doe's case, the nude search—made by two women in the school nurse's office—had been undertaken because a dog continued to give an alert even after Doe had emptied her purse. No marijuana was found on Doe, however.

Doe's lawsuit was based on the Constitution's Fourth Amendment, which bans "unreasonable searches and seizures." In general, courts have interpreted this to mean that authorities need a warrant from a judge, as well as probable cause to believe that the law has been violated, before they can search someone.

The lawsuit came before U.S. District Judge Allen Sharp, who on August 30, 1979, issued a landmark ruling that upheld the constitutionality of the drug inspection in every respect, except for the nude searches. Four major questions were raised in Doe's lawsuit and what follows is a look at how the judge answered each of them in arriving at his decision.

1. Was the drug inspection "a mass detention and deprivation of freedom in violation

*A summary of the case. For the court's complete opinion, see 475 F.Supp. 1012.

of the Fourth Amendment" as Doe claimed? The judge said it wasn't. School officials, he ruled, have the right to restrict student movement and regularly do so in scheduling classes and other activities. "Plaintiff [Doe] will not be heard to say that because she was made to stay in her classroom an extra 1½ hours [for the drug inspection], she was denied a constitutionally protected freedom from unreasonable seizure," Sharp said. "No evidence was presented at trial that shows plaintiff was in any way discomforted by the mere fact of being made to continue her class work for an extra 95 minutes."

2. Was the sniffing of the trained dogs in itself a search and thus permitted only with a warrant? Again, the judge's answer was "no." He noted that in ordering the drug inspection, school officials were simply carrying out their responsibility under the law to care for "the health and welfare of the entire student population.... The use of the dog in this operation was an aid to the school administrator and as such its use is not considered a search." Sharp added that his ruling did not mean students lost their constitutional rights "upon entering the school house doors." But he said that "in matters concerning the reasonable exercise of supervision and authority by school officials, this Court recognizes that a certain balancing occurs between an individual student's rights and the school administrator's need to protect all students and the educational process."

3. Did the search of students' pockets or purses, which was done without a warrant, violate their fourth amendment rights? Sharp said it did not. Much of his ruling on this point was based on the doctrine of *in loco parentis* (Latin for "in the parent's place"). This doctrine gives school officials the legal right to act on parents' behalf in certain circumstances. Sharp ruled that this "limited *in loco parentis* relationship modifies the student's Fourth Amendment guarantee of a sphere of privacy.... While there is a core of privacy so vital to a student's personhood that it must be respected by school officials ... that sphere of privacy ... can usually be invaded by a school official standing *in loco parentis* without a warrant ... upon reasonable cause to believe that the student has violated or is violating school policy." And in the case of the pocket and purse searches, the judge said, they "were conducted in furtherance of the school's legitimate interest in eliminating drug trafficking within the school." However, Sharp added that had the searches been made for the purpose of gathering evidence for criminal prosecutions, then a warrant might have been required.

4. Did the nude search of Doe violate her constitutional rights? Sharp ruled that it did. "Subjecting a student to a nude search is more than just the mild inconvenience of a pocket search," the judge said. "Rather, it is an intrusion into an individual's basic justifiable expectation of privacy." He said school officials can conduct a nude search only if they have specific information that gives them reasonable cause to believe the student actually possesses drugs. Sharp said the alert of a trained dog, which is what prompted the search of Doe, does not provide the kind of specific information needed to justify a nude search. "The animal reacts only to the scent or odor of the marijuana plant, not to the substance itself," Sharp said. "Therefore, the alert of the dog alone does not provide the necessary reasonable cause to believe the student actually *possesses* the drug."

The nude searches of Doe and three other students were, however, the only flaws Sharp found in the drug inspection plan. Summing up, the judge said: "This Court finds no constitutional fault with the basic plan and program as executed.... The effect (of the inspection) was anything but a gestapo-like effort run by gestapo-like people. To suggest anything approaching that idea is to do an extreme disservice to a group of dedicated people who carry heavy legal and moral obligations for public education."

SUGGESTED ACTIVITY

Brief the case of *Doe* v. *Renfrow* using the model and format discussed in this chapter.

VOCABULARY

Briefing
Citation
Defendant
Plaintiff
Versus

SUGGESTED READING

Ronald A. Gerlach and Lynne W. Lamprecht, "Legal Reference Materials," *Teaching About the Law.* Cincinnati: W. H. Anderson Company, 1975, pp. 127-146.

SECTION II

THE CITIZEN-STUDENT AND THE SCHOOL

CONTENTS

5

The Citizen-Student and the Legal Setting of the School

The law requires young people to go to school. This section will try to explain the rules governing school attendance, the consequences of failing to attend school, and the kinds of activities within the school that may have undesirable results.

In general, the state has an obligation to furnish a free education to all its young citizens, people under a certain age have an obligation to attend school, and their parents have an obligation to allow them to attend school.

Students in school are subject to reasonable discipline; if they fail to obey the rules and the offense is serious enough, or if they cause a disruption, they may be suspended for a short period of time or expelled permanently. But students do not lose their rights simply by going to school; the school administration cannot be unreasonable in its handling of students.

What are the sources of law affecting students?

The law governing the rights of students comes from a variety of sources, including state and federal constitutional provisions, state and federal laws, and court decisions. In recent years, legislation has been enacted at both the state and federal levels governing such areas as the education of handicapped children, the privacy of student records, bilingual education, and discrimination. In addition, state and federal courts, including the U.S. Supreme Court, have addressed an ever increasing number of questions involving the legal and constitutional rights of students in the public school setting.

Does the Wisconsin constitution have anything to say about education?

Yes. The Wisconsin constitution grants to each child in Wisconsin the right to a free public education in the district in which he or she resides. Article X, Section 3, of the Wisconsin constitution provides in part:

> The legislature shall provide by law for the establishment of district schools, which shall be as nearly uniform as practicable; and such schools shall be free and without charge for tuition to all children between the ages of 4 and 20 years. . . .

When a student exercises this right, he or she also has a responsibility to act in such a way that the rights of others to an education are not infringed.

Is it constitutional for the state to require me to attend school?

Yes. In *Wisconsin* v. *Yoder,* 406 U.S. 205, 213 (1972), the U.S. Supreme Court held that a state has the power to "impose reasonable regulations for the control and duration of basic education." However, the Court also carved out a narrow exception to this power in the case of *Wisconsin* v. *Yoder.* In that case, the Court held that the state of Wisconsin could not compel Amish parents to send their children to school beyond the eighth grade because it violated their first amendment right to free exercise of their religion.

What does Wisconsin law say about required school attendance?

The law requires all persons having under their control children who are between certain ages to send their children to a public or private school during the period the school is in session. (Wis. Stat. 118.15)

What must my parent or guardian do, under the law, to ensure that I attend school?

The following new statutes spell out the law in Wisconsin.

> **118.15 (1) (a)** Unless the child is excused or has graduated from high school, any person having under control a child who is between the ages of 6 and 18 years ... shall cause ... the child to attend school regularly during the full period and hours, religious holidays excepted, that the public or private school in which the child should be enrolled is in session until the end of the school term, quarter or semester of the school year in which the child becomes 18 years of age.
>
> **(b)** *Upon the child's request of the school board and with the written approval of the child's parent or guardian,* any child who is 16 years of age or over *may* attend, in lieu of high school or on a part-time basis a vocational, technical and adult education school. Where such *request* is made *and approved by the school board,* the district board of the vocational, technical and adult education district in which the child resides must admit the child and must enter into the contract. . . . Every district board must offer day class programs satisfactory to meet the requirements of this paragraph and sub. (2) as a condition to the receipt of any state aid.

When and under what conditions may I leave school?

118.15 (1) (c) Upon the child's request and with the written approval of the child's parent or guardian, any child who is 16 years of age or over shall be excused by the school board from school attendance. A child who is excused from school attendance under this paragraph shall be informed by the school board of his or her right to be readmitted to school upon request. The school board may specify when the child will be excused or readmitted after being excused from school attendance.

What other attendance options are available, under the law, to me, my parents or guardian?

Wis. Stat. 118.15 says that any child's parent or guardian, or the child if the parent or guardian is notified, may ask the school board to provide the child with program or curriculum modifications, including but not limited to:

1. Modifications within the child's current academic program.

2. A school work training or work study program.

3. Enrollment in any alternative public school or program located in the school district in which the child resides.

4. Enrollment in any nonsectarian private school or program, located in the school district in which the child resides, which complies with the requirements of 42 USC 2000d. Enrollment of a child under this

> subdivision shall be pursuant to a contractual agreement which provides for the payment of the child's tuition by the school district.
>
> 5. Home-bound study, including nonsectarian correspondence courses or other courses of study approved by the school board or nonsectarian tutoring provided by the school in which the child is enrolled.
>
> 6. Enrollment in any public educational program located outside the school district in which the child resides. Enrollment of a child under this subdivision may be pursuant to a contractual agreement between school districts.
>
> Any decision made by a school board or a designee of the school board in response to a request for program or curriculum modifications shall be reviewed by the school board upon request of the child's parent or guardian. The school board shall render its determination upon review in writing, if the child's parent or guardian so requests.

Under what circumstances may I be legally absent from school?

You may be legally absent from school if:

1. You are physically or mentally unable to attend school—in other words, if you are ill.
2. You have completed the full four-year high school course.
3. You are exempted from school attendance by the school board for good cause (for example, school-approved field trip, religious instruction).
4. You are over 16 years of age and are excused to participate in an approved work-study program.

How legal are some of the practices used by schools to discourage non-attendance?

Because the compulsory attendance and **truancy** laws specifically set forth the procedures to be followed by a school district in dealing with truancy, the following practices by a school are probably illegal:

1. Withholding course credit for excessive absences.
2. Lowering grades for unexcused absences.
3. Suspending or expelling for truancy.

However, if you are absent from a course without excuse and as a result miss work which would have been counted as part of your grade, the grade can legitimately be lowered.

What is truancy?

The compulsory attendance law requires you to be in school. Since you must attend school, the state creates another law defining your unexcused absences as truancy.

118.16 School attendance enforcement. (1) In this section:

(a) "School attendance officer" means an employee designated by the school board to deal with matters relating to school attendance and truancy.

(b) "Truancy" means any absence of part or all of one or more days from school during which the school attendance officer, principal or teacher has not been notified of the legal cause of such absence by the parent or guardian of the absent pupil, and also means intermittent attendance carried on for the purpose of defeating the intent of s. 118.15.

(2) The school attendance officer:

(a) Shall determine daily which pupils enrolled in the school district are absent from school and whether that absence is excused under s. 118.15.

(b) Annually, on or before August 1, shall determine how many pupils enrolled in the school district were absent in the previous year and whether the absences were excused under s. 118.15 and shall notify the state superintendent of the determination.

(c) Shall notify the parent or guardian of a child who has been truant of the child's truancy and direct the parent or guardian to return the child to school no later than the next day on which school is in session or to provide an excuse under s. 118.15. The notice under this paragraph must be given before the end of the 2nd school day after receiving a report of an unexcused absence and may be made by personal service, mail or telephone call of which a written record is kept.

(d) May visit any place of employment in the school district to ascertain whether any minors are employed there contrary to law. The officer shall require that school certificates and lists of minors who are employed there be produced for inspection, and shall report all cases of illegal employment to the proper school authorities and to the department of industry, labor and human relations.

(e) Shall have access to information regarding the attendance of any child between the ages of 6 and 18 who is a resident of the school district or who claims or is claimed to be in attendance at a private school located in the school district.

(3) All private schools shall keep a record containing the information required under ss. 115.30 (2) and 120.18. The record shall be open to the inspection of *school attendance* officers at all reasonable times. When called upon by any *school attendance* officer, such teachers shall furnish such information in regard to any child between the ages of 6 and 18 *who is a resident of the school district or* who claims or is claimed to be in attendance at *the school.*

(4) The school board shall establish a written attendance policy specifying the reasons for which pupils may be permitted to be absent from a public school under s. 118.15 and shall require the teachers employed in the school district to submit to the school attendance officer daily attendance reports on all pupils under their charge. No public school may deny a pupil credit in a course or subject solely because of the pupil's unexcused absences from school. The school board may establish policies which utilize detention as a deterrent to truancy. The school

> board shall provide each pupil enrolled in the public schools in the district with a copy of the school attendance policy established under this subsection and shall file a copy of the policy in each school in the district. In addition, the school board shall make copies available upon request.
>
> (5) Prior to any proceeding being brought against a child under s. 48.13 (6) or against the child's parent or guardian under s. 118.15, the school attendance officer shall provide evidence that appropriate school personnel in the school or school district in which the child is enrolled have, within the school year during which the truancy occurred:
>
> (a) Met with the child's parent or guardian to discuss the child's truancy or have attempted to meet with the child's parent or guardian and been refused.
>
> (b) Provided an opportunity for educational counseling to the child to determine whether a change in the child's curriculum would resolve the child's truancy and have considered curriculum modifications under s. 118.15 (1) (d).
>
> (c) Evaluated the child to determine whether learning problems may be a cause of the child's truancy and, if so, have taken steps to overcome the learning problems.
>
> (d) Conducted an evaluation to determine whether social problems may be a cause of the child's truancy and, if so, have taken appropriate action or made appropriate referrals.
>
> (6) Any school district administrator, principal, teacher or attendance officer who violates this section shall forfeit not less than $5 nor more than $25.

Are there any special circumstances in which the school must take action to ensure student attendance?

Yes. The law provides for low-income or needy students in Wisconsin Statutes 118.17:

> The principal or teacher in charge of any public school shall report to the authority administering general relief for the municipal unit wherein the school is situated the name and address of any child in the school whose parent, guardian, or other person having control, charge, or custody of the child is without sufficient means to furnish the child with food or clothing necessary to enable the child to attend school.

What does the law require your teachers to do?

The law requires teachers to provide accurate records of all students:

> Every teacher shall record the names, ages, and studies of all pupils under his or her charge and their daily attendance and such other facts or matters relating to the school as the state superintendent or school board requires. Any teacher who fails to comply with this section shall forfeit his wages during the time of such failure. (Wis. Stat. 118.18)

What is suspension and who can be suspended?

Section 120.13(1) of the Wisconsin Statutes authorizes school boards to make rules for the government of the schools, including rules about the conduct of students. In addition, the statute also provides that, with the school board's consent, the superintendent or any principal or teacher named by him or her may make rules. A student may be suspended for a violation of reasonable and lawful school rules or for conduct while at school or under the supervision of a school authority which endangers the health, safety, or property of others.

Are there any limits to how long I can be suspended from school?

Yes. A school **suspension** cannot last longer than three school days unless an **expulsion** notice has been sent, in which case the suspension may last up to seven school days. After a three-day suspension, a student is entitled to return to school, even if his or her parents have not had a conference with a school administrator.

What procedures must the school follow to suspend me?

To suspend you, the school must follow these procedures:

1. Advise you prior to the suspension of the reason for the proposed suspension.

2. Make a determination that you are guilty of the violation charged, and that the suspension is reasonably justified.

3. Give prompt notice to the parent of the suspension and the reason for it.

4. Provide you with the opportunity to take any quarterly, semester, or grading period examinations missed during the suspension period.

5. Afford you and your parents an opportunity for a conference with the district administrator within five school days. The district administrator may appoint someone else to conduct this conference, but it must not be someone from the suspended student's school. The purpose of the conference is to give the administrator or his/her substitute an opportunity to review the facts surrounding the suspension to determine if it was fair, just, and appropriate. If it is determined that the suspension was unfair, unjust, or inappropriate, references to the suspension must be removed from your school records.

Can I appeal a suspension to the state superintendent of public instruction?

No. There is no statutory right to do this.

What criteria must school rules meet before I can be suspended?

School rules must be clearly defined, and the students, teachers, and parents must be given notice regarding what is prohibited or what constitutes unacceptable behavior. You cannot be expected to comply with rules that you do not know about. School rules must also have legitimate educational purposes. A school has no authority to issue a rule, such as requiring each student to carry in a stick of wood, which is not related to the educational process. Finally, the school

At this Wisconsin school, individuals may anonymously notify teachers of student misconduct.

cannot enforce rules which interfere with your constitutional rights.

What is expulsion from school?

Section 120.13(1) of the Wisconsin Statutes grants school boards the authority to expel students in certain situations. By definition, an expulsion would be an exclusion from school for longer than three school days.

Who may expel me from school and for what reasons?

Under the law, only a school board may expel a student and it can do so only after a due process hearing has been held before the board.

A school board may expel a student in two situations:

1. If it finds you guilty of repeated refusal or neglect to obey school rules.

2. If it finds that the student engaged in conduct while at school or under the supervision of school authorities which endangers the health, safety, or property of others.

In addition, the law states that the school board must be ". . . satisfied that the interest of the school demands the expulsion."

What procedures must the school board follow to expel me?

To expel a student under the state law, the school board must adhere to the following procedures:

1. Send written notice to the student and the student's parents of the expulsion hearing.

2. Hold a hearing at which the student and the student's parents may be represented by counsel.

3. After the hearing, if the school board orders an expulsion of the student and, if he is a minor, send written orders to the parent or guardian as well.

Is it possible for me to appeal an expulsion order?

Yes. The law provides that you or your parents may appeal the expulsion to the State Superintendent. A decision of the State Superintendent may be appealed to the circuit court.

Can I be disciplined, suspended, or expelled for conduct which did not occur either at school or while under the supervision of a school authority?

Yes.

If action is taken to suspend or expel me as a student what does due process in the school setting look like?

See Fig. 5.1 for a suggested model for procedural due process.

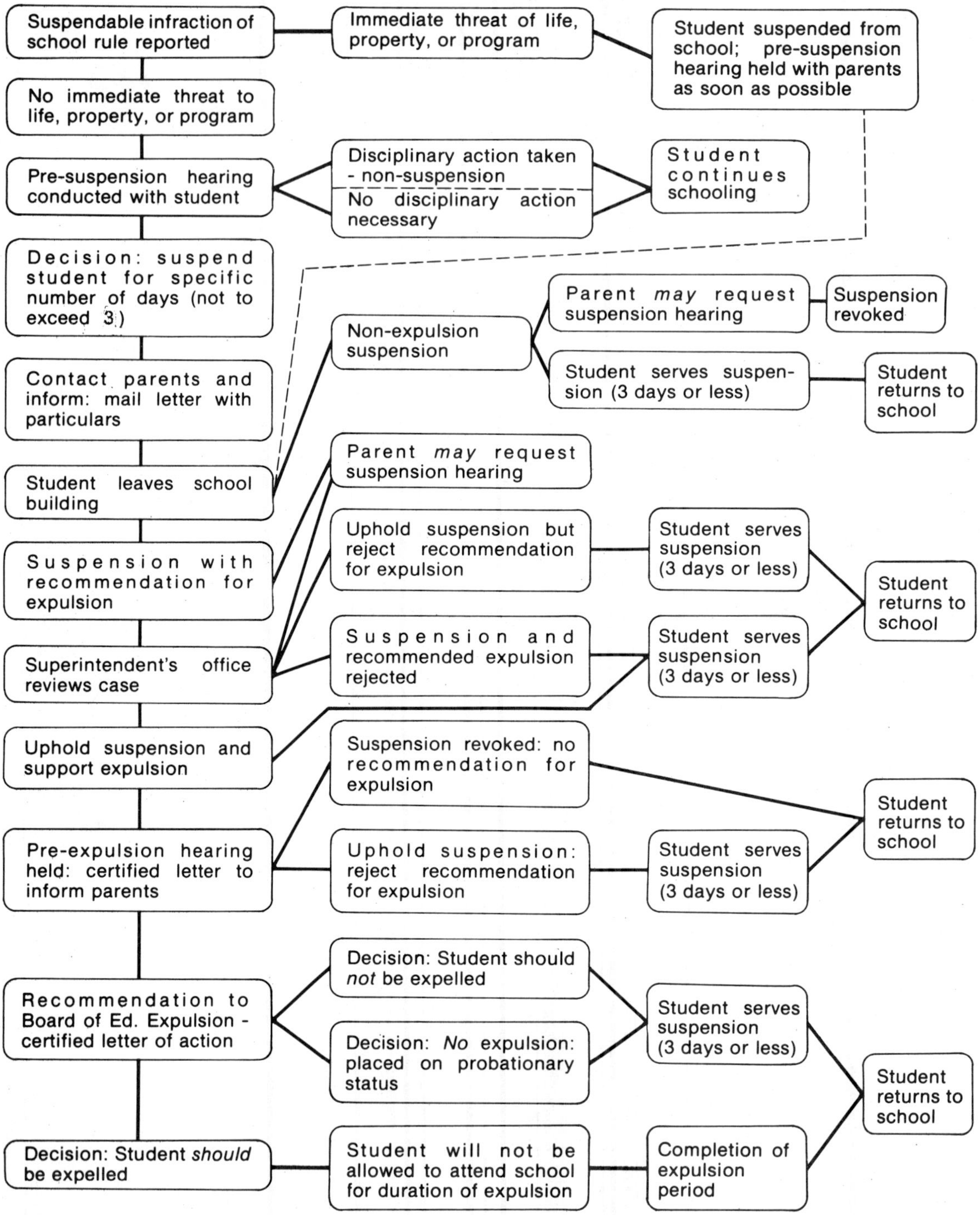

FIGURE 5.1. A suggested model for procedural due process which reflects current Wisconsin law. Source: R. W. MacFeeley, Phi Delta *KAPPAN,* September, 1975. Reprinted by permission.

CASE STUDY*
Wisconsin v. Yoder

For more than 300 years, the Amish people have lived a life apart from the rest of the world. The Amish—a religious sect with several communities in this country—believe that their very salvation depends on leading a life free from worldly influences. Stressing a simple way of life tied to the land, the Amish shun modern devices, preferring to use horses to plow their fields and get them from place to place.

As part of their beliefs, the Amish hold that children should not be overeducated. They believe that a basic education in reading and writing, such as that provided at a typical elementary school, is adequate for youngsters. Once out of eighth grade, Amish children are then given vocational training at home to prepare them for work in the community.

But the Amish approach to education eventually came in conflict with state compulsory school attendance laws, which generally require youngsters to stay in school until age 16. In the late 1960s, in Green County, Wisconsin, this conflict led to a legal battle that was eventually to go all the way to the U.S. Supreme Court. What happened in Green County was that school officials took three Amish men to court because they refused to send their children, ages 14 and 15, to the local high school. The men were subsequently convicted of violating the compulsory attendance law and fined $5 each.

The three Amish fathers—among them a man named Jonas Yoder—immediately appealed to the Wisconsin Supreme Court, arguing that their right to freedom of religion under the first amendment had been violated. The men won their case, but the state of Wisconsin then appealed to the U.S. Supreme Court, which in 1972 issued a landmark ruling in favor of the Amish families. That ruling said in essence that the Amish people's right to freedom of religion takes precedence over a state's legitimate interest in enforcing compulsory school attendance laws.

The Supreme Court's decision, written by Chief Justice Warren Burger and from which one justice dissented, began by noting that states do have a genuine responsibility for educating their citizens. But the court said that "a state's interest in universal education, however highly we rank it, is not totally free from a balancing process when it impinges on other fundamental rights, such as those specifically protected ... by the First Amendment and the traditional interest of parents with respect to the religious upbringing of their children." Religious freedom is so important, the court said, that "only those interests of the highest order" can take precedence over it.

The court went on to note that the religious convictions of the Amish affect all aspects of their lives. Moreover, the court said those religious values would be threatened if Amish children were forced to attend a public high school. "The values and programs of the modern secondary school are in sharp conflict with the fundamental mode of life mandated by the Amish religion," the court said. "Secondary schooling, by exposing Amish children to worldly influences ... and by substantially interfering with the religious development of the Amish

---

*A summary of the case. For the court's complete opinion, see 406 U.S. 205, 92 S.Ct. 1526, 32 L.Ed.2d15 (1972.)

child and his integration into the way of life of the Amish community, contravenes the basic tenets and practice of the Amish people." As a result, the court said, enforcement of the compulsory attendance law "would greatly endanger if not destroy the free exercise of the [Amish families'] religious beliefs."

In its arguments to the court, the state of Wisconsin had contended that compulsory school attendance laws are vitally important for two reasons: (1) they help insure that all the nation's citizens will be educated enough to take part in the political process of democracy, and (2) they help guarantee that individuals will have the education and training they need to be self-reliant. But the Supreme Court noted that these concerns do not really apply to the Amish, who have long emphasized self-sufficiency and who have proven themselves to be "productive and very law-abiding members of society." The court also pointed out that "the Amish alternative to formal secondary education (at-home vocational training) has enabled them to function effectively in their day-to-day life . . . and to survive and prosper in contemporary society. . . . In itself this is strong evidence that they are capable of fulfilling the social and political responsibilities of citizenship without compelled attendance beyond the eighth grade at the price of jeopardizing their free exercise of religious belief."

Another of the state of Wisconsin's arguments was that Amish children have the right to a high school education regardless of their parents' religious beliefs. The court majority, however, did not agree. In the first place, the court said, there was nothing to suggest that the children of the three Amish men disagreed with their fathers about the need for further education. And even if there were such a disagreement, the court said, it would raise issues that would have to be dealt with in a separate lawsuit. Moreover, the court said parents in this country traditionally have had the final say in determining the religious upbringing of their children. "It seems clear that if the State is empowered ... to 'save' a child from himself or his Amish parents by requiring an additional two years of formal high school education," the court said, "the State will in large measure influence, if not determine, the religious future of the child."

The one dissenting vote in the Yoder decision came from Justice William O. Douglas, who said two of the Amish children in the case were never given a chance to testify as to whether they agreed with their parents' views on education. Douglas said it was important for the children to be heard because their lives, not their parents', would be most affected by the court's ruling. "It is the student's judgment ... that is essential if we are to give full meaning to what we have said (in previous decisions) ... about the right of students to be masters of their own destiny," Douglas said in his dissent. "If he is harnessed to the Amish way of life by those in authority over him and if his education is truncated, his entire life may be stunted and deformed. The child, therefore, should be given an opportunity to be heard before the State gives the exemption (from compulsory school attendance) which we honor today."

QUESTIONS FOR DISCUSSION

1. What do you feel are the major constitutional legal issues in the Yoder case?

2. Do you think the Yoder family interests were more valid than the state of Wisconsin's interests?

3. Why have other religious groups not petitioned for exclusion from compulsory attendance in the State of Wisconsin?

4. Do you think there should be restriction on religious freedom? If so, under what circumstances?

5. In light of challenges to school policy, rules, and regulations what should a high school handbook for students contain?

Because students today need to be aware of school regulations, some high schools have routinely prepared handbooks for all students. The handbook of Mt. Horeb High School, Mt. Horeb, Wisconsin, is a model of a contemporary handbook style.

AGE OF MAJORITY

Mt. Horeb Area Schools recognizes that when a student reaches the age of majority (s.990.01), they are afforded all the rights and privileges of adulthood. Eighteen-year old students are subject to the same school rules as other students, except as enumerated below:

1. Students 18 and older may be excused from school attendance without parental consent. They must, however, follow the same guidelines as those set up for parents by state law (s.118.15).
2. Individuals who have attained the age of 18, if suspended, may negotiate their own readmission.
3. Eighteen-year olds have the right to examine their records without parental approval.
4. The school administration can control the drinking of intoxicating beverages or other behavior while students are at school, while under the supervision of a school authority, or while engaged in a school activity. School personnel may also remove or cause to be removed individuals whose behavior indicates they may be under the influence of alcohol or other behavior altering substances. This can be done regardless of whether a student is 18 or not.

A student upon attaining the age of 18 becomes legally responsible for his or her report card, records, attendance and all other school related procedures and activities. If a student wishes to have copies of his or her report card and other records provided to his or her parents, the student must notify the office in writing of this desire.

ALCOHOL

The state statues (s.176.31) prohibit any student under the age of eighteen from procuring, seeking to procure, knowingly possessing or consuming intoxicating liquor in public. The Board of Education also prohibits the above activities as well as being under the influence of alcoholic beverages when students are engaged in school activities, are representing Mt. Horeb High School, or are under the jurisdiction of school officials.

TOBACCO

Students are not allowed to use cigarettes, cigars, pipes, or any other tobacco products in school buildings at any time. The use of these items is also prohibited on school grounds during school hours between 8:00 a.m. and 3:30 p.m.

DRUGS

The possession or use of controlled substances (e.g. marijuana, amphetamines, LSD, barbiturates, cocaine etc. is a violation of law (s.161.41). Students who possess controlled substances at school, while under the supervision of school authority, or while engaged in a school activity are subject to a suspension and referral to appropriate legal authorities. Students are required to obey the same laws on school grounds as off related to the use of controlled substances referred to in s.161.41. Repeated violations or the sale of these substances to others may result in expulsion.

ATTENDANCE POLICY

All students, parents and staff in the Mt. Horeb Area Schools are required to observe the compulsory school attendacne law (s.118.15) Regular school attendance is one of the first essentials to school success and is an important part of the high school record each student is establishing. Its importance emphasizes the basic attempt to nurture two major objectives: 1) to instill in each student a willingness to accept the responsibility related to his daily attendance, and 2) to create in students the desire to successfully complete courses in which they enroll. All students are required to be in their scheduled class or study hall each period. School attendance is the responsibility of the students **and the parents or guardians. It is the responsibility of the parents or guardians to telephone the high school office at 437-5516 or 437-5517 before 9:00 a.m. on the day of the absence to inform school officials of the absence and the the reason for it.** On occasions when it is necessary for the student to be absent an attempt will be made to determine whether the absence is excused or unexcused. The following reasons for absence are considered justified and the students will be permitted to make up work missed:

1. Illness on the part of the student.
2. Serious illness or death in the immediate family.
3. Regular medical and dental visits.
4. Special circumstances (e.g. college visitations, job interviews, family vacations in which an individual child is excused for good cause according to the provisions outlined in the state statutes) provided an anticipated absence form is picked up from the high school office and completed in advance of the trip.
5. Absence resulting from acts of nature which cause serious problems to the economic status of the family.

Students have one week from the time of an absence to have the absence excused. It is recognized that school field trips and co-curricular activities will occasionally cause a student to miss a class. These absences will not be considered as missing school. However, all work missed must be made up. If all work is not made up by the conclusion of the marking period, the student will receive an incomplete. Incompletes must be eliminated within two (2) weeks after each of the first three grading periods or an F will be given for work not completed. This F would then be included in computing a final grade for the class. All work for the fourth quarter must be completed by the end of the quarter. The following reasons for class absence are not and cannot under state law (s.118.16) be considered justified and excusable:

1. Truancy (including leaving school during the day without checking out through the high school office, skipping an individual class without prior arrangements, hunting and fishing, and shopping trips even though sanctioned by parents or with parents).

A student having an unexcused absence will receive a zero for the work missed, and it may be recommended that the student make up the time and/or the work missed by individual teachers in an attempt to help the student understand the concepts missed in order to successfully pass the course.

Suspension or expulsion from school is not a justified and excusable absence. However, a suspended student shall be permitted to take any quarterly, semester or grading period exams missed during the suspension and these scores will be averaged into the final course grade.

Students will receive one unexcused absence from a particular class for the third unexcused tardy and an additional unexcused absence after each subsequent unexcused tardy.

Consistent violations of the school attendance policies could result in suspension from school.

DISMISSAL FROM CLASS

If a teacher finds it necessary to send you from a classroom because of willful and persistent disruptive misbehavior to the students, and, or refusal to obey the teacher in the room, you are to report immediately to the office. To be reinstated in the class, you must confer with a building administrator and the teacher concerned. Your parents will be informed. If a second dismissal from the same class occurs, a conference must be held with a building administrator, the teacher and your parents. If a third dismissal occurs, you will be dropped from that class for the duration of the semester.

FIRE DRILLS AND ALARMS

Fire drills at regular intervals are required by law and are an important safety precaution (s.118.07). It is essential that when the first signal is given, everyone clears the building by the prescribed route as quickly as possible. The classroom teacher will give the students instructions. Students will be suspended and/or referred to appropriate authorities for interferring with the school's fire fighting equipment (s.941.12) and for intentionally setting off a false alarm (s.941.13).

SEARCH BY SCHOOL PERSONNEL

School lockers are the property of the Board of Education and are provided for the convenience of students. Each student will be assigned a locker the first day of school. Students should not share lockers with friends and should not let others know their locker combinations. The school retains the right to conduct both announced and unannounced locker searches. Among the reasons are suspicion of concealing alcohol, drugs, material of a disruptive nature, stolen property, weapons, or other items which pose a danger to health and/or safety. If your locker is damaged in any way during the school year, report this damage immediately to the office. If damage is not reported, the student to whom the locker was assigned will be held accountable. Students should not put anthing in their locker or carry anything in their possession that they would not want the police to know about. Discovery of illegal materials may result in suspension and/or referral to appropriate authorities.

STUDENT VALUABLES

Students, not the school, are responsible for their personal property. Do not leave valuable items and money in your locker. When it is necessary to bring large and valuable items to school you are encouraged to check these into the office. A list containing the exact items must be submitted with the items.

SUSPENSION

State statutes permit the suspension of students (s. 120.13(1)(b). In Mt. Horeb students can be suspended for the reasons listed below:

1. Noncompliance with the school rules related to disruptive behavior, alcohol, tobacco, drugs, fire drills and alarms, attendance policy and searches defined elsewhere in this handbook.
2. assault and battery – A student causing bodily harm to another by an act done with intent to cause bodily harm to that person harmed is guilty of a misdemeanor (s.940.19).
3. vandalism – Any student who intentionally causes damage to the school building and, or school property without the consent of the school district is guilty of a misdemeanor (s.943.01).
4. slander/libel – The statutes (s.942.01) prohibit intentionally defaming another whether a student or a staff member. This involves anything which exposes the other to hatred, contempt, ridicule or digrace in their line of work.
5. disorderly conduct – Students who engage in violent, abusive, indecent, profane, boisterous, unreasonably loud, or otherwise disorderly conduct in which such conduct tends to cause or provoke a disturbance is guilty of disorderly conduct (s.941.01).
6. obscenity – A student who imports, prints, advertises, sells, has in his possession for sale, or publishes, exhibits, or transfers commercially any lewd, obscene or indecent written matter, picture, sound recording, or film or who has in his possession with intent to transfer to a person under 18 years of age any of the above materials or whoever makes any lewd, obscene or indecent drawings or writings in school is guilty of a felony by state statutes (s.944.21 and s.944.23).

The procedures for the implementation of suspensions are defined in (s.120.13(1)(b). The school district administrator or any principal or teacher designated by him . . . may suspend a pupil for not more than 3 days, or, more than a total of 7 consecutive school days for non-compliance with . . . school board rules, or for conduct by the pupil while at school or while under the supervision of a school authority, which endangers the property, health or safety of others. Prior to any suspension, the pupil shall be advised of the reason for the proposed suspension. The pupil may be suspended if it is determined that he is guilty of noncompliance with such rule, or of the conduct charged, and that his suspension is reasonable justified. The parent or guardian of a suspended minor pupil shall be given prompt notice of the suspension and the reason therefor. The suspended pupil or his parent or guardian may, within 5 school days following the commencement of the suspension, have a conference with the school district administrator or his designee who shall be someone other than a principal, administrator, or teacher in the suspended pupil's school. If the school district administrator or his designee finds that the pupil was suspended unfairly or unjustly, or that the suspension was inappropriate given the nature of the alleged offense, or that the pupil suffered undue consequences or penalties as a result of the suspension, reference to the suspension on the pupil's school record shall be expunged. Such finding shall be made within 15 days of said conference. A pupil suspended under this paragraph shall not be denied the opportunity to take any quarterly, semester, or grading period examination missed during the suspension period.

EXPULSION

The school board may expel a pupil from school whenever it finds him guilty of repeated refusal or neglect to obey the rules, or finds that a pupil knowingly conveyed or caused to be conveyed any threat or false information concerning an attempt or alleged attempt being made or to be made to destroy any school property by means of explosives, or finds that he engaged in conduct while at school or while under the supervision of a school authority which endangers the property, health or safety of others, or finds that a pupil while not at school or while not under the supervision of a school authority engaged in conduct which endangered the property, health or safety of others at school or under the supervision of a school authority, and is satisfied that the interest of the school demands his expulsion (s. 120.13(1)(c). Prior to such expulsion, the school board shall hold a hearing thereon. Not less than 5 days' written notice of the hearing shall be sent to the pupil and, if the pupil is a minor, to his parent or guardian, specifying the particulars of the alleged refusal, neglect or conduct, stating the time and place of the hearing and stating that the hearing may result in the pupil's expulsion. The pupil and, if the pupil is a minor, his parent or guardian may be represented at the hearing by counsel. The school board shall keep written minutes of the hearing, Upon the ordering by the school board of the expulsion of a pupil, the school district clerk shall mail a copy of the order to the pupil and, if the pupil is a minor, to his parent or guardian, The expelled pupil or, if the pupil is a minor, his parent or guardian may appeal the expulsion to the state superintendent. An appeal from the decision of the state superintendent may be taken within 30 days to the circuit court of the county in which the school is located. This paragraph shall be printed in full on the face or back of the notice.

NAME______________________________LOCKER_________

PROGRAM

Period	Subject	Room Number	Teacher
1			
2			
3			
4			
5			
6			
7			

DANCES

Dances may begin at 8:00 p.m. and the doors in will close one and one half (1½) hours after the dance starts. If you leave after the one and one half hour time limit, you may not return. Special arrangements can be made before the dance with a chaperone to let you in after the one and one half hour time limit if you work at a job that does not end until after that time.

A social hour after a football or basketball game will begin immediately after the game and end at 11:30 p.m. The doors in will be closed one half hour after the end of the game. All dances and social hours will be open to any students of high school age. All students who attend are subject to Mt. Horeb High School rules.

GUIDANCE

Guidance services are available for every student in the school. These services include assistance with educational planning, interpretation of test scores, occupational and career information, study helps, assistance with home, school and/or social concerns, or any questions the student may feel he would like to discuss with the counselor.

LOST AND FOUND

Students who find lost articles are asked to take them to the office, where they can be claimed by the owner.

PROGRESS REPORTS

Parents of students who are doing unsatisfactory or failing work are mailed reports to this effect approximately five weeks after the beginning of each quarter. Teachers have been encouraged to mail a report to a parent at any time during the quarter when unsatisfactory work is being done. It is strongly recommended that parents seek a conference with the teacher of the course where unsatisfactory work is being done. These conferences can be arranged by calling the high school at 437-5516.

WEATHER ANNOUNCEMENTS

In the event severe weather conditions require school to be called off before starting or through early dismissal, this information can be gained by listening to radio stations WIBA, WISM and WTSO, Madison or WDMP, Dodgeville.

TEXTBOOKS

Students are responsible for the care of the textbooks which they are using. Because books are expensive items, all students are urged to take care of them. Students are to sign their name and the date loaned in ink on the nameplate in the front of their books. At the beginning and end of the school year teachers will evaluate the books. If a book is damaged due to obvious carelessness or deliberate mutilation a fine will be assessed. If a book is lost, students will be assessed the replacement cost. Transfer students and freshmen are assessed a $1.00 fee per student for textbook rental.

VISITORS

The school welcomes visits from parents at any time, but if a conference is desired with a teacher or administrator, it is best to make an appointment.

Student guests are not encouraged at Mt. Horeb High School. Student visitors must secure a pass in the office. The student must accompany his guest throughout the day and is responsible for his conduct. Present the pass to each teacher at the beginning of each period.

WORK PERMITS

Wisconsin laws require that all persons under 18 years of age must secure a work permit for each new job in which they are engaged after school hours, Saturdays and Sundays and during vacation. Permits may be obtained in the office any time during the year upon presentation of a birth or baptismal record for proof of age. You also need a letter from the prospective employer promising employment and a letter from parent or guardian consenting to employment. Finally, there is a $1.00 fee to be paid by the employer.

WITHDRAWAL AND TRANSFER

The first step in withdrawing or transferring is to secure a withdrawal or transfer note from your parent or guardian. Obtain appropriate forms from the office. Have the forms filled out by teachers; return all school books and property, and make sure all fees are paid. Then take completed forms to the office. Students under the age of 18 must seek Board of Education approval before withdrawing.

FIGURE 5.2. Student handbook from Mt. Horeb High School, Mt. Horeb, Wisconsin. Source: Mt. Horeb High School, Mt. Horeb, WI. Reproduced by permission. Printed by COLAD, Inc., Buffalo, NY.

SUGGESTED ACTIVITY

Develop a fictitious case involving the expulsion of a student from your school. Follow the state requirements for an administrative hearing in the school setting.

1. Develop the case record against the student.
2. Develop the due process guidelines.
3. Assign specific roles and tasks for citizen-student participants.
4. Conduct a simulated school board hearing for the expulsion of the student.
5. Follow the basic quasi-legal adversary requirements unique to a school expulsion hearing.

VOCABULARY

Compulsory	**Suspension**
Expulsion	**Truancy**

RELATED LEGAL CASES

Burpee v. *Burot* (1878) 45 Wis. 150 (corporal punishment)

Pacyna v. *Board of Education Joint School District No. 1, City of Stevens Point,* 57 Wis.2d 562, 204 N.W.2d 671 (1973). (child cannot insist on right to attend school if excluded for immaturity or other reasons)

Wisconsin v. *Yoder,* 406 U.S. 205, 92 S.Ct. 1526, (overriding state interest required to compel attendance past eighth grade)

Truancy Opinion, Attorney General, July 25, 1969. (any reasonable excuse should be considered by school authorities in order to permit absenteeism)

Breen v. *Kahl,* 419 Fed.2d 1034. (hair regulation not sufficient for expulsion)

Keller v. *Fochs,* 385 F. Supp. 262. (student entitled to notice of charges and hearing on expulsion)

LeBoyd v. *Jenkins,* 381 So.2d 908 (teacher has immunity from civil liability if spanking is reasonable)

Tinker v. *Des Moines Independent Community School District,* 393 U.S. 503. (students possess same rights as "persons" under Constitution)

SUGGESTED READING

"Climate of Fear: Crime and Violence in the Schools" Los Angeles: Constitutional Rights Foundation, *Bill of Rights in Action,* February 1977, vol. 11, no. 1, pp. 11-14.

SUGGESTED RESOURCES

Statutes of Wisconsin Relating to Elementary and Secondary School, 1979. A current statutory copy is available from the Department of Public Instruction, Madison, Wisconsin.

Students' Rights in Wisconsin Public Schools Elementary and Secondary Education. 1977 Wisconsin Department of Public Instruction, Madison, Wisconsin.

Louis Fischer, David Schimmel, and Cynthia Kelly, *Teachers and The Law.* New York: Longman, Inc., 1981.

OMRO
47
FOOTBALL

6

Students' Rights, Responsibilities, and Limitations in the School

Since 1968 the courts at all levels in the United States have been forced by ever increasing case loads to define students' rights, responsibilities, and limitations. These cases have changed the relationship between the citizen-student and the school.

Students are no longer considered second-class citizens simply because they attend school. The courts have consistently said they would prefer not to interfere with the operation of the school. They have been forced, however, to make it clear that when the school seeks to deny constitutional protections to the citizen-student they are compelled to clarify what constitutes rights, responsibilities, and limitations to constitutional guarantees as well as to examine the intent of legislation when it concerns the student.

This chapter presents the types of **litigation** (lawsuits) that affect you as a citizen-student in Wisconsin. Many of the cases referred to in this chapter are from states other than Wisconsin but the application of those principles has the impact of the rule of law for you.

How have U.S. Supreme Court decisions affected my rights as a student?

Some recent U.S. Supreme Court decisions have dealt with the rights of students in the public school setting. Three important decisions are:

1. A 1967 case, *In re Gault,* 387 U.S. 1 (1967), while not involving a student in the public school setting, did see the Supreme Court declare that "... neither the Fourteenth Amendment nor the Bill of Rights is

for adults alone." The Court concluded that a juvenile in a juvenile proceeding had the right to due process of law, including the right to notice of the charges, the right to counsel, the right to be advised that he need not incriminate himself, and the right to confront and cross examine his accuser.

2. In 1969, in *Tinker* v. *Des Moines,* the Supreme Court held that public school students could not be suspended for wearing black armbands to school to protest the war in Vietnam, because this would violate their first amendment right of free speech.

3. In 1975 the Supreme Court held, in *Goss* v. *Lopez,* 419 U.S.565 (1975), that once a state has granted to a student the right to an education, the student could not then be deprived of that right, even for a short period of time via a suspension, without some procedural due process.

CONSTITUTIONAL ISSUES

The first amendment to the United States constitution provides that:

> Congress shall make no law respecting an establishment of religion, or prohibiting the free exercise thereof; or abridging the freedom of speech, or of the press; or to the right of the people to peaceably assemble, and to petition the Government for a redress of grievances.

Do I surrender my first amendment right to free expression when I attend school?

No. In the case of *Tinker* v. *Des Moines,* some public school students were suspended for wearing black armbands to school to protest the war in Vietnam. They wore the armbands to school despite a school policy against them. The U.S. Supreme Court held that the students had a right to express their opinions by wearing armbands, and the school could not infringe on their constitutional right to do so unless there were facts "... which might reasonably have led school authorities to forecast substantial disruption of or material interference with school activities. ..." The court went on to say that fear on the part of school authorities that some disruption might occur was not enough to ban wearing of the armbands. Thus, the court concluded, "... undifferentiated fear or apprehension of disturbance is not enough to overcome the right of freedom of expression. ... In order for the State in the person of school officials to justify prohibition of a particular expression of opinion, it must be able to show that its action was caused by something more than a mere desire to avoid the discomfort and unpleasantness that always accompany an unpopular viewpoint." Thus, the *Tinker* decision made it clear that some substantial evidence must exist that disruption or interference with school activities will occur or is occurring in order for a school to curtail the exercise of first amendment rights.

Must I get advance approval to distribute literature on school property?

It depends. In the case of *Fujishima* v. *Board of Education,* 460 F.2d 1355 (1972), the Seventh Circuit Court of Appeals held that a school could not keep students from distributing literature on the school property unless they first got approval of the superintendent. In the Fujishima case, three students were suspended for distributing literature or leaflets without prior approval. The court said it was unconstitutional to have a rule which required administrative approval of student publications. If, after distribution began, substantial disruption occured or was reasonably expected to occur, then under the *Tinker* rule the literature could be prohibited.

The Court of Appeals in *Fujishima* said a school could have reasonable regulations governing the time, place, and manner of distributing written materials and it could discipline students who violated these rules. However, the school board would have to inform students of any rules regarding the time, place, and manner of distributing written materials and it could not require students to apply for approval of the time or the place each time they wished to distribute something.

Do I have a right to publish or distribute obscene materials on school grounds?

No. Obscene or **libelous** (injury to a person's character by written or printed word) material is not protected by the first amendment. Schools can have a rule prohibiting obscene material and discipline students for publishing or distributing it.

Legally, obscenity is defined as: that which relates to depicting or describing sexual conduct in a patently offensive way, which appeals to the **prurient** interest in sex, and which, taken as a whole, does not have serious literary, artistic, political, or scientific value. *(Miller* v. *California,* 413 U.S. 15, 1973) In the case of *Jacobs* v. *Board of School Commissioners* (349 F. Supp. 605 (S.D. Ind. 1972, aff'd 490 F.2d 601 (7th Cir. 1973), the Seventh Circuit Court said:

> A few earthy words relating to bodily functions and sexual intercourse are used in the copies of the newspaper in the record. Usually they appear as expletives or at some similar level. One cartoon depicts a sequence of incidents in a bathroom. This material amounts only to a very small part of the newspapers, which are tabloid size containing eight or twelve pages. These issues contain no material which is in any significant way erotic, sexually explicit, or which could plausibly be said to appeal to the prurient interest of adult or minor.

Are prayer and bible reading forbidden in school?

Yes. These activities have been held to be unconstitutional even though participation by students is voluntary. (See *Engle* v. *Vitale,* 370 U.S. 421 (1962), and *Abington School District* v. *Schempp,* U.S. 203, 1963).

What is the fourth amendment?

The fourth amendment of the constitution, ratified in 1791 as one of the ten Bill of Rights amendments, reads:

> The right of the people to be secure in their persons, houses, papers, and effects, against unreasonable searches and seizures, shall not be violated, and no Warrants shall issue, but upon probable cause, supported by Oath or affirmation, and particularly describing the place to be searched, and the persons or things to be seized.

Am I protected from unreasonable searches and seizures by school officials?

Yes, to some extent. The fourth amendment provides that people have the right to be free of unreasonable searches and seizures. (*Weeks* v. *United States,* 232 U.S. 383, (1914); *Mapp* v. *Ohio,* 367 U.S. 643, 1961). Thus, the fourth amendment prohibits state and federal governmental officials from subjecting persons to unreasonable searches of their persons or property.

What is an unreasonable search?

As a general rule, a search is unreasonable if the official does not first have a search **warrant.** To obtain a warrant the official must show probable cause to justify the search. There are some exceptions to the requirement that a search warrant be obtained. For example a search warrant is not needed if the person consents to the search or if there are some emergency or other extenuating circumstances which would justify a warrantless search.

In order to put teeth into the fourth amendment's prohibition of unreasonable searches, the U.S. Supreme Court has held that evidence obtained through illegal searches is not admissible evidence against a person in a criminal proceeding.

What are the consequences for school officials of an unreasonable or illegal search of a student?

1. Any evidence found may be excluded from evidence in a criminal proceeding against the student.

2. Evidence found during such a search would have to be excluded from evidence in a school proceeding against the student (for example, an expulsion hearing).

3. A civil suit or criminal prosecution might be instituted for a violation of the student's privacy. (Robert E. Phay and George T. Register, Jr., "Searches of Students and the Fourth Amendment," *Journal of Law and Education,* vol. 5, pp. 57-73, 1976.)

The right to privacy in the school needs to be balanced between the students' Fourth Amendment rights and school officials' legal responsibilities to care for the welfare of all students.

Are school officials held to the same standards as other public officials in search and seizure issues?

No. Most courts which have considered the issue have held that the fourth amendment requirement that there be probable cause and a search warrant does not necessarily apply to protect students in a public school setting. For example, one New York case held that there does not need to be probable cause to believe that a rule or law is being violated before a student can be searched, although there does need to be some reasonable suspicion to justify searching a student. (*People* v. *D.*, 34 N.Y.S. 483, 1974)

Is my school locker immune from searches?

Probably not. The reasoning for this is that the school administrators have control over student lockers, that the lockers are loaned to the students for certain specified purposes only, and that the student cannot have a reasonable expectation of privacy about the contents of his or her locker. (Kelly Frels, "The Status of Search and Seizure in Public Schools," *New Directions in School Law,* pp. 78-95, 1975.)

Courts in general have been reluctant to grant very much fourth amendment protection to students, although a few courts have gone farther in that direction than most. Courts will generally view a search of a student's person as a more serious intrusion than a search of a locker or other property. The law in this area is probably not settled, but it appears that at least for the present most courts, in judging whether a search is legal, are not going to hold school officials to the same standards required for other kinds of searches.

Can school officials administer corporal punishment to me?

There is no state law which either expressly permits or prohibits corporal punishment. However, school boards, under their broad rulemaking authority, could adopt a policy which prohibits corporal punishment. If such a policy were adopted in a particular school district, corporal punishment would not be permissible in that district. If corporal punishment is not prohibited by school board policy, then it is probably permissible, subject to certain limitations.

The constitutional basis for these limitations is found in the eighth amendment:

> Excessive bail shall not be required, nor fines imposed, nor cruel and unusual punishment inflicted.

Are there any limitations to corporal punishment?

Yes. If corporal punishment is permitted, only reasonable force may be used. Teachers or administrators who misuse this privilege may be subject to civil or criminal liability. (Wis.Stat. 939.45 (5))

DISCRIMINATION

The fourteenth amendment of the constitution, ratified in 1868, guarantees all citizens equal rights:

> All persons born or naturalized in the United States, and subject to the jurisdiction thereof, are citizens of the United States and of the State wherein they reside. No State shall make or enforce any law which shall abridge the privileges or immunities of citizens of the United States; nor shall any State deprive any person of life, liberty, or property, without due process of law; nor deny to any person within its jurisdiction the equal protection of the laws.

Are public schools forbidden to segregate students based on race?

Yes. In 1954, the U.S. Supreme Court held in the case of *Brown* v. *Board of Education* that segregation of children in public schools solely on the basis of race was a violation of the equal protection clause of the fourteenth amendment. In addition, Title VI of the Civil Rights Act of 1964 prohibits discrimination against students on the basis of race or national origin in all programs receiving federal funds.

May the school discriminate against students based on sex?

Title IX and regulations for Title IX of the Education Amendments of 1972 prohibit discrimination on the basis of sex in any education program or activity receiving federal financial assistance. In addition, all courses must be offered on a coeducational basis, including such things as home economics, physical education, and industrial arts.

There are only three exceptions to this requirement:

1. Portions of classes in elementary and secondary schools which deal exclusively with human sexuality may be conducted separately for boys and girls.

2. Vocal music classes may group students by vocal range or quality which may result in choruses of one sex.

3. Students may be separated by sex in portions of physical education classes during participation in bodily contact sports (wrestling, boxing, rugby, ice hockey, football, and basketball). In addition, students may be grouped by ability in physical education classes, and this might result in classes of one, or predominantly one, sex.

Are there areas other than course work where sex-segregation is forbidden?

Yes. Title IX prohibits, among other things:

1. different school rules for boys and girls,
2. different graduation requirements for boys and girls,
3. different treatment of married or pregnant students,
4. counseling services which are sex-biased,
5. unequal opportunity, based on sex, to compete in athletics in a meaningful way.

What can I do if I believe there is a practice at school which discriminates against me because of my sex?

1. Talk to the Title IX coordinator for the school district.
2. File a complaint according to the school's grievance procedures.
3. File a complaint with the Office for Civil Rights in Washington, D.C.

Wisconsin also has a state law (118.13) which prohibits exclusion of or discrimination against any person in a public school on the basis of race, sex, religion, national origin, physical condition, or developmental disability.

Is it permissible for a school to discriminate against married or pregnant students?

No. Title IX of the Education Amendments of 1972 prohibits discrimination on the basis of sex in educational institutions or activities which

In Wisconsin, married students do not lose any of their education rights.

receive federal financial assistance. In addition, Section 118.13 of the Wisconsin Statutes states that no person may be discriminated against on the basis of sex in obtaining the advantages, privileges, or courses of study of a public school. Section 118.15(4m) states that no school board, nor any person employed by the school, may force a pregnant girl to withdraw from her regular education program. Finally, under subchapter IV of Chapter 115 Wisconsin Statutes, a pregnant student may be found to have exceptional educational needs and may therefore be entitled to special education to supplement or replace regular education.

When recently confronted with the issue, courts have fairly consistently held that students may not be treated differently because of their marital status or because of pregnancy.

RELATED ISSUES

What is the statutory basis for school rules regulating my conduct as a student?

The legislature has granted school boards authority of a broad nature to supervise and manage the affairs of the school district (Wis.Stat. 120.12) and to make rules for the government of the schools in the district, including rules regarding student conduct. (Wis.Stat. 120.13(1)(a)). Thus, students can be expected to obey reasonable school rules.

Is the school board's authority to make rules boundless?

No. The Wisconsin Supreme Court, in an old case, has said that the school's rules must be reasonable and necessary for the government, good order, and efficiency of the schools. (State ex rel. *Bowe* v. *Board of Education of City of Fond du Lac,* 63 Wis 234, 23 N.W. 102, 1885) In that case, a school rule required each student to bring in a stick of wood after recess for the fire. The court said the school had no authority to make and enforce such a rule, because it had nothing to do with the education of students.

In addition to the state constitutional and statutory framework within which school boards and administrators must function, the U.S. constitution guarantees school students certain constitutional rights and protections.

Aren't dress and grooming codes by public schools illegal?

Not necessarily. While the Wisconsin Statutes (120.13) do grant school boards the power to make rules "... including rules pertaining to conduct and dress of pupils. . . ." court decisions have limited the kinds of rules and standards which might be validly made. In addition, each state comes within the jurisdiction of a federal circuit court of appeals. About half of these courts have held that students have a constitutionally protected right to wear their hair as they choose, and about half of these courts have held that there is no constitutionally protected right in this area. The U.S. Supreme Court has not ruled on this issue, so federal district courts in each state are governed by the circuit court decision for their district. Wisconsin is located in the Seventh Circuit.

The Seventh Circuit, in 1969, decided a case called *Breen* v. *Kahl,* 419 F.2d 1034 (1969) which involved a school rule attempting to regulate the length of male students' hair and resulting in expulsion of students for noncompliance with that rule. The Court of Appeals for the Seventh Circuit held that "The right to wear one's hair at any length or in any desired manner is an ingredient of personal freedom protected by the United States Constitution." The court went on to say that before a school board could enact and enforce a rule which limited or curtailed this right, it must have a substantial justification for such a rule. Thus a serious health, safety, or disruption problem must exist before a school board can take action to regulate students' dress or grooming.

CASE STUDY*
Soglin v. Kauffman

Student protests were a common sight at the University of Wisconsin in the 1960s, when opposition to the war in Vietnam was at its height. One group that took part in many of those campus protests was the Madison chapter of Students for a Democratic Society (SDS). Members of this group, which strongly opposed the war, sometimes used tactics that got them in trouble with the university administration. That's exactly what happened on October 18, 1967, when about ten SDS members staged a protest against the Dow Chemical Company, which made napalm for use in Vietnam. Dow representatives had come to the Madison campus that day to interview students seeking jobs with the company. But the SDS members, as part of their protest, allegedly blocked the doorway to the interviewing room in an effort to disrupt the company's activities on campus.

A day later, some of the SDS members were notified by mail that the university was considering disciplinary action against them because of their alleged "misconduct" on October 18. The SDS members were also told that by blocking the doorway they had violated a university regulation guaranteeing all students the right to "freedom of speech" and "peaceable assembly." Faced with possible expulsion from the university, the SDS members—led by a student named Paul Soglin—brought suit in federal court to challenge the university's disciplinary policies.

At a hearing before U.S. District Judge James E. Doyle, the students argued that a standard as vague and all-inclusive as "misconduct" could not be used as the sole reason for disciplining them. The students said any disciplinary action based on such a standard would violate their rights under the Fourteenth Amendment to the Constitution. That amendment says, among other things, that no citizen can be deprived of "life, liberty, or property without due process of law." The students also contended that their First Amendment rights to free speech would be violated if they could be disciplined for something as broad and subjective as "misconduct."

University officials argued in response that academic institutions traditionally have been given a great deal of latitude by the courts in disciplining students. They admitted that the term "misconduct" would be unconstitutionally vague if used as a standard in, for example, criminal law. But university regulations, they said, carry less weight than criminal laws and so cannot be held to the same standards. Moreover, university officials pointed out that the SDS members were warned before the October 18 protest that they would be disciplined if they disrupted the Dow interviews. This warning, university officials contended, was the same as giving the students "fair notice," which is generally required as part of due process of law.

Judge Doyle's decision, handed down in December of 1968, proved to be an important ruling that significantly extended the rights of students. "A standard of 'misconduct,' without more, may not serve as the sole foundation for the imposition of the sanction of expulsion,

---

*A summary of the case. For the court's complete opinion, see 295 F.Supp. 978 (1968). At the time of this case, Joseph F. Kauffman was the Dean of Student Affairs at the University of Wisconsin (Madison campus).

or the sanction of suspension for any significant time, throughout the entire range of student life in the university," Doyle said.

In reaching his decision, Doyle stressed the fact that universities cannot be viewed as places isolated from the mainstream of American life. He said the University of Wisconsin is a huge institution whose power and influence extend throughout the state. As a result, Doyle said, the university's policies should be subject to the same kind of judicial review as those of any other large public institution. Moreover, Doyle said, the relationship between a university and its students cannot be viewed the way it once was. "The facts of life have long since undermined the concepts, such as *in loco parentis,* which have been invoked historically for conferring upon university authorities virtually limitless disciplinary discretion."

Doyle also pointed out that expulsion is a severe penalty in a society that places a high value on a college education. "In the present day, expulsion from an institution of higher learning . . . may well be, and often is in fact, a more severe sanction than a monetary fine or a relatively brief confinement imposed by a court in a criminal proceeding," Doyle said. Because of this, he said, university regulations cannot be "wholly immune" from the constitutional requirement that laws be neither overly vague nor overly broad.

Another argument advanced in the case was that attending a university is a privilege and not a right. But Doyle said previous court rulings had made it clear that "whether the opportunity to attend a state institution of higher learning is viewed as a right or as a privilege, it may not be conditioned on the student's acceptance of a regime in which procedural due process is abdicated or in which substantive rules flatly restricting free expression are enforced." The judge concluded: "It cannot presently be contended that in order to enjoy the 'privilege' of higher education, one may be obliged to consent that he may be expelled without specification of charges, notice, or hearing, or to consent to remain silent on the political and social issues of his time."

Milwaukee students demonstrate against racial violence.

QUESTIONS FOR DISCUSSION

1. Do you think the *Soglin* v. *Kauffman* decision has affected your written school rules and regulations?

2. How would you as a citizen-student go about helping to improve your school rules and regulations?

EXTRACURRICULAR ACTIVITIES

Extracurricular activities are school-sponsored activities in which a student can participate but which are not offered for course credit. Extracurricular activities might include participation in school-sponsored clubs or organizations or participation in interscholastic athletics.

Are school rules regulating my conduct in school-sponsored extracurricular activities legal?

It depends. The Wisconsin Statutes (120.13) grant to school boards, administrators, and teachers the power to make rules governing conduct of students. This rulemaking authority would include the power to make reasonable rules governing your conduct while participating in school-sponsored extracurricular activities.

The problem emerges when you come to the kinds of rules governing students in extracurricular activities. For example, because Wisconsin is in the Seventh Circuit, which has held that students have a constitutional right to wear their hair as they choose, schools in Wisconsin would probably have to be able to support with substantial justification a rule governing the hair length of students participating in extracurricular activities.

Are rules of conduct which exclude me from participating in interscholastic athletics for violating athletic codes legal?

This area of the law is unsettled. While the following case is not binding on Wisconsin courts, the reasoning in the decision may give you some indication of what a court might look at when judging rules governing extracurricular activities.

An Iowa case dealt with rules of conduct for boys participating in interscholastic athletics. The Iowa High School Athletic Association had a rule which excluded a boy from interscholastic athletic competition if he was found guilty of using alcoholic beverages or if he was found guilty of being in a car in which he knew alcoholic beverages were being transported. The student in that case was excluded from the football team because during the previous summer he was found riding in a car in which beer was being transported. The student admitted he knew the beer was in the car, but there was no evidence or admission that he drank any of it. The Iowa Supreme Court held that a school had no authority to make such a rule. The rule covered students outside the football season, beyond the school year (during the summer months), and even if there were no improper use of beer. The Court said that such a rule was beyond the permissible scope of school rules. It pointed out that a school rule must relate to and affect the management of the school and its efficiency. The court did intimate that a school rule could declare students who drank beer during the football season to be ineligible and probably could validly prohibit beer drinking during the summer months. However, the court felt that the rule in question went beyond those permissible kinds of prohibitions. In addition to finding the rule beyond the scope of the school's authority, the court also found the rule to be unreasonable, and unreasonable rules will not be upheld by a court. (*Bunger* v. *Iowa High School Athletic Association,* 197 N.W. 2d 555, 1972)

Would an athletic code written and enforced (in part) by students have to meet the burden of "reasonableness?"

Yes. See *Arnold* v. *Carpenter,* 459 F.2d 939, 7th Cir. (1972).

What should due process look like for athletics?

Figure 6.1 is a good example of the chain of events in a dispute over an athletic code violation. The process begins with a written notice

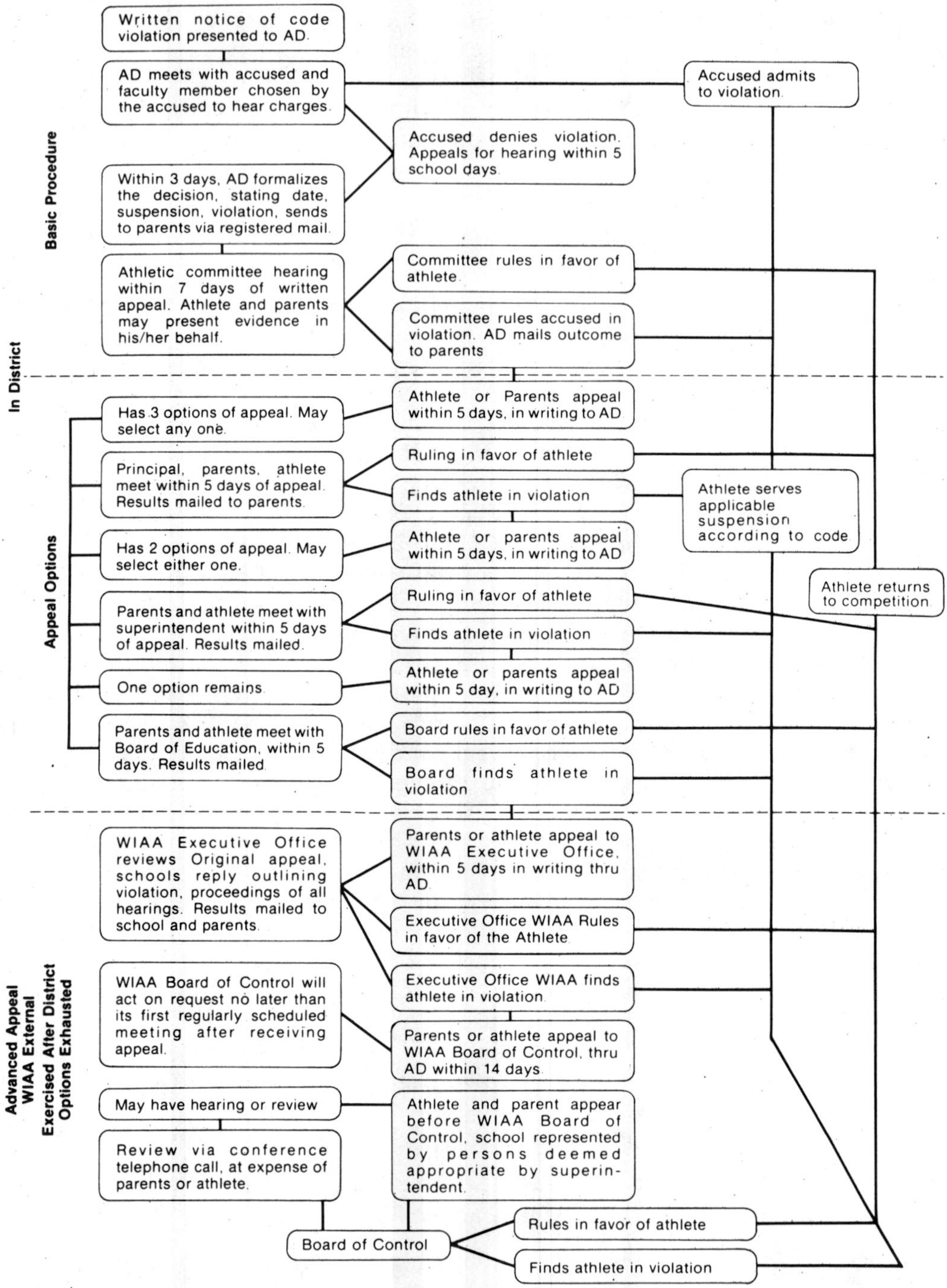

FIGURE 6.1. Due process when a violation of the athletic code is suspected. Ron Wunrow, Athletic Director, River Falls Public Schools, 1978. Source: Ron Wunrow, River Falls, Wisconsin. Reproduced by permission.

of a violation presented to the AD or Athletic Director. (WIAA means the Wisconsin Interscholastic Athletic Association.)

STUDENT RECORDS

Are there any laws which govern access to my student records?

Yes. Both state law (Wis. Stat. 118.125) and federal law (20 U.S.C. sec. 1232g) govern access to and confidentiality of student records. The federal law is also known as the Family Educational Rights and Privacy Act.

What do these laws provide for and prohibit?

Both laws:

1. Require that a parent or an adult student be allowed to inspect or review records kept on the student by the school.

2. Prohibit disclosure of information from a student's record to third parties, except in specifically enumerated situations, without the written consent of the parent or the adult student.

3. Require the school board to adopt a written policy governing access to and release of student records which is consistent with the law.

4. Require that once a student is 18 years old or, under the federal law, is attending an institution of post-secondary education, the student is entitled to see his or her own records and to decide when they should be released to third parties. The parent no longer has these rights.

Is there any way to have inaccurate, inappropriate, or misleading information amended in my school records?

Yes. The federal law provides that a school must adopt a policy whereby a parent or an adult student has a chance to request that records or a portion of them be amended (changed). The parent or student is entitled to a hearing, and if it is determined not to amend the record, the parent or the adult student must be given the opportunity to place their own explanation in the file.

Does the term records also apply to personal notes of teachers?

No. However, the parents and the student under the records laws are clearly entitled to copies of the student's grades.

CASE STUDY*
Breen v. Kahl

In the 1960s, long hair on males was very fashionable in a lot of places. But in the small community of Williams Bay, Wisconsin, long hair was viewed with disfavor, especially in the local high school. And to make sure that male students didn't let their locks grow too long, the Williams Bay School Board in 1967 passed a regulation to that effect. The regulation said boys' hair could not hang below the collar or over the ears. Boys were also required to be clean shaven and could not have long sideburns.

But in the fall of 1968 two boys—16-year-old Thomas Breen and 17-year-old James Anton—showed up at the high school with hair that was clearly longer than allowed by the regulation. The two refused to have their hair cut and were promptly expelled from school. However, Anton did get his hair cut shortly after being expelled and was allowed to return to school. But Breen, backed by his parents, refused to go to the barber. Instead, he appealed his expulsion to the Wisconsin Superintendent of Public Education, who upheld the school officials in Williams Bay. Breen and his parents, joined by Anton, then took their case to federal court.

In a hearing before U.S. District Judge James E. Doyle, Breen and Anton argued that the hair-length regulation violated the due process clause of the Fourteenth Amendment. As a result, they asked the judge to issue an injunction that would prohibit school officials from enforcing the regulation.

Williams Bay school officials countered by arguing that schools traditionally have had the right to set standards of conduct for their students. Moreover, they argued, Anton and Breen's long hair distracted other students from their school work. The school officials also contended that students whose appearance conforms to community standards do better in school than students who don't conform. A more extreme argument was offered by a high school principal from a school district near Williams Bay. The principal said that long hair on boys "symbolizes something that I feel is not in the best interests of good citizenship.... Whenever I see a long-hair youngster he is usually leading a riot, he has gotten through committing a crime, he is a dope addict or some such thing."

Doyle handed down his decision on February 20, 1969, and it turned out to be a major ruling on the rights of students. For the judge ruled that the hair-length regulation did indeed violate the constitution.

In reaching that conclusion, Doyle dealt with two major questions: (1) whether there is a constitutional right to wear long hair, and (2) whether that right extends to high school students as well as to adults. On the first question, Doyle said there is no question that something as personal as hair length is protected by the Constitution. He noted that if a city tried to pass an ordinance banning beards or requiring all men to wear short hair, that ordinance would quickly be thrown out by the courts. "In my view, with respect to adults, freedom to wear one's hair at a certain length or to wear a beard is constitutionally

*A summary of the case. For the court's complete opinion, see 296 F.Supp. 702 (1969). At the time of this case, William C. Kahl was State Superintendent of Public Instruction for the State of Wisconsin.

protected, even though it expresses nothing but individual taste," Doyle said. The judge went on to say that any effort to regulate hair length must bear "a substantial burden of justification, whether the attempted justification be in terms of health, physical danger to others, obscenity, or 'distraction' of others from their various pursuits."

Doyle then turned to the question of whether the right to wear long hair applies to high school students as well as to adults. He noted that the Williams Bay school officials had argued against any judicial intervention in the case, claiming this would only serve to undermine their authority and thus cause further disruption in the schools. But Doyle said expulsion from school is such a serious matter that the courts must intervene if students' rights are being violated. "It must not be forgotten, however small the community ... that when a school board undertakes to expel a public school student, it is undertaking to apply the terrible organized force of the state, just as surely as it is applied by the police, the courts, the prison warden, or the militia," Doyle said. As a result, he said, school regulations simply cannot be "immune from ... constitutional scrutiny by the courts."

As for the argument that the school's disciplinary powers might be undermined by an unfavorable court ruling, Doyle said: "It is important for [students] to appreciate the present vitality of our proud tradition that although we respect government in the exercise of its constitutional powers, we jealously guard our freedoms from its attempts to exercise unconstitutional powers." Moreover, Doyle said it is especially important that students be protected by the courts because students have no political power. "The students who are subjected to these regulations do not vote in school board elections," Doyle noted. "Political redress of their grievances is not open to them; theirs is a situation in which judicial vindication of constitutional protections has been considered particularly appropriate." The judge added: "Cautious counsel to avoid judicial involvement in serious constitutional issues merely because they concern younger people ... is neither prudent, expedient, or just. It is time to broaden the constitutional community by including within its protections younger people whose claim to dignity matches that of their elders."

Having determined that students have a constitutional right to wear long hair, Doyle then turned to the question of whether the hair-length regulation still could be justified on the grounds that Anton and Breen's long locks somehow distracted other students. Doyle found that this simply was not the case. "There is no direct testimony that such distraction has occurred," he said. "There has been no offer of the results of any empirical studies on the subject by educators, psychologists, psychiatrists, or other experts." Doyle thus concluded that "defendants [the school board] have fallen far short of showing that the distraction caused by male high school students whose hair length exceeds the Board standard is so aggravated, so frequent, so general, and so persistent that this invasion of their individual freedom by the state is warranted."

QUESTIONS FOR DISCUSSION

1. Does your school have dress and grooming rules? What are they?

2. The United States Supreme Court has refused to hear cases and arguments dealing with hair, grooming, and dress. Why do you think they have?

3. Are dress and grooming issues in the school constitutionally protected?

4. When and under what circumstances does the school have the right and responsibility to govern your personal dress and grooming habits?

SUGGESTED ACTIVITIES

1. Work through your student government in cooperation with your school administration to seek ways to improve your school's student handbook and athletic codes and present your findings and suggestions to your school board.

2. Review in other school law resources related dress and grooming cases and develop a list of the pro and con arguments relative to dress and grooming regulations. Determine from the facts of those cases why dress and grooming regulations seem to be so controversial (if they are) for your school, your parents, and your community.

VOCABULARY

Discipline
Injunction
Libelous
Litigation
Prurient
Unconstitutional
Warrant

RELATED LEGAL CASES

First Amendment:
1. *West Virginia State Board of Education* v. *Barnette,* Supreme Court of United States 319 U.S. 624 (1943)

2. *School District of Abington Township* v. *Schempp,* Supreme Court of United States 374 U.S. 203 (1963)

3. *Guzick* v. *Drebus,* U.S. Court of Appeals 431 F.2d 594 (6th Cir. 1970)

4. *Hernandez* v. *School District #1 Denver Colorado,* U.S. District Court 315 F.Supp. 289 (D. Colo. 1970)

5. *Trachtmen* v. *Anker,* U.S. Court of Appeals 2nd Circuit (1977), 563 F.2d 512 cert. denied 98 S.Ct. 1491 (1978)

Fourth Amendment:

1. *People* v. *Overton,* Ct. Appeals of New York (1967), 24 N.Y.2d 522 249 N.E.2d 366, 301 N.Y.S.2d 479 (1969)

2. *People* v. *Jacobson,* Supreme Ct. Appellate Term, First Dept., 65 — Misc.2d 909, 319 N.Y.S.2d 731 (1971)

3. *State* v. *Baccino,* Superior Court of Delaware, New Castle, 282 A.2d 869 (1971)

4. *In Re Scott K.,* 155 Cal. Rptr. 671 (May 25, 1979) *Search and seizure.* In re: L.L. LL, 280 N.W.2d 343 (1979) (Wisconsin). Must be reasonable suspicion that student has a dangerous or illegal item in his possession.

Fifth Amendment:

1. *Goldberg* v. *Kelly* 90 S.Ct. 1011 (1970)

Eighth Amendment:

1. *Ingraham* v. *Wright,* Supreme Court of the United States, 430 U.S. 651, 97 S.Ct. 1401 (1977)

2. *Baker* v. *Owen,* 395 F.Supp. 294 (1975) Affirmed 96 S.Ct. 210 (1975)

3. *Goss* v. *Lopez,* 419 U.S. 565, 95 S.Ct. 729, L.Ed.2d 725 (1975)

4. *Kersey* v. *Harvin,* 531 S.W.2d 76 (1975)

Fourteenth Amendment:

1. *Brown* v. *Board of Education,* Supreme Court of the United States, 347 U.S. 483 (1954)

2. *Hobsen* v. *Hansen,* United States Court of Appeals, 269 F.Supp. 401 (D.D.C.) (1967)

3. *San Antonio Independent School District* v. *Rodriquez,* Supreme Court of the United States, 411 U.S. 11 (1973)

4. *Lau* v. *Nichols,* Supreme Court of the United States, 94 S.Ct. 786 (1974)

SUGGESTED READINGS

"Firm, Fair, and Consistent: Classroom Activities on School Discipline," *Bill of Rights in Action,* September 1978, vol. 12, no. 3, pp. 17-19.

"Violent School or Safe School—How Does Your School Rate?" *Bill of Rights in Action,* September 1978, vol. 12, no. 3, p. 4.

SUGGESTED RESOURCES

Statutes of Wisconsin Relating to Elementary and Secondary Schools, August 1979 by Wisconsin Department of Public Instruction.

Louis Fisher and David Schimmel, *The Civil Rights of Students.* New York: Harper and Row, 1975.

Alan Sussman, *The Rights of Young People,* ACLU Handbook. New York: Avon Books, 1977.

Alexander Kern, *School Law.* St. Paul, MN: West Publishing, 1980.

SUGGESTED ORGANIZATIONS

Youth Policy and Law Center, Inc., 30 West Mifflin Street, Madison, Wisconsin 53703

Children's Legal Rights Information and Training Program, 2008 Hillyer Place, N.W. Washington, D.C. 20009

National Organization Legal Problems Education (NOLPE), 825 Western Avenue, Topeka, Kansas 66606.

SECTION III

THE CITIZEN-STUDENT, PARENTS, AND MARRIAGE

CONTENTS

7

The Citizen-Student and the Family

For the first eighteen years or more of your life you will probably live with your parents. When you are young they will provide food and clothing and a place for you to live, but as you grow older you may assume some of these responsibilities yourself. If you become a parent before you reach the **age of majority** (18 years of age), you will have the same responsibilities as an adult parent, no matter how old you are.

The relationship between parents and children is a very special one and is subject to many rules of both statutory and case law. Each has certain obligations toward the other. The state also has an interest in protecting young people, particularly children who are unable to protect themselves. Therefore, if parents fail to discharge their responsibilities to their children, the state may step in and go so far as to remove the children from the parents' **custody,** if that seems best for the child.

The material in this section is designed to point out some of the problems that arise from the parent-child relationship and suggest ways that the law deals with these problems.

What are my parents' duties and my duties?

Parents have a duty to provide their minor children with support, education, and protection and the children have a duty to render obedience and services to their parents.

What does my parents' duty to support me mean?

In general, they must provide you with necessary shelter, food, medical care, and education. Of course, they don't have to buy anything that is very expensive; they simply have to give you those things that you really need and that they can afford to provide. (Wis. Stat. 48.40)

Parents are required by law to provide their children with food, shelter, and other support.

What does my parents' duty to educate and protect me mean?

This does not just mean that they must send you to school, but they must also provide you with normal parental attention, care, and instruction. The amount of care a parent must give depends on the age of the child; naturally, a small child requires more attention than does a teenager. However the parents of teenagers must provide some care and must not create an atmosphere which is detrimental to the physical, mental, or moral health of their children. (Wis. Stat. 48.40)

What will happen if my parents don't do these things?

If your parents fail to support you when they can afford to do so, if they abandon you, if they fail to care for you and protect you, or if they create an unhealthy or immoral atmosphere in your home, the juvenile court can end your parents' rights and take custody away from them. (Wis. Stat. 48.40). The juvenile court could say that you were "neglected" or "dependent" and could:

1. leave you in your own home under the supervision of the county welfare board or a child-placing agency, or

2. transfer legal custody to a child-placing agency, or

3. order your parents to provide any special care or treatment you may need. (Wis. Stat. 48.35)

Can my parents be arrested if they don't support me?

If you are under 18 and are needy it is a **misdemeanor,** punishable by up to nine months in jail or a fine of $10,000, if your parents can afford to support you and intentionally fail to do so.

Do I have to obey my parents?

Yes. If you are under 18 and if your parents can't control you or you are habitually disobedient, the juvenile court could say that you are a "delinquent child." (Wis. Stat. 48.12) The judge might simply counsel you and your parents, but the court might, if it thought it was necessary, put you under the supervision of a probation officer, transfer custody to a child-placing agency, a foster home, or the Department of Health and Social Services.

What can happen if I run away from home?

If you are under 18, a police officer can take you into custody immediately, without a warrant, if you have run away from your parents or if the officer reasonably believes that you have. (Wis. Stat. 48.991) No arrest warrant is necessary because this is not an arrest; the police only take you into custody to stop you from running away. (Wis. Stat. 48.28)

A young father shares in the caring for his child.

What can the police do with me after they pick me up?

Your parents will be notified immediately and you may be released to go home with them if they agree to bring you to court in case that is necessary. However, you can be kept for twenty-four hours in a detention home, a foster home, or any other suitable place if your welfare requires it or if it is necessary for the "protection of the community." The authorities cannot keep you for more than forty-eight hours without the permission of the juvenile court judge. (Wis. Stat. 48.29, .30)

What if I run away to another state?

Your parents can still get you back. Wisconsin, along with 41 other states and the District of Columbia, belongs to the "Interstate Compact of Juveniles." This means that the governments of all these states have agreed to return runaway **minors** to their homes in other states. (Wis. Stat. 48.991)

How does this work?

The procedure is complicated, but usually it begins when your parents ask a court in the state of Wisconsin to send a requisition (request) to the other state for your return. They must show the court that you are not an independent minor and that by running away you have endangered your own welfare or that of others. When the courts or governor of the other state get the requisition, the police there may take you into custody. The courts of that state will then decide whether the requisition is legal and, if it is, return you to Wisconsin. (Wis. Stat. 48.991)

Can my parents hit me or punish me physically if I don't obey them?

Yes. Parents may use reasonable force to "restrain a child" in the exercise of their lawful authority over the child.

What does this mean?

This applies to any person under eighteen years old or to any school pupil. Not only parents and legal guardians but also step-parents can use physical punishment if they have supported the child and treated the minor as a member of the family.

How much force can my parents use?

"Reasonable force" does not include so much force that you would be severely injured. If you parents really injure you they may be guilty of child abuse, a **felony,** or aggravated battery, also a felony, depending on how badly you are hurt. (Wis. Stat. 490.201) In Wisconsin, minors have a right to sue their parents for neglect or injurious conduct. *(Goller* v. *White,* 20 Wis.2d 402, 122 N.W.2d 193, 1963)

What should I do if I suspect that a friend of mine is being physically abused?

The law in Wisconsin expresses a public policy to protect the neglected or abused child. It requires certain individuals (teachers, doctors, police officers, and social workers) to report to their local authorities cases of child abuse. Although you, as students, are not required to report these cases, it may be a good idea to tell a school official if you sincerely believe that a classmate or friend of yours is being abused or neglected by his or her parents. (Wis. Stat. 49.981, 940.201)

If I have a job do my parents have a right to my earnings?

Yes. Your parents are entitled to your "services" because they support you. However, if a parent refuses to provide for your support, your earnings are your sole property in Wisconsin. (Wis. Stat. 48.987)

If my parents' marriage is dissolved, can I decide which one I want to live with?

The court has the power to decide custody of all minor children. Wisconsin law requires the judge to follow certain rules in deciding which parents should have custody: the judge must consider all the facts, the judge must not give custody to the mother or father simply because of their sex, and the judge must make the decision that is in the best interests of the child. (Wis. Stat. 247.23, .24) The court will often allow older children to live with the parent they prefer.

If I live with one parent can I visit the other parent?

Yes. The court may only deny visitation rights to the parent who does not have custody if it is in your best interest not to see that parent. In Wisconsin, an attorney is required to be appointed to represent the minor in every case involving custody disputes. The clearest statement of this position was made by the Supreme Court of Wisconsin, which declared that legal representation "is due the children who are not to be buffeted around as mere chattels in a divorce controversy, but rather are to be treated as interested and affected parties whose welfare should be the prime concern of the court in its custody determination." (*Wendland* v. *Wendland,* 29 Wis.2d 145, 138 N.W.2d 185, 191, 1965)

Can I get medical care without my parents' consent?

A minor can get certain kinds of medical care in some cases without parental consent; usually however, the parents' consent is required. The exceptions to the general rule are as follows:

1. Minors living separately from their parents and managing their own money, where their parents neglect or refuse to support them, may obtain any kind of medical and health care. (Wis. Stat. 48.99)

2. Any minor who has been married or who has had a child may consent to any kind of medical or other health care. (Wis. Stat. 880.26)

3. Any minor may give consent to medical care to determine the presence of or to treat venereal disease. (Wis. Stat. 143.07)

If I get medical care under these rules, will the doctor tell my parents?

Not necessarily. In Wisconsin and in every other state, communications between a doctor and patient are considered "privileged," that is, information communicated to or discovered by a physician cannot be disclosed to anyone other than the patient or to persons authorized by the patient. Recent judicial interpretations of the doctor-patient privilege indicate that when the patient is a minor, the privilege is extended just as securely as if he or she were an adult.

What is emancipation?

Emancipation refers to the ending of the legal ties between parent and child. Wisconsin law does not provide any exact definition. In general parents give up their right to the child's services and their right to control the child; on the other hand, their duty to support the child is ended.

Emancipation does not have to be complete; it can be partial or limited. For example, the parents' right to services and control may end, but they still may have the duty to support the child. Or, there may be complete emancipation even though the child still lives with his parents.

Packing up to start school or a job away from home may represent an informal kind of emancipation.

CASE STUDY*
In re Phillip B.

Parents in this country traditionally have had a great deal of freedom in raising their children, a freedom that the courts have protected many times. But this freedom is not absolute because the state also has an interest in children's welfare. Sometimes the interests of the parents and the state collide, as happened in California in 1979 with a 12-year-old boy named Phillip (last names are not used in juvenile court proceedings). The dispute over Phillip's welfare led to a lengthy court battle that centered on the question of whether the state of California could require the boy to have an operation against his parents' wishes.

Phillip, who had lived in a special residential-care facility since birth, suffered from a genetic disorder known as Down's syndrome or mongolism. Because of this, Phillip was mentally retarded and also suffered from various physical ailments often associated with the disorder. Phillip's most serious problem was a congenital heart defect that caused his heart to work three times as hard as the average person's. As a result, the boy's blood pressure was extremely high. Moreover, the defect was gradually damaging his lungs, which doctors said eventually would be unable to supply oxygen to his bloodstream. When that happened, Phillip would die.

As early as 1973, doctors who examined Phillip had recommended certain medical tests to learn more about his heart problem. At first, his parents would not allow the tests. However, in 1977 they finally consented to the tests, which showed that Phillip's problem was a hole between the right and left ventricles or chambers of his heart. The doctors agreed that surgery would be required to correct the problem. But the doctors also said that surgery would be dangerous because Down's syndrome children have a higher than average risk of post-operative complications. In Phillip's case, the doctors said, there was a five to ten percent chance that he would die on the operating table. But without the surgery, they said, Phillip would slowly waste away and die within twenty years.

Despite that diagnosis, Phillip's parents refused to authorize the surgery. It was then that California juvenile officials moved in. They filed a petition asking that Phillip be declared a special dependent of the court so that he could have the operation. The petition was based on a California law that allows state officials to act on behalf of a child whose parents have failed to provide him with the "necessities of life." But after holding a hearing on the case, a juvenile court judge dismissed the state's petition. The judge said the state had not provided "clear and convincing evidence" that Phillip's parents, by refusing to permit the operation, had in fact denied him the necessities of life. Following the judge's ruling, the state took its case to the California Court of Appeal, which on May 8, 1979, upheld the lower court decision.

In its ruling, the appeals court began by noting that other courts have stated time and again that "parental authority is constitutionally protected." The appeals court said that "inherent in this preference for parental autonomy is a commitment to diverse lifestyles,

---

*This is a summary of the case. For the court's complete opinion, see 92 Cal.App.3d 796, 156 Cal. Rptr. 48 (1979). The U.S. Supreme Court denied certiorari (or refused to consider hearing the case) in 1980 when the state of California brought an appeal to that court.

including the right of parents to raise their children as they think best." Yet the court also pointed out that "parental autonomy is not absolute. The state is the guardian of society's basic values ... [and] has a right, indeed, a duty, to protect children." As a result, the court said, "where parents fail to provide their children with adequate medical care, the state is justified to intervene." But the court said that in such cases, the state "has a serious burden of justification before abridging parental autonomy by substituting its judgment for that of the parents."

The appeals court went on to say that a number of "relevant factors" must be considered before the state can require a child to receive medical treatment that is opposed by the parents. Among those factors, the court said, are: (1) the seriousness of the medical problem facing the child; (2) the evaluation of the child's doctors; (3) the risks of any proposed medical treatment; and (4) the wishes of the child himself. In Phillip's case, the court said, the testimony of medical experts was inconclusive as to the benefits and risks of surgery to repair his heart defect. The court mentioned the testimony of one doctor, who said at the juvenile court hearing that surgery on Phillip would be especially difficult because the boy had already suffered some damage to his blood vessels as a result of his heart condition. Another doctor at the hearing also pointed out that surgery might damage some of the nerves controlling the boy's heart. If that happened, the doctor said, Phillip would have to have a pacemaker implanted to control his heartbeat.

In view of all this, the appeals court concluded: "We cannot say as a matter of law that there was no substantial evidence to support the decision off the [juvenile] court." Thus no operation could be performed on Phillip's heart without the consent of his parents.

The case of Phillip B. did not end with the decision of the California court of appeals. Pat and Herb Heath, a couple unrelated to Phillip, but who know him well, have sought to obtain legal guardianship of Phillip through the courts. This action is currently being contested in California and to date no final decision has been reached in the courts.

QUESTIONS FOR DISCUSSION

1. Do you agree with the court's reasoning that the rationale for denying life-sustaining surgery is that Phillip's parents may not live long enough to care for him in his later years?

2. What are the implications for persons who are emotionally unstable or physically infirm if life-sustaining surgery can be denied on the grounds that they might not be able to "make it" on their own as adults?

3. At what point do you think the state should intervene to protect minors from arbitrary and capricious decisions of parents that will result in the death of their children?

4. Do you know of any new developments in this case that have been reported in the newspapers or on television?

When does emancipation occur?

It is difficult to tell when emancipation occurs. You are automatically emancipated when you become eighteen, although it can happen earlier. Parent and child don't have to have a written or oral agreement for emancipation to occur. Normally you can tell if a minor is emancipated by looking at his or her conduct and that of his or her parents. Marriage and membership in the armed forces usually emancipate a child automatically, even when he or she is below the age of majority and even if no court has granted a decree.

SUGGESTED ACTIVITIES

1. Invite a family relations lawyer to visit the classroom to discuss cases and situations he or she has dealt with of parents' activity within or abusing their legal authority.

2. Arrange for a visit to or a visit from a person in the Wisconsin Department of Health and Social Services. A family case worker could discuss the procedures that are followed when a case of child neglect is reported.

3. Try to arrange a visit with a family court judge. Ask about procedures followed in the hearing of a neglect case and what the judge looks for in reaching a decision.

VOCABULARY

Age of majority
Consent
Custody
Emancipation
Felony
Minor
Misdemeanor

SUGGESTED READINGS

David Schimmel and Louis Fisher, *The Rights of Parents.* Columbia, MD: The National Committee for Citizens in Education, 1977.

"What is Child Abuse?" *Bill of Rights in Action* Los Angeles: Constitutional Rights Foundation, February, 1979, vol. 13, no. 1, p. 11.

"Cases on the Parent-Child Relationship," *Update,* Fall, 1977, vol. 2, no. 2, pp. 26-27.

Children and The Law. St. Paul, MN: West Publishing, 1981.

"What Do You Think Should be Done?" *Bill of Rights in Action.* Los Angeles: Constitutional Rights Foundation, April 1979, vol. 13, no. 2, p. IXXX.

SUGGESTED RESOURCES

Department of Health and Social Services. Madison, Wisconsin

Wisconsin Statutes

Children's Legal Rights Journal, Children's Legal Rights Information and Training Program, 2008 Hillyer Place, N.W., Washington, D.C. 20009.

Looking Glass (monthly newsletter), Youth Policy and Law Center, 30 W. Mifflin St., Room 904, Madison, Wisconsin 53703.

Mock Trials: Scripts for Wisconsin Lawyers and Teachers. Published by Wisconsin Department of Public Instruction in cooperation with The Wisconsin Bar Foundation. Bulletin No. 0166, 1980.

Mock trials include: automobile accident, landlord-tenant, drunk driving, homicide, burglary, and child abuse scripts.

RELATED LEGAL CASES

Opinion Attorney General June 1, 1977 (liability for torts resulting from failure of parent to exercise control over child when parents know or should have known that absence of control would cause injury)

Wendland v. *Wendland,* 29 Wis.2d 145, 138 N.W.2d 185, at 191 (1965).

Goller v. *White,* 20 Wis.2d 402, 122 N.W.2d 193 (1963).

State ex rel Lewis v. *Lutheran Social Services of Wisconsin and Upper Michigan,* 68 Wis.2d 36, 227 N.W.2d 643 (1975); *Marquette Law Review,* vol. 59, no. 2, p. 347 (termination of parental rights)

Morotz v. *Morotz,* 259 N.W.2d 524 (1977). *Delchambre* v. *Delchambre,* 86 Wis.2d 538, 273 N.W.2d 301 (1979). (review of custody allowed if substantial change in circumstances)

Niesen v. *Niesen,* 38 Wis.2d 599, 157 N.W.2d 660 (1968). (interest of putative father protected by law)

Stanley v. *Illinois,* 405 U.S. 645 (1972). (when child was self-supporting parents released of obligation to support) 386 Southern 2d 472 (1980)

Erdmann v. *Erdmann,* 67 Wis.2d 116 (1975). *Miller* v. *Miller,* 67 Wis.2d 435 227 N.W.2d 627. (support obligation limited to minor children only)

MARRIAGE
LICENSES

8

The Citizen-Student and Marriage

Marriage is obviously a serious undertaking. Marriage gives rise to many legal obligations and rights which are enforceable in a court of law. These rights and obligations are of concern not only to the person directly involved but to the people of the state of Wisconsin as well. Accordingly, the state has established rules closely governing the process of marrying and dissolving marriages and the rights of the parties during the marriage relationship.

GETTING MARRIED

When can I get married?

1. If you are eighteen years of age or older, you can get married without your parents' consent whether you are a young man or young woman. (Wis.Stat. 765.02)

2. If you are sixteen or seventeen years old, you may marry if you have the written consent of your parents or guardian. (Wis.Stat. 765.02)

3. If you are younger than sixteen years of age, you may not marry even if you have the written consent of your parents. (Wis.Stat. 765.02) This requirement cannot be waived for any reason by anyone.

How do I get a marriage license?

You must apply for the license from the county clerk in the county where one of the parties has resided for the preceding thirty days. Under oath, you must tell the clerk your name, address, age, and if you have ever been married before. You must wait for five days to get the license after filling out the application. The clerk may refuse

to give you a license if you are too young, if you are already married, if you are applying to marry a relative closer than a second cousin, or if you are incompetent (unable to function alone). (Wis.Stat. 765.03, .09)

What can happen if we lie about our ages to get married?

1. If either of you is so young that you could not be married at all, the marriage is absolutely void. The law will treat you as if you had never gone through a marriage ceremony.

2. If you were married without the consent of your parents and consent was necessary, the marriage is voidable. This means that the person who was underage at the time of the marriage may go to court and have the marriage ended by **annulment.** (Wis.Stat. 767.02)

3. Lying under oath is called **perjury** and is a very serious crime. If you lie to the clerk of court about your age after having sworn to tell the truth you might be prosecuted or declared delinquent. (Wis.Stat. 765.30)

Do I have to get a blood test to get married?

Yes. Within at least twenty days before applying for a license, a blood test is required for syphillis and venereal disease. (Wis.Stat. 765.06)

Who can perform a marriage ceremony?

Any judge or licensed or ordained minister may perform a marriage ceremony. (Wis.Stat. 765.16)

If I go to another state to get married, will that marriage be recognized in Wisconsin?

There is a general rule of law, recognized in Wisconsin, that if the marriage is **valid** under the laws of the state in which it is performed, it is valid everywhere. The marriage first has to be valid in the state where it is performed. For example, an Ohio marriage is recognized as valid in Wisconsin, if it was valid under Ohio law when performed there. (Wis.Stat. 765.04)

What legal obligations result from a valid marriage?

Marriage is a kind of personal contract between two consenting parties of the opposite sex. That means that each of the two people involved has certain duties toward the other partner. The state has an interest in this kind of contract and the partners cannot decide to end the marriage unless the state agrees and dissolves the marriage. (Wis.Stat. 765.001) Each spouse has a duty to support the other spouse and children, and to pay for their necessities. Even if the marriage is dissolved, each spouse must continue to support his or her children and may have to provide for his or her former spouse through **mainte-**

nance payments or property division. (Wis.Stat. 767.08) The reasons for **dissolution** (breaking up a marriage) indicated below also give you an idea of some of the legal obligations of marriage. For example, since a reason for dissolution is continuous separation of one year or more, it follows that your legal obligation is to stay with and support your spouse as much as you can.

DISSOLVING THE MARRIAGE

It's been said that marriage is not a state to be lightly entered into. One of the most important reasons for this statement is the legal and emotional complexity of the process of dissolving the marriage. The dissolution, of a marriage or divorce, has been likened to attempting to unscramble eggs!

The Wisconsin Statutes (Chapter 105, Laws of 1977) were recently revised not with the intention of making divorce, **annulment,** or legal **separation** easier to obtain, but rather for the purpose of promoting fair and reasonable settlement of the economic and custodial issues involved in marriage relationships.

What are the grounds for annulment of a marriage?

A court may annul a marriage entered into under the following circumstances:

1. One person lacks the ability to consent to the marriage at the time the marriage was solemnized, either because of age, mental incapacity or infirmity, or because of the influence of alcohol, drugs, or other incapacitating substances, or a person entered into a marriage by force

Every couple considering dissolution of their marriage is encouraged to seek counseling.

CASE STUDY*
Kraemer v. Kraemer

Edward and Ellen Kraemer of Calumet County, Wisconsin, had been married for more than 12 years when, in 1973, Mrs. Kraemer filed for divorce. By the time their case got to court, the couple had already divided much of their property in anticipation of the final divorce decree. However, there was one very important issue they could not agree on, and that was who would get custody of their 4-year-old son. It was thus up to Calumet County Judge David H. Sebora, who presided over the Kraemers' case, to decide which parent should have custody of the boy.

The judge made his decision in August 1973, granting Mrs. Kraemer, then 31, a divorce and awarding her custody of their son. In his order, the judge gave no basis for his decision on the custody question, although it was common practice at that time to award custody to the mother rather than the father. As part of the divorce decree, Edward Kraemer was given the right to visit his son at least once a week, with more frequent visitations permitted during the summer months. Kraemer was also required to pay a certain amount weekly toward support of the boy.

Mr. Kraemer was dissatisfied with the custody ruling and other aspects of the divorce decree, so he appealed to the Wisconsin Supreme Court. Among other things, Kraemer claimed that Judge Sebora had abused his discretion by awarding custody to Mrs. Kraemer without giving any reason for his decision. Custody must be awarded on the basis of what is in the child's best interests, Kraemer argued, and not on the basis of the parent's sex.

The Wisconsin Supreme Court, in a decision handed down in March 1975, agreed with Kraemer's arguments. While upholding most provisions of the divorce decree, the court said that Judge Sebora's ruling on the custody issue was based on inadequate findings of fact. "On the matter of the custody of the minor child, there is no finding of fact by the trial court as to what the best interests of the child are," the Supreme Court said. "The trial court merely awards custody to the mother.... There is no reference to the basis of the trial court's decision. It is therefore impossible for this court to determine on review whether the trial court ruled properly on the basis of the best interests of the child, which is always the controlling consideration."

The Supreme Court went on to say that "sex alone cannot be used as the sole basis for making a custody award." As a result, the court sent the case back to Judge Sebora, ordering him to make findings as to what would be in the son's best interests before awarding custody to either parent.

In line with the Supreme Court's ruling, Judge Sebora ordered a hearing on the custody issue to be held in August 1975. Following that hearing, the judge instructed the Calumet County Social Services Department to make a custody study to help determine what would be in the child's best interest. The Social Services Department completed its report in September 1975, but as it turned out, the report wasn't needed. For, in the interim, Edward Kraemer had decided to drop his efforts to gain custody of the boy. In November 1975, Judge Sebora then issued his final order in the case of *Kraemer v. Kraemer*, ruling once again that the boy should stay with his mother.

---

*This is a summary of the case. For the court's complete opinion, see 67 Wis.2d 319, 227 N.W.2d 61 (1975).

QUESTIONS FOR DISCUSSION

1. What do you think the difference in approach would be in 'determining the best interests of the child' if the child were six years old? twelve years old? or seventeen years old?

2. Kraemer establishes that the sex of the parent alone cannot be used as the sole basis for making a custody award. Why is this important to you now and in the future?

---

or duress, or by fraud involving the essentials of marriage. Suit may be brought by either person, or by the legal representative of a person lacking the capacity to consent, no later than one year after he or she finds out about the described condition.

2. One person lacks the capacity to consummate the marriage by sexual intercourse, and at the time the marriage was solemnized the other party did not know of the incapacity.

3. One person was sixteen or seventeen years of age and did not have the consent of his or her parent or guardian or judicial approval, or a person sixteen years of age. Suit may be brought by the underaged party or by a parent or guardian at any time prior to the party's attaining the age of eighteen years, but a parent or guardian must bring the suit within one year of finding out about the marriage.

4. The marriage is prohibited by the laws of this state. Suit may be brought by either party within ten years of the marriage. (Wis.Stat. 767.03)

When may a court grant a judgment of divorce or legal separation?

A court can grant a judgment of divorce or legal separation if:

1. The requirements for residence and marriage assessment counseling have been complied with.

2. The court finds that the marriage is irretrievably broken as provided under the law.

3. The court has considered, approved, or made provision for child custody, the support of any child of the marriage entitled to support, the maintenance of either spouse, the support of the family, and the disposition of property. (Wis.Stat. 767.07)

What is the purpose of marriage assessment counseling for divorce, separation, and annulment actions?

In every action for annulment, divorce, or legal separation, the family court commissioner must inform the parties of the availability of coun-

seling for marriage assessment, divorce, and separation as well as referral services offered by the family court. The purpose of the counseling is to explore the possibility of **reconciliation,** to enable the parties to adjust to the status of being unmarried persons, to prepare the parties to live separate lives, and, finally, to assist the parties in planning for the needs of their minor children (if any). (Wis.Stat. 767.081)

When is a marriage "irretrievably broken?"

If both the parties, by petition or otherwise, have stated under oath that the marriage is irretrievably broken, or if the parties have voluntarily lived apart continuously for twelve months or more just before beginning the divorce action and one party has so stated, the court, after hearing, must find that the marriage is irretrievably broken.

If the parties have not voluntarily lived apart for at least twelve months just before beginning the action and if only one party has stated under oath that the marriage is irretrievably broken, the court will consider all relevant factors, including the circumstances that give rise to filing the petition and the prospect of reconciliation. The court then has two choices:

1. If the court finds no reasonable prospect of reconciliation, it will make a finding that the marriage is irretrievably broken.

2. If the court finds that there is a reasonable prospect of reconciliation, it will continue the matter for further hearing within sixty days, and may suggest to the parties that they seek counseling. At the adjourned hearing, if either party states under oath that the marriage is irretrievably broken, the court will make a finding whether the marriage is irretrievably broken. (Wis.Stat. 767.12-2)

What factors do the courts use to determine custody of children?

The law requires that in making a custody determination the court must "consider all facts in the best interest of the child and shall not prefer one potential custodian over the other on the basis of the sex of the custodian." (Wis.Stat. 767.24) Factors taken into considering in making a determination of child custody are:

1. The wishes of the child's parent or parents as to custody.

2. The interaction and interrelationship of the child with his or her parent or parents, siblings, and any other person who may significantly affect the child's best interest.

3. The child's adjustment to the home, school, religion, and community.

4. The mental and physical health of the parties, the minor children, and other persons living in a proposed custodial household.

5. The availability of public or private child-care services.

In determining custody, the best interests of the child come first.

6. Such other factors as the court may in each individual case determine to be relevant. (Wis.Stat. 767.24 1m)

Are divorced parents entitled to visitation rights?

Yes. The law makes it clear that a parent is entitled to reasonable visitation rights unless the court finds, after a hearing, that visitation would endanger the child's physical, mental, or emotional health. Also, visitation may not be denied for failure to pay alimony or child support.

In addition, wherever the court grants visitation rights to a parent, the other parent must obtain the written approval of the parent with visitation rights or permission of the court in order to establish legal residence outside Wisconsin or to remove the child from Wisconsin for a period of time exceeding 90 days. (Wis.Stat. 767.245)

Who is required to provide child support in cases of annulment, divorce, or legal separation?

The court may order either or both parents to pay an amount reasonable or necessary for support of a child, after considering the following:

1. The financial resources of the child.

2. The financial resources of both parents.

3. The standard of living the child would have enjoyed had the marriage not ended.

4. The desirability of the parent who has the child remaining in the home as a full-time parent.

5. The cost of day care if the parent with the child works outside the home, or the value of child-care services performed by that parent if she or he remains in the home.

6. The physical and emotional health needs of the child.

7. The child's educational needs.

8. The tax consequences to each party. (Wis.Stat. 767.25)

How is the property divided when a marriage is dissolved?

The law requires the court to presume that all property except gifts and inherited property is to be divided equally between the parties— although a portion of the property may be set aside by the court in a trust fund for the support, maintenance, education, and general welfare of the children.

The court may, however, not divide the property equally between the parties after considering:

1. The length of the marriage.

2. The property brought to the mariage by each party.

3. The contribution of each party to the marriage, giving appropriate economic value to each party's contribution in homemaking and child-care services.

4. The age and physical and emotional health of the parties.

5. The contribution of one party to the education, training, or increased earning power of the other.

6. The earning capacity of each party.

7. The desirability of awarding the family home or the right to live therein for a reasonable period to the party having custody of any children.

8. Other economic circumstances of each party, including pension benefits.

9. The tax consequences to each party.

10. Any written agreement made by the parties before or during the marriage concerning any arrangement for property distribution is binding upon the court. (Wis.Stat. 767.255)

What factors determine who pays alimony or "maintenance payments?"

The court may order either party to make maintenance payments for a limited or indefinite length of time after considering the following:

1. The length of the marriage.

2. The age and physical and emotional health of the parties.

3. The distribution of property.

4. The educational level of each party at the time of marriage and at the time the action is commenced.

5. The earning capacity of the party seeking maintenance.

6. The feasibility that the party seeking maintenance can become self-supporting at a standard of living reasonably comparable to that enjoyed during the marriage and, if so, the length of time necessary to achieve this goal.

7. The tax consequences to each party. (Wis.Stat. 767.26)

How long does one have to pay alimony?

As long as the court orders. However, if the payee has remarried, the court will on application of the payer and upon proof of remarriage, cancel the order requiring **alimony** payments. (Wis.Stat. 767.32)

What can happen if a person fails to pay child support or alimony?

There are a number of options available to the court to deal with a party who has a financial obligation as a result of dissolution of a marriage.

1. He or she may be held in contempt of court and put in jail. (Wis.Stat. 767.305, 295.02)

2. The employer can be ordered to withhold enough salary to meet maintenance payments, child support, or family support payments.

Is it possible for the wife to have her maiden name restored?

Yes. This is most often granted by the courts if the wife requests it when she brings the dissolution petition. (Wis.Stat. 767.20)

CASE STUDY*
Marvin v. Marvin

In 1964, while filming a movie, actor Lee Marvin met a woman named Michelle Triola. Marvin, at that time separated from his wife, was a successful actor who had starred in many Hollywood movies. Triola, on the other hand, was a not very successful singer whose movie career had been limited to a few bit parts. Soon after meeting, Marvin and Triola began seeing each other daily and having frequent sexual relations. As time went on, the two became almost constant companions. Triola accompanied Marvin to the South Seas, Europe, and other movie locales. She also shared a beach house with him in the posh California community of Malibu. All told, the two lived together off and on for more than six years. But they never seriously considered marriage, which Marvin was strongly opposed to. In about 1970 the relationship began to sour and Marvin finally kicked Triola out. That action set the stage for a landmark lawsuit on the issue of what financial obligations, if any, a man has to a woman he has lived with but never married. (The word "palimony," a combination of "pal" and "alimony," was soon coined to describe any payments a man might owe in such a situation.)

In her lawsuit, Triola claimed that since she had performed all the duties of a wife she was entitled to half of the $3.6 million Marvin earned during the period they lived together. (Under California's community property law, almost all property acquired by a man and woman during their marriage must be divided equally at the time of divorce.) Triola said Marvin had promised to take care of her financially if they ever broke up. "What I have is yours and what you have is mine," Triola quoted Marvin as saying shortly after their relationship began. These words, Triola contended, amounted to an express contract (one based on something spoken or written) between her and Marvin. Triola also claimed that she had an implied contract (one based on a person's acts or conduct) with Marvin because he had treated her as a wife during the six years they lived together.

Marvin, however, denied that he had ever promised Triola anything or that their relationship was one of husband and wife. He said their relationship was primarily sexual and that he viewed Triola as a live-in lover, not a wife. As a result, Marvin said, there had never been a contract—either express or implied—between them.

Triola's lawsuit first came before Los Angeles County Superior Court Judge William Munnell, who listened to six weeks of testimony before ruling in Marvin's favor. Munnell granted what is known as judgment on the pleadings, which means he ruled that Triola did not have a legitimate cause of action to bring before a jury. The judge based his ruling on a finding that Triola's relationship with Marvin was essentially a sexual one. Munnell's decision reflected the traditional reluctance of judges to enforce a contract between unmarried persons because of the belief that to do so would seriously damage the institution of marriage.

Triola quickly appealed to the California Supreme Court, which in December of 1976 reversed Munnell's ruling and said Triola did have legal grounds to sue Marvin. In its ruling,

*This is a summary of the case. For the court's complete opinion, see 18 Cal.3d 660, 134 Cal. Rptr. 815, 557 P.2d 106 (1976) and Judge Arthur K. Marshall's unpublished memorandum opinion in Case No. C23303 of April 18, 1979.

the court said that "adults who voluntarily live together and engage in sexual relations are . . . as competent as any other persons to contract respecting their earnings and property rights. Of course, they cannot lawfully contract to pay for the performance of sexual services, for such a contract is, in essence, an agreement for prostitution and unlawful for that reason." But in Triola's case, the court said, her relationship with Marvin clearly involved more than sexual services. Moreover, the court said Triola could sue not only on the grounds that she had an express contract with Marvin, but also on the grounds that there was an implied contract between them. The court's ruling in this respect was precedent setting because up until then courts had refused to enforce implied contracts between unmarried couples.

As part of its ruling, the Supreme Court remanded the case back to a lower court for a trial on the issue of whether Triola did indeed have an express or implied contract with Marvin that entitled her to half of his property. The trial was held in 1979 before Los Angeles Superior Court Judge Arthur K. Marshall. More than sixty witnesses were called during the lengthy trial, and the transcript of their testimony filled over 8,000 pages.

Marshall finally issued his decision in April of 1979, ruling that Triola had failed to prove that she had either an express or implied contract with Marvin. Among other things, Marshall found that Marvin could not have intended to make an express contract with Triola when he allegedly told her in late 1964 that "what I have is yours and what you have is mine." Marshall noted that "in 1964 defendant [Marvin] was married; he had considerable unresolved financial problems; he had repeatedly informed plaintiff [Triola] that he did not believe in marriage because of the property rights which a wife thereby acquires. Plaintiff could not have understood that phrase ['what I have is yours'] to accord the same rights to one who was *not* defendant's wife." The judge went on to say that "it is more reasonable to conclude that the declaration was simply hyperbole typical of persons who live and work in the entertainment field. It was defendant's way of expressing his affection for the plaintiff."

As for an implied contract, Marshall said the conduct of Marvin and Triola during their six years together did not suggest that they believed some sort of contract existed between them. Moreover, Marshall noted that Triola herself once told an interviewer that she and Marvin "'were always very proud of the fact that nothing really held us. We both agreed . . . that you work harder at a relationship when you know that there is nothing really holding you.'" Because of this and other testimony, Marshall concluded that Marvin and Triola "came together because of mutual affection and not because of a mutual consent to a contract."

Triola (who in 1970 changed her name to Marvin) did not come out of her long court battle empty-handed, however. For Marshall did order Marvin to pay her $104,000 "for rehabilitation purposes so that she may have the economic means to re-educate herself and to learn new, employable skills . . . so that she may return from her status as a companion of a motion picture star to a separate, independent but perhaps more prosaic existence."

Subsequently Lee Marvin appealed Judge Marshall's decision to award $104,000 to Michele Triola. The California Court of Appeal overturned the monetary award on the grounds that it "is without support in either equity or law." Triola has since countered with her own appeal to the California Supreme Court.

QUESTIONS FOR DISCUSSION

1. The *Marvin* case creates a burden of proof necessary to make a claim of support to one party after a period of time together. How does this compare to Wisconsin law?

2. In light of the *Marvin* case, do you think the Wisconsin law is fair to both parties?

3. Do you know of any new developments in this case that have been reported in the newspapers or on television?

SUGGESTED ACTIVITY

Assume that you have decided to get married. You have parental consent if you are sixteen or seventeen or you have reached the age of majority, eighteen.

You decide that before the ceremony you and your chosen partner will sit down and draft a prenuptial agreement.

The agreement should include:

1. Why you have decided to get married.
2. A listing of his responsibilities in the marriage.
3. A listing of her responsibilities in the marriage.
4. A listing of both your mutually shared responsibilities in the marriage.
5. Mutually agreed upon remedies or due process in event of a conflict. How you would resolve disagreements.
6. View this agreement as a contract which both would sign prior to marriage.

You may wish to do this on an individual basis or pair with a member of the opposite gender.

VOCABULARY

Alimony
Annulment
Dissolution
Incompetant
Maintenance
Perjury
Reconciliation
Separation
Valid

SUGGESTED READING

"The Best Interest of the Child," *Bill of Rights in Action*. Los Angeles: Constitutional Rights Foundation, February, 1979, vol. 13, no. 1, pp. 17-18.

SUGGESTED RESOURCES

Wisconsin Department of Health and Social Services, Bureau of Children, Youth and Families. 534 WS State Office Building, Madison 53702.

Wisconsin Statutes

SECTION IV

THE CITIZEN-STUDENT AND THE COMMUNITY

CONTENTS

9

The Citizen-Student and Personal Responsibilities

This chapter deals with rights and responsibilities which are initiated or pursued primarily from the home. You will notice that these are mostly recreational in nature and of major interest at this time in your life.

DRIVER'S LICENSE

Am I entitled to a driver's license as soon as I reach legal age?

No. A driver's license is a privilege extended by the state to its citizens and not a right. You must meet certain requirements to be licensed to drive a motor vehicle. Then you must obey the rules and conditions under which your license is granted, or the state can take away that privilege.

How can I get a regular driver's license?

1. Fill out an application.

2. Pay the required fee.

3. Prove that you are sixteen years old and have successfully completed an approved driver education course, or prove that you are eighteen years old.

4. Pass a vision test.

5. Pass a test showing that you can read and understand highway signs and that you know the traffic laws.

6. Pass a driving test showing that you can control a car or a motorcycle properly. (Wis.Stat. 343.05, .06, .07, .08, .085, .09)

Do I need a special license to drive a motorcycle?

Your license to drive a car will be marked to show that you may also drive a motorcycle. When you take your automobile driving test, the examiner will give you another test to see if you can drive a motorcycle skillfully. (Wis.Stat. 343.05, .16)

Are there special regulations for motorcycles?

The law requires that driver and passenger wear eye-protective devices (unless the motorcycle has a windscreen). Cyclists are also required to use their headlights both night and day while their vehicle is in operation. (Wis.Stat. 347.485(2))

What should I do if I lose my license?

You must prove that you have lost it, fill out a form, and pay a fee. You will then get a new duplicate license. (Wis.Stat. 343.19)

What should I do if I move?

Within 10 days after moving you must notify the Division of Motor Vehicles in writing of the old and new address and the number of your license. You also must do this if you change your name—when a girl gets married, for example. (Wis.Stat. 343.22)

What are the limits on the use of my driver's license?

It is illegal to:

1. Possess a canceled, revoked, suspended, fictitious, or altered license.

2. Lend your license to anyone else.

3. Borrow anyone's license and use it as your own.

4. Change or alter your license or make a counterfeit license. (Wis.Stat. 343.43)

What will happen if I do any of these things?

Violations of the above rules are treated as misdemeanors, and you will have to appear in court. Criminal and civil courts have exclusive jurisdiction against people who violate the motor vehicle code. (Wis.Stat. 345.20)

What can happen if I take a friend's driving test or written exam for him?

Both of you have committed a misdemeanor. You will have to appear in court. (Wis.Stat. 343.16(4))

What can happen if I drive without a license?

This is illegal. You will have to appear in court. (Wis.Stat. 343.18)

MOTOR VEHICLES

What is a motor vehicle?

A motor vehicle is any self-propelled vehicle that can carry people or property. In other words, motorcycles, scooters, minibikes, go-carts, and similar small vehicles must follow the same rules as automobiles. (Wis.Stat. 340.01 - 35)

Can a minor own a motor vehicle?

Yes. Minors may purchase any automobile provided they submit to the seller a statement verified before a person authorized to administer oaths and signed by their parents that the purchaser has parental consent to purchase a vehicle. (Wis.Stat. 218.01 - 7b)

What is a certificate of title?

A certificate of **title** is an official form used by the Division of Motor Vehicles for keeping records of motor vehicles and their owners. Whenever a car is sold, the buyer and seller must send their names, addresses, the serial number of the vehicle, and other information to the DMV so that a new title certificate can be issued. When you buy a car it is very important to have the title changed so that you can later prove that you own the car. It is also very important to transfer title to the buyer when you sell your car. Otherwise, you would remain the owner of the car for all legal purposes and you could be held liable if the buyer gets into trouble with "your" car. (Wis.Stat. 341.08)

Can I get into trouble if I customize my car with certain types of mufflers, multiple spotlights, and similar equipment?

Some of these items are probably illegal. The law requires normal mufflers and it forbids cut-outs, by-passes, and similar devices. (Wis. Stat. 347.39) There is also a legal limit on the amount of noise a vehicle can make, regardless of the kind of muffler it has, and the owner is responsible for keeping down the noise level to comply with the law. (Wis.Stat. 347.39) Three or more spotlights, flashing lights, or colored lights are also forbidden. (Wis.Stat. 347.26) So are horns which make any sounds other than those normally made by a horn. (Wis.Stat. 347.38) Violating these rules is a misdemeanor. (Wis.Stat. 347.50)

Must I wear seat belts?

At the present time, there is no law requiring you to wear your seat belt. However, it is the law that all cars built after 1962 must have seat belts on the left and right front seats. (Wis.Stat. 347.48)

What is the "open bottle" law?

This is a statute which makes it a misdemeanor to have an open bottle or can of hard liquor or beer in a moving vehicle on a highway. (Wis.Stat. 346.935)

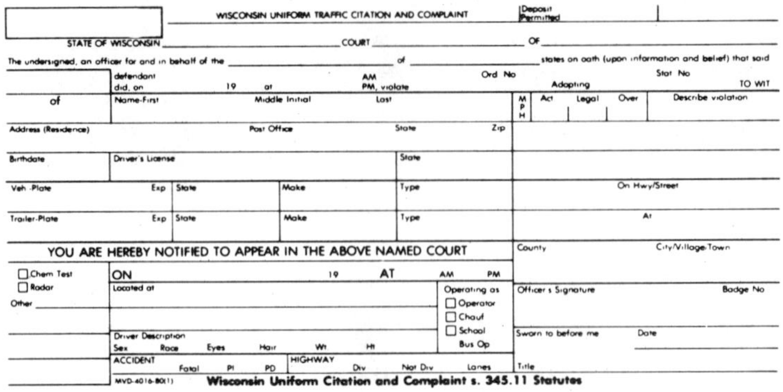

WISCONSIN UNIFORM TRAFFIC CITATION AND COMPLAINT
Deposit Permitted
STATE OF WISCONSIN ______ COURT ______ OF ______
The undersigned, an officer for and in behalf of the ______ of ______ states on oath (upon information and belief) that said defendant did, on ______ 19 ______ at ______ AM PM, violate ______ Ord No ______ Stat No ______ Adopting ______ TO WIT
of
Name-First | Middle Initial | Last
M P H | Act | Legal | Over | Describe violation
Address (Residence) | Post Office | State | Zip
Birthdate | Driver's License | State
Veh.-Plate | Exp | State | Make | Type
On Hwy/Street
Trailer-Plate | Exp | State | Make | Type
At
YOU ARE HEREBY NOTIFIED TO APPEAR IN THE ABOVE NAMED COURT
County | City/Village-Town
☐ Chem Test
☐ Radar
Other ______
ON ______ 19 ______ AT ______ AM PM
Located at
Operating as ☐ Operator ☐ Chauf ☐ School Bus Op
Officer's Signature | Badge No
Driver Description: Sex | Race | Eyes | Hair | Wt | Ht
Sworn to before me | Date
ACCIDENT: Fatal | PI | PD
HIGHWAY: Div | Not Div | Lanes
Title
MVD-4016-80(1) Wisconsin Uniform Citation and Complaint s. 345.11 Statutes

Figure 9.1a. Page one of a sample of Wisconsin traffic ticket.

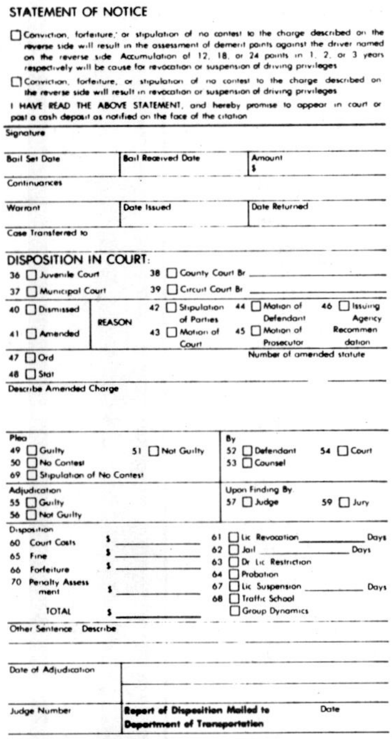

STATEMENT OF NOTICE
☐ Conviction, forfeiture, or stipulation of no contest to the charge described on the reverse side will result in the assessment of demerit points against the driver named on the reverse side. Accumulation of 12, 18, or 24 points in 1, 2, or 3 years respectively will be cause for revocation or suspension of driving privileges.
☐ Conviction, forfeiture, or stipulation of no contest to the charge described on the reverse side will result in revocation or suspension of driving privileges.
I HAVE READ THE ABOVE STATEMENT, and hereby promise to appear in court or post a cash deposit as notified on the face of the citation.
Signature
Bail Set Date | Bail Received Date | Amount $
Continuances
Warrant | Date Issued | Date Returned
Case Transferred to
DISPOSITION IN COURT:
36 ☐ Juvenile Court 38 ☐ County Court Br ______
37 ☐ Municipal Court 39 ☐ Circuit Court Br ______
40 ☐ Dismissed 41 ☐ Amended REASON 42 ☐ Stipulation of Parties 43 ☐ Motion of Court 44 ☐ Motion of Defendant 45 ☐ Motion of Prosecutor 46 ☐ Issuing Agency Recommendation
47 ☐ Ord 48 ☐ Stat Number of amended statute
Describe Amended Charge
Plea: 49 ☐ Guilty 50 ☐ No Contest 69 ☐ Stipulation of No Contest 51 ☐ Not Guilty
By: 52 ☐ Defendant 53 ☐ Counsel 54 ☐ Court
Adjudication: 55 ☐ Guilty 56 ☐ Not Guilty
Upon Finding By: 57 ☐ Judge 59 ☐ Jury
Disposition: 60 Court Costs $ ______ 65 Fine $ ______ 66 Forfeiture $ ______ 70 Penalty Assessment $ ______ TOTAL $ ______
61 ☐ Lic Revocation ______ Days 62 ☐ Jail ______ Days 63 ☐ Dr Lic Restriction 64 ☐ Probation 67 ☐ Lic Suspension ______ Days 68 ☐ Traffic School ☐ Group Dynamics
Other Sentence Describe
Date of Adjudication
Judge Number | Report of Disposition Mailed to Department of Transportation | Date

FIGURE 9.1b. Page two of a sample Wisconsin traffic ticket.

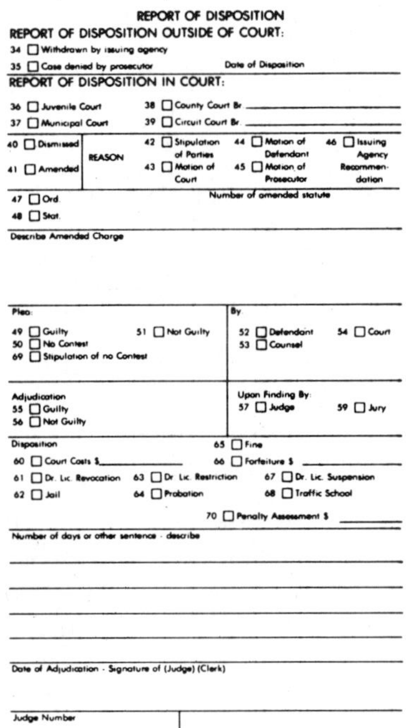

REPORT OF DISPOSITION
REPORT OF DISPOSITION OUTSIDE OF COURT:
34 ☐ Withdrawn by issuing agency
35 ☐ Case denied by prosecutor Date of Disposition
REPORT OF DISPOSITION IN COURT:
36 ☐ Juvenile Court 38 ☐ County Court Br. ______
37 ☐ Municipal Court 39 ☐ Circuit Court Br. ______
40 ☐ Dismissed 41 ☐ Amended REASON 42 ☐ Stipulation of Parties 43 ☐ Motion of Court 44 ☐ Motion of Defendant 45 ☐ Motion of Prosecutor 46 ☐ Issuing Agency Recommendation
47 ☐ Ord. 48 ☐ Stat. Number of amended statute
Describe Amended Charge
Plea: 49 ☐ Guilty 50 ☐ No Contest 69 ☐ Stipulation of no Contest 51 ☐ Not Guilty
By: 52 ☐ Defendant 53 ☐ Counsel 54 ☐ Court
Adjudication: 55 ☐ Guilty 56 ☐ Not Guilty
Upon Finding By: 57 ☐ Judge 59 ☐ Jury
Disposition: 60 ☐ Court Costs $ ______ 65 ☐ Fine 66 ☐ Forfeiture $ ______
61 ☐ Dr. Lic. Revocation 63 ☐ Dr. Lic. Restriction 67 ☐ Dr. Lic. Suspension
62 ☐ Jail 64 ☐ Probation 68 ☐ Traffic School
70 ☐ Penalty Assessment $ ______
Number of days or other sentence - describe
Date of Adjudication - Signature of (Judge) (Clerk)
Judge Number

FIGURE 9.1c. Page three of a sample Wisconsin traffic ticket.

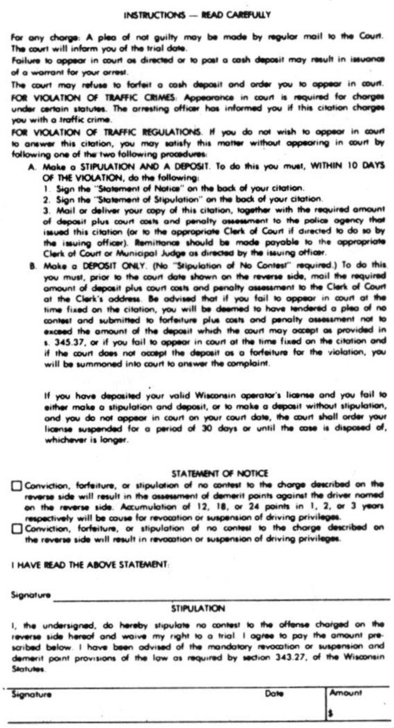

INSTRUCTIONS — READ CAREFULLY
For any charge: A plea of not guilty may be made by regular mail to the Court. The court will inform you of the trial date.
Failure to appear in court as directed or to post a cash deposit may result in issuance of a warrant for your arrest.
The court may refuse to forfeit a cash deposit and order you to appear in court.
FOR VIOLATION OF TRAFFIC CRIMES: Appearance in court is required for charges under certain statutes. The arresting officer has informed you if this citation charges you with a traffic crime.
FOR VIOLATION OF TRAFFIC REGULATIONS. If you do not wish to appear in court to answer this citation, you may satisfy this matter without appearing in court by following one of the two following procedures:
A. Make a STIPULATION AND A DEPOSIT. To do this you must, WITHIN 10 DAYS OF THE VIOLATION, do the following:
1. Sign the "Statement of Notice" on the back of your citation.
2. Sign the "Statement of Stipulation" on the back of your citation.
3. Mail or deliver your copy of this citation, together with the required amount of deposit plus court costs and penalty assessment to the police agency that issued this citation (or to the appropriate Clerk of Court if directed to do so by the issuing officer). Remittance should be made payable to the appropriate Clerk of Court or Municipal Judge as directed by the issuing officer.
B. Make a DEPOSIT ONLY. (No "Stipulation of No Contest" required.) To do this you must, prior to the court date shown on the reverse side, mail the required amount of deposit plus court costs and penalty assessment to the Clerk of Court at the Clerk's address. Be advised that if you fail to appear in court at the time fixed on the citation, you will be deemed to have tendered a plea of no contest and submitted to forfeiture plus costs and penalty assessment not to exceed the amount of the deposit which the court may accept as provided in s. 345.37, or if you fail to appear in court at the time fixed on the citation and if the court does not accept the deposit as a forfeiture for the violation, you will be summoned into court to answer the complaint.
If you have deposited your valid Wisconsin operator's license and you fail to either make a stipulation and deposit, or to make a deposit without stipulation, and you do not appear in court on your court date, the court shall order your license suspended for a period of 30 days or until the case is disposed of, whichever is longer.
STATEMENT OF NOTICE
☐ Conviction, forfeiture, or stipulation of no contest to the charge described on the reverse side will result in the assessment of demerit points against the driver named on the reverse side. Accumulation of 12, 18, or 24 points in 1, 2, or 3 years respectively will be cause for revocation or suspension of driving privileges.
☐ Conviction, forfeiture, or stipulation of no contest to the charge described on the reverse side will result in revocation or suspension of driving privileges.
I HAVE READ THE ABOVE STATEMENT:
Signature ______
STIPULATION
I, the undersigned, do hereby stipulate no contest to the offense charged on the reverse side hereof and waive my right to a trial. I agree to pay the amount prescribed below. I have been advised of the mandatory revocation or suspension and demerit point provisions of the law as required by section 343.27, of the Wisconsin Statutes.
Signature | Date | Amount $

Figure 9.1d. Page four of a sample Wisconsin traffic ticket. Notice that you sign the ticket on the first line labeled "signature."

What is the "basic speed" law?

This law simply says that you may not drive faster than is "reasonable and prudent" under existing conditions regardless of any specific speed limit. It also says that you must drive as slowly as is necessary to avoid hitting a pedestrian or other vehicle that is also obeying the

law. This means that you must drive slower than the posted speed limit if the roads are slippery or snowy or if there are any other conditions that might make it dangerous to go faster. (Wis.Stat. 346.57)

Do I have to sign a traffic ticket even if I am not guilty?

Yes. When you sign a traffic ticket you do not admit that you are guilty. Your signature only means that you promise to appear in traffic court. If you refuse to sign, the police officer may not release you and you may be taken into custody immediately. (Wis.Stat. 345.23) See figure 9.1 for a sample traffic ticket.

What are the "rules of the road?"

These are all the laws that describe the way in which automobiles and other motor vehicles may be driven. They govern speed, right-of-way, and many other matters. There are too many of these laws to describe here. Copies of the rules can be obtained from the Division of Motor Vehicles. You must know these rules to get a driver's license. (Wis.Stat., Ch. 346)

What additional activities are prohibited by law while operating a vehicle?

Wis.Stat. 346.94 lists these other forbidden activities:

1. **Driving on sidewalk.** The operator of a vehicle shall not drive upon any sidewalk area except at a permanent or temporarily established driveway unless permitted to do so by the local authorities.

2. **Racing.** No operator of a motor vehicle shall participate in any race or speed or endurance contest upon any highway.

3. **Leading animal from motor vehicle.** No person shall lead any animal upon a highway from a motor vehicle or from a trailer or semitrailer drawn by a motor vehicle.

4. **Throwing missile in vehicle.** No person shall throw any missile, circular, or pamphlet at the occupants of any vehicle or throw or place any missile, circular, or pamphlet in or on any vehicle, whether or not the vehicle is occupied.

5. **Placing injurious substance on highway.** No person shall place or cause to be placed upon a highway any foreign substance which is or may be injurious to any vehicle or part thereof.

6. **Debris on public or private property.** No person shall throw or deposit any type of debris or waste material on or along any highway or on any other public or private property.

7. **Permitting throwing of debris on highway.** No operator of any vehicle shall permit to be thrown or deposited from such vehicle any type of debris or waste material.

8. **Spilling loads of waste or foreign matter.** The operator of every vehicle transporting waste or foreign matter on the highways of this state shall provide adequate facilities to prevent such waste or foreign matter from spilling on or along the highways.

9. **Transporting persons in mobile homes or boats.** No person shall operate a motor vehicle towing any mobile home or boat on a trailer upon a highway when any person is in such mobile home or boat.

10. **Alighting from or boarding moving vehicle.** No person shall alight from or board any vehicle when such vehicle is in motion.

11. **Clinging to moving vehicle.** No person riding upon a motor driven cycle shall attach the same or himself to any other moving vehicle upon a highway.

12. **Towing sleds, etc.** No person shall operate any vehicle or combination of vehicles upon a highway when such vehicle or combination of vehicles is towing any toboggan, sled, skis, bicycle, skates, or toy vehicle bearing any person.

What is the Wisconsin traffic violation "point system"?

An explanation of the point system is found in Figure 9.2.

WISCONSIN'S POINT SYSTEM

State of Wisconsin

Department of Transportation

Division of Motor Vehicles

This handy wallet card is a guide to Wisconsin's point system and how it affects your driving privilege. The point system began Aug. 1, 1956, and is revised periodically to keep it a modern, effective device in traffic accident prevention.

HERE'S HOW IT WORKS

The Division of Motor Vehicles receives a record of all convictions for moving traffic violations, from the court. Demerit points for violations are entered on the drivers' record. Twelve points in one year, 18 in two or 24 in three years subjects the licensee to suspension or revocation. In determining actions, records are reviewed from date of violation.

The point total may be reduced by 3 for attending driver improvement counseling, approved traffic safety school or modified defensive driving course, provided other requirements for point reduction are met. Only one reduction is allowed in a five year period. Ask the local License Examiner or Driver Improvement Analyst about assignment to an approved course. No point reduction is permitted if a person accumulates sufficient points to require suspension or revocation or if the court has ordered course attendance in lieu of revocation for conviction of operating while intoxicated.

Revocation is required when a driver is convicted of an offense which caused an accident resulting in death of another.

Revocation of operating privilege is required, upon conviction for operating under the influence of intoxicants or drugs except that a driver may be assigned to a traffic safety school in lieu of revocation when it's a first conviction. In all cases 6 points are assigned to the driving record.

Demerit points will be reduced by one-third after one year without a violation, the remaining points reduced by one-half after two years without violation, and all remaining points will be wiped out after three consecutive years without a moving violation.

VIOLATIONS	POINTS
Reckless driving or racing	6
Speeding 20 mph or more over limit	6
Attempt to elude an officer (mandatory 6 months revocation)	6
Operating under influence of intoxicant	6
Failure to perform duty after accident	6
Speeding in excess – 20 mph or more over speed limit	6
Illegal passing	4
Operating with license expired more than six months or without any license	4
Imprudent driving, too fast for conditions, failure to have vehicle under control	4
Passing school bus when red lights flashing	4
Deviating from a traffic lane	4
Speeding Intermediate 11-19 mph over speed limit	4
Arterial or traffic control violation	3
Failing to give proper signal	3
Failing to yield right of way	3
Driving wrong way on one-way or wrong side two way	3
Failing to yield to emergency vehicle	3
Following too closely	3
Improper brak : or lights	3
Prohibited or :gal turn	3
Failing to dir ghts	3
Inattentive driving	3
Speeding up to 10 mph over limit	3
Operating with license expired less than six month or not on person	2
Parking on highway in traffic lane	2
No registration plate light	0
Other moving violations not listed	2
MOTORCYCLE	
Riding side saddle (operator)	2
Head lamps not lit (Daylight hours 0 points)	3
No protective headgear (operator)	0
No eye protection (operator)	2
Defective or repaired handlebars	0
Illegal muffler	0
More than 2 riders (operator)	2
Deprive traffic lane	2
No cycle validation	4

"Any person who holds a probationary license (or to whom such license would have been issued had proper application been made) will be assigned DOUBLE THE DEMERIT POINTS shown on above schedule FOR THE SECOND AND ALL SUBSEQUENT CONVICTIONS."

The following graduated scale for speeding violations will be in effect for all convictions of speeding violations occurring on or after 7-1-80:

(in a 3 yr. period)	1st offense	2nd offense	3rd offense	4th offense	5th offense & Subsequent
0 thru 10 mph over speed limit	3	4	5	6	7
11 thru 19 mph over speed limit	4	6	8	10	12
20 mph & more over speed limit	6	8	10	12	14

After serving a period of revocation a driver may be reinstated upon making application, passing the written, vision and road test given by a state driver license examiner, paying the $30 reinstatement and $5 exam fee, and showing proof of financial responsibility. In addition reinstatees may be required to meet with a Driver Improvement Analyst prior to reinstatement. Upon reinstatement the number of points on the driving record is reduced to six.

To Reinstate a license after a period of suspension:

1. Meet with a Driver Improvement Analyst if required by the Division of Motor Vehicles.
2. Pay a $20 fee.

Traffic laws represent the will of the people. They are the rules that society, through its legislature, has enacted for its own protection. Violations of these laws cause accidents; obedience prevents accidents.

The point system is a method of evaluating the quality of your driving. The division may notify you when your point total reaches six or more. When your point total is more than six, but less than twelve you may be required to meet with a driver analyst to help improve your driving. Before this happens, for your own sake and for the sake of others, examine your driving habits and correct those that you find deficient. It is your surest means of avoiding a traffic accident.

FIGURE 9.2. The Wisconsin traffic violation "point system."

Involvement in an accident requires that a driver stop at the scene. Failure to do so is a misdemeanor.

What should I do if I have an automobile accident?

You must stop immediately at the scene of the accident or as close as you can without blocking traffic. You are required by law to stop even if the damage done is very slight. If anyone is injured in the accident you must give help and call the police. If there is any damage to property or any injury you must give the other driver your name and address and the registration number of your automobile. If you damage a parked car or some other kind of property you must attempt to find the owner and notify him. Failure to stop and do these things is a misdemeanor and you will not be given a ticket, but will actually be taken into custody by the police if you are caught. (Wis.Stat. 346.67, .68, .69, .70) If the accident causes death, personal injury, or property damage of $400 or more you must also fill out a written accident report and submit it to the Division of Motor Vehicles. (Wis.Stat. 346.74) See figure 9.3 for an example of the Wisconsin Motor Vehicle Accident Report which the officer will fill out at the scene of an accident and figure 9.4 for a sample of the Wisconsin Driver's Report of Accident, which must be submitted within 10 days of an accident.

WISCONSIN MOTOR VEHICLE ACCIDENT REPORT
MVD-4000 3-73

Document No. 2312878

County | ☐ City ☐ Village ☐ Township | Name

ACCIDENT: Day of Wk. | Mo.-Day-Yr. | Time of Acc.
NUMBER: Killed | Inj. | Veh Inv
1. Less than $200 2. $200 or more

ON Give Name of Street or Highway Number

AT Intersecting Street or Highway Number

OR Ft. Mi. | North S E W | Show Nearest Intersecting St./Hwy. Of

AND Ref. Pt. | State Highway Network | Ref. Pt.
From | ☐ Feet ☐ Miles | Toward

POLICE NOTIFIED: Mo.-Day-Yr. | Time Notified | Time Arrived | Site Cleared | Hit & Run

TYPE OF ACCIDENT: 1. On Roadway 2. Off Roadway — Enter one

1. Motor veh on other road.
2. Motor veh in transport.
3. Parked motor vehicle.
4. Maintenance veh. or equip.
5. Railway train
6. Fixed object
7. Other object
8. Farm equip.
9. Pedestrian
10. Pedal cyclist
11. Deer
12. Other animal
13. Overturning
14. Other Non-coll.

Enter one

Driver - Veh. No. 1 First | M.I. | Last | Phone No. — Driver 2 or Ped First | M.I. | Last | Phone No.

Address | City and State | Zip — Address | City and State | Zip

Date of Birth | Driver's License - No. - State - Exp. Yr. | Sex — Date of Birth | Driver's License - No. - State - Exp. Yr. | Sex

Vehicle ID Number | Valid Insp. Sticker Y=Yes N=No — Vehicle ID Number | Valid Insp. Sticker Y=Yes N=No

Year & Make of Vehicle | Model | Body Style | Color — Year & Make of Vehicle | Model | Body Style | Color

License Plate No. | State | Exp. Year | Odometer Reading — License Plate No. | State | Exp. Year | Odometer Reading

Owner First | M.I. | Last — Owner First | M.I. | Last

Address | City and State | Zip — Address | City and State | Zip

Liability Insurance - Name of Company — Liability Insurance - Name of Company

Veh Damage Class -1 | Veh Damage Class -2 — Veh Damage Class - 1 | Veh Damage Class - 2

Vehicle Removed To | By: — Vehicle Removed To | By:

Non-Inj. Occupants B= Belt Used H= Harness Used N= None Used | Seating Position | 1 | 2 | 3 | 4 | 5 | 6 | Other 7 | 1 | 2 | 3 | 4 | 5 | 6 | Other 7 | Ejected Y= Yes N= No P= Partial | Cycle Safety B= Eye Protect. H= Helmet N= None Used
Enter Code

Injured Unit No. | Name First | M.I. | Last | Age | Sex | Address | City and State | Zip
Injury Severity - A-B-C-K: Head | Trunk Int. | Trunk Ext. | Arm | Leg
Nature of Injury | Eject. | Safety | Seat Code | Pos

Injured Unit No. | Name First | M.I. | Last | Age | Sex | Address | City and State | Zip | Nature of Injury | Eject. | Safety | Pos

Injured Unit No. | Name First | M.I. | Last | Age | Sex | Address | City and State | Zip | Nature of Injury | Eject. | Safety | Pos

Injured Unit No. | Name First | M.I. | Last | Age | Sex | Address | City and State | Zip | Nature of Injury | Eject. | Safety | Pos

Seat Code: Front Left to Right 1 2 3; Back Left to Right 4 5 6; Cycle Oper 1; Pass 2; All Other 7

Injured Taken To: | By: | Amb. Called | Time Arr. Scene | Arrived Hosp

Damage to any property other than vehicle, including highway signs and structures | Amount $

Owner: First | M.I. | Last | Address

LIGHT CONDITION: 1. Daylight 2. Dawn/Dusk 3. Dark - no street light 4. Dark - street lighted

WEATHER: 1. Clear 2. Cloudy 3. Raining 4. Sleeting 5. Snowing 6. Fog/Mist

ROAD
SURFACE (Unit 1, 2): 1. Concrete 2. Asphalt 3. Unpaved 4. Other
CONDITIONS (Unit 1, 2): 1. Dry 2. Wet 3. Snowy/Icy 4. Loose gravel 5. Oily 6. Muddy 7. Slush 8. Other
Horizontal Character (Unit 1, 2): 1. Straight 2. Curve
Vertical Character (Unit 1, 2): 1. Level 2. On grade 3. Hillcrest

PAVEMENT MARKING (Unit 1, 2): 1. Marked traffic lane 2. No passing zone 3. Edge stripe 4. Other

Reporting Officer at Scene Y= Yes N= No | Photos Taken By | Citation Issued To Driver Owner or Pedestrian | UNIT No. 1: Citation No. | Charge; 2: Citation No. | Charge

Officers Rank & Name | Badge No. | Dist. No. | Department | Date of Report

Location | Date | Dist. No. | Accident No.

FIGURE 9.3a. Page one of a sample Wisconsin Motor Vehicle Accident Report.

TYPE OF ROAD

Unit 1 2

1. One lane
2. Two lane
3. Three lane
4. Four or more

5. Divided
6. Undivided

7. One way
8. Two way

9. Parking lot
0. Other

Under Const.
Y = Yes

DIRECTION OF TRAVEL
Enter 1 or 2 letters for each

Codes
N=North
S=South
E=East
W=West
NE=Northeast, etc.

UNIT 1
UNIT 2

Visibility Obscured By

Skidmarks to Impact
Unit 1 Unit 2
Ft. Ft.

Distance Traveled After Impact
Unit 1 Unit 2
Ft. Ft.

Draw Diagram of Accident
Indicate North by Arrow

NARRATIVE:

Fixed Object Struck

Distance from edge of pavement Ft.

TRAFFIC CONTROL

Unit 1 2

1. Traf sig norm oper
2. Traf sig flasher oper
3. Stop sign
4. Stop sign/flasher
5. Yield sign
6. Warning
7. Warn sign/yellow flash
8. Police officer
9. RR crossing gates
10. RR crossing signals
11. No control
12. Other

MANNER OF COLLISION

Leave blank if accident did not involve a collision of 2 or more vehicles.

1. Turning maneuver
2. Rear end
3. Head on
4. Sideswipe vehicle in opposite direction
5. Sideswipe vehicle in same direction
6. Cutting in
7. Merging
8. Angle
9. Unknown
10. Other

Enter one only

WHAT DRIVERS WERE DOING

1. Making right turn
2. Making left turn
3. Making U turn
4. Going straight ahead
5. Slowing down or stopping
6. Overtaking on left
7. Overtaking on right
8. Parking maneuver
9. Changing lanes
10. Backing
11. Stopped in traffic
12. Parked
13. Legally parked
14. Other

Unit 1 2

Enter one only for each unit

PEDESTRIAN ACTION

1. In near crosswalk
2. In far crosswalk
3. In intersection, not in crosswalk
4. In midblock crosswalk
5. Crossing not at intersection
6. Walking in roadway
7. Walking in roadway against traffic
8. Standing in roadway
9. Getting on or off vehicle
10. Pushing or working on vehicle
11. Other working in roadway
12. Playing in roadway
13. Other in roadway
14. Not in roadway

Enter one only

Pedestrian Clothes: Color

1=Light
2=Dark

RELATIONSHIP TO JUNCTION
Enter no. 1, only if none of others apply.

1. Non junction related
2. Intersection
3. Intersection related
4. Intersection with alley
5. Driveway access
6. Railroad crossing

SUPPLEMENTARY INFORMATION

1. Skidding out of control
2. Tire blowout
3. Avoiding vehicle, object, animal or pedestrian
4. Wind caused loss of control

SPEED Unit 1 2

Posted speed

Estimated safe speed

NAME-Witness	Address	Phone No.	Age	Sex
NAME-Witness	Address	Phone No.	Age	Sex

DRIVER — PEDESTRIAN CONDITIONS

Unit 1 2

1. Had not been drinking
2. Had been drinking
3. Had been using non-prescription drugs
4. Had been using prescription drugs
5. Ability impaired
6. Ability not impaired

1. Apparently asleep
2. Fatigued
3. Other

4. Appeared normal

List Physical Disability

Unit 1

Unit 2

None apparent

DESCRIBE POSSIBLE CONTRIBUTING CIRCUMSTANCES

VEHICLE FACTORS

Unit 1 2

1. Steering
2. Stop lamps
3. Tail lamps
4. Head lamps
5. Turn signals
6. Brakes
7. Disabled in prior acc
8. Other disabled
9. Smooth tires
10. Other

HIGHWAY FACTORS

Unit 1 2

1. Unplowed snow
2. Debris/prior accident
3. Other debris
4. Signs/obscured-missing
5. Soft shoulder
6. Low shoulder
7. Narrow shoulder
8. Narrow bridge
9. Rough pavement
10. Other

DRIVER FACTORS

Unit 1 2

1. Improper overtaking
2. Improper turn
3. Left of center
4. Following too close
5. Passed stop sign
6. Disregard signal
7. Inattentive driving
8. Speed too fast/condition
9. Fail to yield right of way
10. Other

FIGURE 9.3b. Page two of a sample Wisconsin Motor Vehicle Accident Report.

440648 432

WISCONSIN
DRIVER'S REPORT OF ACCIDENT

State of Wisconsin/Department of Transportation
DIVISION OF MOTOR VEHICLES
Safety Responsibility Unit
P. O. Box 7919
Madison, WI 53707

SR-19
MVD-3019
2-79

This report must be completed and forwarded to the above within 10 days of the accident when there is any injury or death and/or the apparent property damage exceeds $200. Type or print, press hard. Do not use felt pen. Read instructions on reverse side.

DO NOT DETACH

DRIVER'S REPORT OF ACCIDENT SR-21 | SR NO. | POLICE REPORT NO.

Accident Date | Month | Day | Year | Day of Week | Hour : ☐ AM ☐ PM | **Accident Location** | County of | City of

Name of Street or Highway Number | Enforcement Agency at Scene | DMV USE ONLY SR 21 Mailed

MY VEHICLE NO. 1

Driver's Full Name | Address | City | State | Zip | **Injury Code** ☐

Driver License Number | Issuing State | Birthdate | Sex | Employer

Owner's Full Name | Address | City | State | Zip | Age

License Plate Number | Year | Issuing State | Make of Vehicle | Type | Year | Color | Identification Number

Repair cost | Parts of Vehicle Damaged

Was an automobile liability policy providing you with at least the minimum limits required by section 344.15(1) Wisconsin Statutes in effect on the date of the accident. If yes, have policy in front of you-Complete all insurance information. ☐ **YES** ☐ **NO**

Exact Name of Insurance Co. (Give Full Legal Name)

Policy Number

Policy Period From (before acc.) Month Day Year To (after acc.) Month Day Year

I certify the statements made on this report are true and correct to the best of my knowledge. (See *Instruction No. 4 on Reverse Side*)

(DRIVER SIGN HERE) X

Insurance Agent Name

Policy Holders Name

Were you issued a ticket for a traffic violation? ☐ Yes ☐ No | If yes, what charge

If you struck a parked vehicle was it legally parked? ☐ Yes ☐ No
If you fail to answer this question it will be assumed it was legally parked.

Number of vehicles involved in this accident
If more than three use additional forms

VEHICLE NO. 2

Driver's Full Name | Address | City | State | Zip | **Injury Code** ☐

Driver License Number | Issuing State | Birthdate | Sex | Employer

Owner's Full Name | Address | City | State | Zip | Age

License Plate Number | Year | Issuing State | Make of Vehicle | Type | Year | Color | Parts Damaged and Repair Costs

VEHICLE NO. 3

Driver's Full Name | Address | City | State | Zip | **Injury Code** ☐

Driver License Number | Issuing State | Birthdate | Sex | Employer

Owner's Full Name | Address | City | State | Zip | Age

License Plate Number | Year | Issuing State | Make of Vehicle | Type | Year | Color | Parts Damaged and Repair Costs

OTHER DAMAGES

1. Describe Property Damage and give Repair Cost | Property Owner's Name and Address
2. Describe Property Damage and give Repair Cost | Property Owner's Name and Address

CODE FOR INJURY A - Serious B - Minor K - Killed | Total No. Killed | Total No. Injured

INJURED or KILLED

Name	Address	City	State	Sex	Age	In Vehicle No.		
1. Name	Address	City	State	Sex	Age	In Vehicle No.	☐ Passenger ☐ Pedestrian ☐ Bicyclist	**Injury Code** ☐
2. Name	Address	City	State	Sex	Age	In Vehicle No.	☐ Passenger ☐ Pedestrian ☐ Bicyclist	**Injury Code** ☐
3. Name	Address	City	State	Sex	Age	In Vehicle No.	☐ Passenger ☐ Pedestrian ☐ Bicyclist	**Injury Code** ☐
4. Name	Address	City	State	Sex	Age	In Vehicle No.	☐ Passenger ☐ Pedestrian ☐ Bicyclist	**Injury Code** ☐

DESCRIBE WHAT HAPPENED

PHONE NUMBER
(See back page Instructions #6)
PRINT DRIVER'S LAST NAME →

FIGURE 9.4. A sample Wisconsin Driver's Report of Accident.

Although hitchhiking is not illegal in Wisconsin, certain rules must be followed.

HITCHHIKING AND PEDESTRIANS

What is hitchhiking?

Hitchhiking is asking the driver of a motor vehicle for a ride. It is hitchhiking whether you use your thumb, knock on car windows, or simply ask the driver.

Is it against the law to hitchhike?

No. It is not against the law to hitchhike, but you must obey these rules:

1. You may not hitchhike while standing on the roadway. In most areas this means that both feet should be on the curb. If there is no curb, you should stand well back off the shoulder of the road, the area beyond the edge of the road. (Wis.Stat. 346.30)
2. You may not hitchhike on "freeways."

What can happen to me if I violate these rules?

If you hitchhike from the roadway you might receive a traffic ticket and forfeit not less than $2.00 nor more than $20.00 for the first offense and not less than $10.00 nor more than $50.00 for the second or subsequent offenses. (Wis.Stat. 346.29)

What is a pedestrian?

The law defines a pedestrian as "any person afoot." (Wis.Stat. 340.01 - 43)

What is jaywalking?

Jaywalking is the popular name for crossing a street in the middle of a block or crossing against the light.

Do pedestrians have to obey traffic lights?

Yes. In general you must obey the signals just as an automobile must. You cannot cross on a red light or a Don't Walk sign. You may start to cross the road on a green light or a Walk sign, and if you do the drivers must give you the right-of-way. (Wis.Stat. 346.23)

When can I cross the street if there is no light?

You may always cross in a marked crosswalk and, if you do, drivers must yield the right-of-way to you. (Wis.Stat. 346.23) If you cross other than at an intersection or a marked crosswalk you must yield the right-of-way to automobiles. (Wis.Stat. 346.25) Even if you are crossing the street illegally, the law requires drivers to be careful to avoid hitting you. (Wis.Stat. 346.18)

Can I walk in the street?

You may not walk along or in the street or road if there are sidewalks that you could use instead. If there are no sidewalks you can walk in the road or along the left shoulder. You must stay close to the left side (facing oncoming traffic) and yield the right-of-way to drivers. (Wis.Stat. 346.28)

BICYCLES

What is a bicycle?

The law defines a bicycle as anything which is propelled by the feet on which a person can ride and which has any two wheels at least 14 inches in diameter. (Wis.Stat. 340.01)

Do I have to get a license for my bicycle?

State law does not require that a bicycle be licensed, although most municipalities do have ordinances (local laws passed by local units of government) that require you to buy a license. If you drive your bicycle without a license in these areas the police may impound it and fine you. Even if your bicycle is not required to be licensed it is a good idea to license it so that if it is stolen the police will know that it is yours and will be able to return it to you. One of the main reasons for licensing laws is to help identify all the lost and stolen bicycles. (Wis.Stat. 349.18)

What equipment must I have on my bicycle?

1. A rear brake which will allow you to make the wheel skid on dry pavement.

2. A red reflector on the rear.

3. If the bike is ridden at night a white light on the front that can be seen 500 feet away and a reflector or rear red light visible from a distance of 500 feet to the rear. (Wis.Stat. 346.81)

Does a bicycle have to obey all traffic laws?

Yes. You must obey all the laws that the driver of an automobile must obey except those laws that would not make sense if applied to a bicycle (for example, a law requiring a certain kind of muffler). (Wis.Stat. 346.02 - 4)

Where can I ride a bicycle?

You can ride on any roads except controlled access roads (freeways); there the speed of the other vehicles is so different from that of a bicycle that the two don't mix. (Wis.Stat. 346.80) If you do drive on the road you must ride as close to the right side of the road as possible. (Wis.Stat. 346.80) You may not ride more than two vehicles abreast on the road. (Wis.Stat. 346.80)

What other laws should I know about when I ride a bike?

1. You must ride astride the seat of the bicycle while driving it.

2. You must not carry any more riders than the bike is equipped to carry (for example, no riders on handlebars or fenders).

3. You may not hitch a ride behind an automobile or other vehicle.

4. You may not carry anything which prevents you from keeping at least one hand on the handlebars. (Wis.Stat. 346.79)

Can I get a ticket if I violate these rules?

Yes. You can get a ticket for any violation of the traffic laws, whether you are driving an automobile, walking, or riding a bike.

GUNS AND WEAPONS

What is a dangerous weapon?

The law says that a dangerous weapon is any firearm (gun) or anything else which is used to hurt people and which could kill or seriously injure someone else. (Wis.Stat. 939.22)

Is it okay to scare people with a gun?

No. It is a misdemeanor to point a gun at another person on purpose even if the gun is unloaded. (Wis.Stat. 941.20)

Can minors own guns?

There is no state law that says that minors cannot own guns but it is unlawful for any person under age sixteen to have in his or her possession any firearms for any purpose unless accompanied by a parent. A person between the ages of fourteen and sixteen who has completed a hunter safety program is exempted from the above age requirement. (Wis.Stat. 29.225)

Are there special laws regarding pistols?

The law limits the use and possession of pistols in the state of Wisconsin. The law states that a person under the age of eighteen cannot possess a pistol unless he or she is in the actual presence of a parent or guardian, for the purpose of target practice or for the purpose of instruction under a qualified instructor. A pistol means any firearm having a barrel less than twelve inches long. (Wis.Stat. 941.22)

Can I carry a gun for protection?

Usually not. Any person except a police officer is prohibited from being armed with a concealed dangerous weapon. (Wis.Stat. 941.23) This means that you may not wear a gun, knife, or any other dangerous weapon under your coat or other clothes.

Can a minor own a switchblade?

No. It is a misdemeanor for anyone, whatever his or her age, to own a switchblade. (Wis.Stat. 941.24)

Do I have to have a license to fish or hunt?

Usually you must have a license to take game or to fish or to trap, but there are some exceptions. You must often get different licenses to take different animals.

When can I hunt or fish without a license?

You do not need a license:

1. to fish, if you are a resident of Wisconsin and are under the age of sixteen.

2. to hunt foxes, raccoons, woodchucks, rabbits, and squirrels at any time except during the period of five days prior to opening date for deer hunting on your parents' land.

How old do I have to be to get a hunting license?

No hunting licenses will be issued to persons under sixteen unless

An officer of the Wisconsin Department of Natural Resources inspects a fish catch.

they have a valid firearm safety permit. Teenagers between twelve and sixteen must have such a permit to hunt. (Wis.Stat. 29.09)

How do I get a certificate?

You must take a special firearms and hunter safety instruction course approved by the Department of Natural Resources. The courses teach safety in hunting and the safe use of firearms. (Wis.Stat. 29.225) Check with your local police department.

How old do I have to be to get a certificate?

You must be at least twelve, although you can start taking the course when you are eleven and graduate when you are twelve. (Wis.Stat. 29.225)

Can I hunt without a certificate?

It is illegal for you to hunt with a gun if you are under sixteen unless your parents are with you or you have a certificate. If you have a certificate you can hunt without your parents and use your gun if you are over fourteen. (Wis.Stat. 29.225) Check with your local rifle association or at your school.

What is hunting season?

Hunting season is a period of time during the year when the law allows hunters to kill certain animals. There are different seasons for different animals. Some seasons are very short if the animals are not numerous. Check yearly to find proper hunting seasons and areas where hunting is permitted in the state.

What are limits?

Because the number of some animals is limited, hunters are allowed to take only a few. For example, each bear hunter can take only one black bear. This allows more people to hunt and controls the number of animals that are taken. (Wis.Stat. 29.174)

Are there any other rules I should know about?

It is illegal to:

1. Shoot wild animals from a car or snowmobile.

2. Hunt with a firearm or bow and arrow while intoxicated or under the influence of narcotics.

3. Hunt deer with explosive or poisonous arrows.

4. Hunt deer unless you are wearing blaze orange on your hat and coat.

5. Shooting at deer by shining your headlights or other lights at them.

What are the penalties for violating these rules?

Most violations are misdemeanors. It is negligence to hunt with a weapon while intoxicated or to shine deer. (Wis.Stat. 941.20)

The conservation officers may confiscate and sell any game or fish illegally taken, as well as all your equipment. For serious offenses, such as shining deer, they may also confiscate your automobile or boat. (Wis.Stat. 29.05)

Is there anything else I should know?

This is just a brief summary of the hunting and fishing laws. They are very complicated. If you plan to hunt or fish you should first apply for a license and obtain more detailed information from the Department of Natural Resources. (Wis.Stat. 29.09)

Do I need a special license to drive a motorboat?

No person under age ten may operate a motorboat. A person between the ages of ten and twelve may operate a motorboat only when accompanied by an adult. A person over twelve but under sixteen must obtain a watercraft operator's permit to operate such a boat without an adult present. There is an educational course and a written test required to obtain a permit. (Wis.Stat. 30.68)

Are there rules for waterskiers and scuba divers?

Yes. It is unlawful to pull a waterskier any time after sunset to sunrise of the following day. When towing waterskiers, another competent person (in addition to the boat's driver) must be in the boat to observe the progress of the person being towed. (Wis.Stat. 30.69, .70) Any person using artificial breathing equipment in the water is required to display a divers flag above the surface of the water.

MOVIES AND PUBLICATIONS

Is it illegal for me to go to an X-rated movie if I'm under 18?

No. But if you are under eighteen, it is illegal for the theater to sell you a ticket to any movie which depicts nudity, sexual conduct, sexual excitement, or sadomasochistic abuse. (Wis.Stat. 944.25)

Can I buy Playboy *or* Playgirl?

It is not a crime for you to buy it but it may be a misdemeanor for someone to sell it to you. The standard for magazines is the same as for movies: it is illegal to sell books or magazines to persons under eighteen if they "predominantly appeal to the prurient, shameful, or morbid interest of minors." (Wis.Stat. 944.21, .25)

CURFEW

What is curfew?

A curfew is a rule which says that people may not be on the street or in public places after a certain time of night. It is usually a law or ordinance requiring teenagers to be home at a specific time at night, but if there is a riot or other civil disturbance, the authorities sometimes set a curfew for people of all ages.

Does Wisconsin have a curfew law for teenagers?

No. There is no state law setting a curfew, but many cities have curfew ordinances.

What do these ordinances say?

Although the details may be different from city to city, most ordinances are probably similar. Typically, they apply to everyone under sixteen and say that you may not "loiter, idle, wander, stroll, or play" in the streets or other public places after XX P.M. or before XX A.M. They also say it is illegal for your parents to allow you to do these things.

FIREWORKS

Is it illegal to shoot off fireworks?

Yes. It is illegal for anyone to sell, use, or explode any fireworks. Cap pistols are not considered fireworks, but small firecrackers, cherry bombs, and some sparklers are included. Naturally, public displays are allowed; these rules apply only to unauthorized use of fireworks. If you violate this law you can be convicted of a misdemeanor and the police may seize the fireworks. (Wis.Stat. 167.10)

DOGS

Do I have to have a license for my dog?

State law does not require you to license your dog but state law requires towns, villages, and cities to pass ordinances that require licenses. If the municipality regulates dogs, county ordinances apply outside municipal limits only. (Wis.Stat. 174)

Can I take my dog out for a walk without a leash?

Again, state law does not require that dogs be leashed, but many villages and cities have ordinances which do require it.

What happens if I don't have a leash or license for my dog?

In Wisconsin, a dog without a license attached to its collar is assumed to be unlicensed and any law enforcement officer may seize the dog and put him in the dog pound. To get the dog back you may have to forfeit money for a pound fee, for the dog's room and board, and for a license if the dog is unlicensed. If you do not reclaim the dog within seven days, it may be destroyed. (Wis.Stat. 174.10)

Is there a limit on the number of dogs I can own?

There is nothing in state law. However, a municipality may limit the number of dogs and cats a person can own.

Can I get in trouble if my dog bites someone?

Yes. If your dog attacks a person in any place where that person has a right to be, you can be sued and made to pay for the damages the dog caused. This is true even though you were not careless and did not know that the dog might bite a person; the law says you are strictly liable. (Wis.Stat. 174.02)

LITTERING

Is it illegal to litter?

Yes. It is a misdemeanor to dump or throw any kind of trash, garbage, or harmful or dangerous things on the streets, highways, waterways, or on private or public land without its owner's consent. The littering offense carries a fine of $200.00.

SUGGESTED ACTIVITY

Role Play

Most children think of running away from home at one time or another, usually because of family problems. Although it is difficult to generalize about runaways, authorities do have some facts. The average age of a runaway is sixteen years. Thirty-six percent of all runaways are boys, although many boys are not reported because of the common assumption that boys can take care of themselves. Most runaways find refuge close to their homes—sometimes in their own community. Many go to runaway centers where counseling, shelter, food, and clothing are available. Girls who run away have special problems. For example, they may meet someone who promises to "take care of them" and find that they are expected to become prostitutes. Both boys and girls who have run away have been the victims of unscrupulous people. Many have gotten hurt and some have been murdered.

Runaways are often found when they are picked up by police for curfew violation or another minor offense. After police identify a runaway, the young person is turned over to a Juvenile Probation Officer. This officer has two days to decide what to do with each runaway who has been picked up. Usually, he or she schedules a family conference to help resolve conflicts which may have led to the child's leaving home. He or she tries to find solutions to the problem.

In the activity which follows, you will have an opportunity to role-play a family meeting with a probation officer.* Members of the class should choose the roles listed in each case and then complete the role-play. After each role-play, the class can discuss what happened using the questions provided at the end of this activity.

How to Proceed

1. Role players should prepare their roles individually by studying the descriptions of their characters.

2. Probation officer calls the conference together. He or she may open the conference by asking a question or inviting the family members to talk.

3. Probation officers should try to discover the conflicts in the family and resolve them by discussion.

4. Probation officers should make a decision in each case.

5. Discuss the role-play using the discussion questions following the lesson.

---

*"Runaway—Simulation," *Crime and Justice, Ten Activities*. Los Angeles, CA: Constitutional Rights Foundation, 1979, pp. 25-28. Reprinted by permission of the publisher.

Probation Officers: Role Description

In each case, probation officers should try to resolve the present conflict concerning the runaway. You will conduct a family conference. Your primary goal is to help the family stay together and to send the runaway home. You must try to make the family feel responsible for solving the problem of the runaway. If it is impossible to send the child home because the parents do not want him or her or because he or she has been abused, or for some other reason, you might try to get the parents to agree to place their child with a relative, in a foster home, or in a group home. If the family refuses to do anything you may have to place the child under the care of the county and detain him or her in a juvenile detention center.

During the family conference, you may ask members of the family such questions as:

Why are you here?
How do you feel about this situation?
When did this problem start?
What have you done in the past that worked?
What do you want to do now?
What do you think would help?

At the close of the conference, inform the family what action you are going to take in the case. You may make any of the following decisions:

1. Send the runaway home with parents. No further action.
2. Send the runaway home with follow-up counseling through the Probation Department.
3. Place the runaway at the home of a relative or friend pending juvenile court disposition.
4. Place the runaway in a foster home pending juvenile court disposition.
5. Place the runaway in a private group home for troubled youth pending juvenile court disposition.

The Families: Role Descriptions

Case #1:	Sylvia (Age 15)	"My parents don't care about me. They never really wanted to have children. They wouldn't even want me back and are glad I am gone."
	Sylvia	Develop your role based on the above information. Try to be as realistic as possible and stay in character during the family conference.
	Sylvia's Mother & Father	Develop your roles according to the above information. Try to be as realistic as possible and stay in character during the family conference. Be prepared to discuss your feelings about your child who has become a runaway.

	Juvenile Probation Officer	See role description above.
Case #2:	John (Age 17)	"My father is an alcoholic. When he comes home he beats me up and pushes me around like a toy. My parents are always fighting. No peace. I can't take it any longer."
	John	Develop your role based on the above information. Try to be as realistic as possible and stay in character during the family conference.
	John's Mother & Father	Develop your roles according to the above information. Try to be as realistic as possible while staying in character during the family conference. Be prepared to discuss your feelings about your child who has become a runaway.
	Juvenile Probation Officer	See role description above.
Case #3:	Emily (Age 16)	"My family won't let me breathe. I can't do anything with my friends. They don't trust me, and are always on my back. Nag, nag, nag, everyone in our house is always fighting."
	Emily	Develop your role based on the above information. Try to be as realistic as possible and stay in character during the family conference.
	Emily's Mother & Father	Develop your roles according to the above information. Try to be as realistic as possible while staying in character during the family conference. Be prepared to discuss your feelings about your child who has become a runaway.
	Emily's Sister	Develop your role according to the above information. Try to be as realistic as possible while staying in character during the family conference. Be prepared to talk about your sister who has run away.
	Juvenile Probation Officer	See role description above.
Case #4:	Dave (Age 15)	"I wanted some adventure. I don't want people running my life, telling me what to do all the time. I want to be on my own—to find out who I really am."
	Dave	Develop your role based on the above information. Try to be as realistic as possible and stay in character during the family conference.

Dave's Mother & Father	Develop your roles according to the above information. Try to be as realistic as possible while staying in character during the family conference. Be prepared to discuss your feelings about your child who has become a runaway.
Dave's Brother	Develop your role according to the above information. Try to be as realistic as possible while staying in character during the family conference. Talk about your brother who has run away.
Juvenile Probation Officer	See role description above.

QUESTIONS FOR DISCUSSION

1. What decisions did the probation officer make in each case? Why? Do you agree or disagree with his or her decision? Why?

2. In your opinion, are any of the youths in these cases delinquent? Why or why not?

3. From your reading and experience, how important would you say family life is in contributing to juvenile delinquency?

4. In your opinion, are there youngsters who would get in trouble no matter what their family life was like? If so, what other factors might account for their getting into trouble?

SUGGESTED ACTIVITY

Mock Trials: Scripts for Wisconsin Lawyers and Teachers. Published by Wisconsin Department of Public Instruction in cooperation with The Wisconsin Bar Foundation. Bulletin No. 0166, 1980.

Mock Trials include Automobile Accident, Land-Lord-Tenant, Drunk Driving, Homicide, Burglary, and Child Abuse scripts.

VOCABULARY

Bond
Citation
Curfew
Forfeiture
Intoxicating
Loiter
Narcotics
Oath
Offense
Probation
Registration
Revoked
Suspended
Title

SUGGESTED READING

Wisconsin Statutes

Bill of Rights in Action. Constitutional Rights Foundation

Update. (Law Related Education) American Bar Association, Chicago, Illinois

SUGGESTED RESOURCES

Local Police Department

County Sheriff or Juvenile Officer

Wisconsin State Patrol, Regional Office

Wisconsin Department of Transportation, Madison

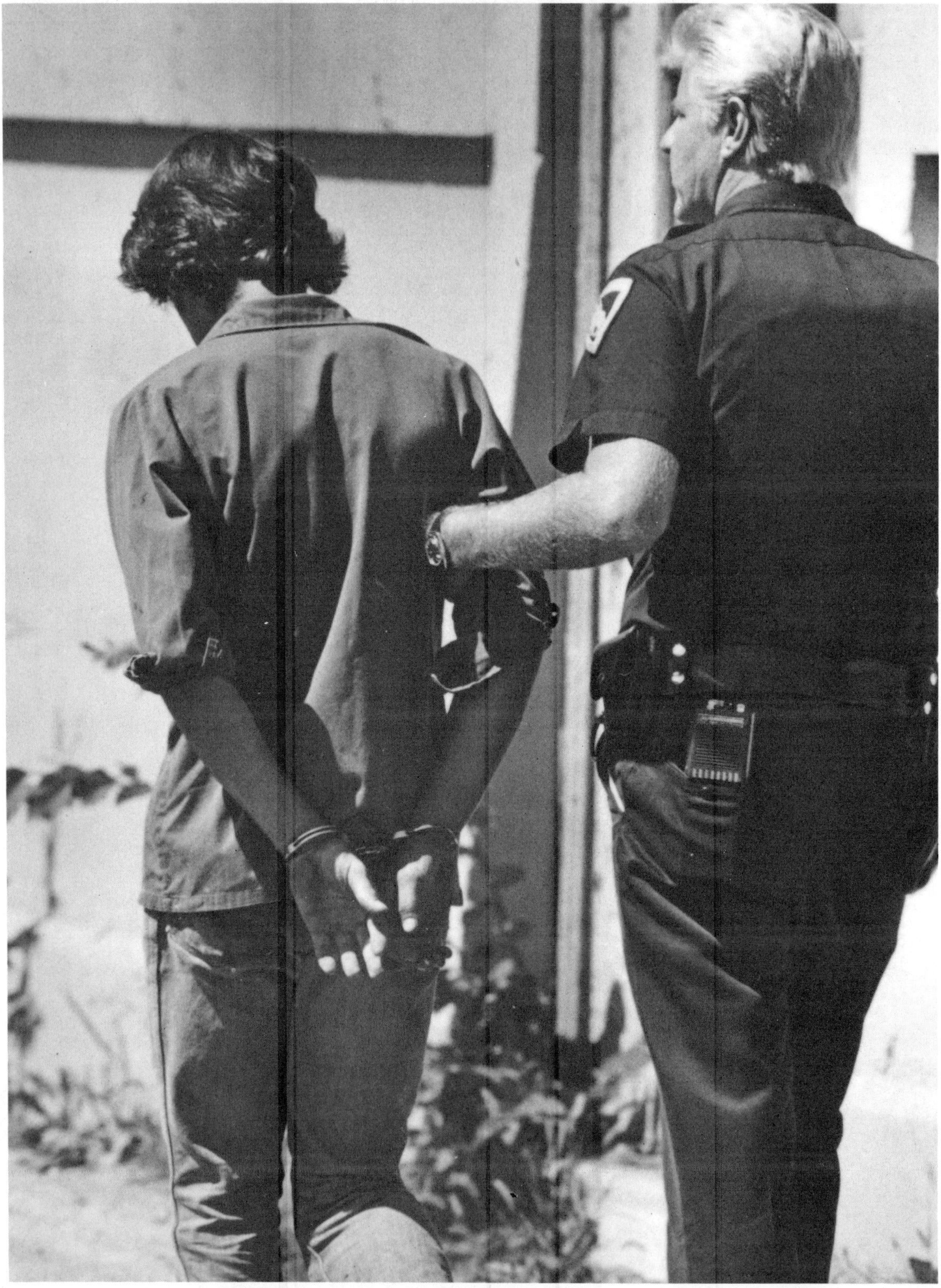

10

The Law and the Juvenile Justice System

Criminal laws have two purposes. First, they seek to regulate the conduct of an individual within society by saying which kinds of behavior society will not tolerate. This protects the interests of the vast majority of citizens who are law-abiding.

Second, criminal laws provide punishment if the individual engages in these forbidden types of activity. If you violate a criminal law, you may be arrested, tried, convicted, and punished by the state. Deciding which activities are to be forbidden is the job of our legislative bodies at the federal, state, and local levels. For example, in Wisconsin an act is not a crime unless a legislative body has said it is. These bodies also provide general guidelines as to the punishment for each offense. The enforcement of these laws is left to the police, the court systems, and the correctional authorities.

This chapter will give you some idea of what is a crime and what can happen when a person is arrested for committing a crime. In criminal law, as in civil law, a young person may be treated the same as anybody else or given certain additional safeguards, depending on the circumstances. The first part of this chapter explains some crimes or unlawful acts young people most frequently become involved in and a chart of adult criminal laws in Wisconsin.

CRIME

What is a crime?

Wisconsin law defines a crime as any conduct which is forbidden by state law and for which a person may be sentenced to prison or fined or both. Conduct punishable only by a **forfeiture** (fine) is not a crime. (Wis.Stat. 939.12) There are two different types of crime:

1. Felonies—crimes punishable by more than one year in prison.

2. Misdemeanors—crimes punishable by a jail sentence of not more than one year or a fine, or both.

Wisconsin has five different kinds of felonies. Each class of felony carries a different penalty. The kinds of felonies and their penalties are:

- Class A felony (life imprisonment)
- Class B felony (imprisonment not to exceed 20 years)
- Class C felony (a fine not to exceed $10,000 or imprisonment not to exceed 10 years, or both)
- Class D felony (fine not to exceed $10,000 or imprisonment not to exceed five years, or both)
- Class E felony (fine not to exceed $10,000 or imprisonment not to exceed two years, or both).

There are three kinds of misdemeanors in Wisconsin. The three classes and their penalties are:

- Class A misdemeanor (fine not to exceed $10,000 or imprisonment not to exceed nine months, or both)
- Class B misdemeanor (fine not to exceed $1,000 or imprisonment not to exceed 90 days, or both)
- Class C misdemeanor (fine not to exceed $500 or imprisonment not to exceed 30 days, or both).

Is it a crime to park in a no parking zone?

No. Minor traffic violations and other minor offenses are not crimes at all.

What happens if a minor breaks a law?

The juvenile court can decide that a person under 18 who has broken a law is a delinquent child. (Wis.Stat. 48.34) Teenagers between the ages of 16 and 18 years may be prosecuted for a crime just like adults if the juvenile court, after a hearing for that purpose, decides that they should be. (Wis.Stat. 48.39) However, unless the juvenile court judge decides to refer the case for criminal prosecution, it will be treated like the case of a younger minor and there will be a delinquency proceeding in the juvenile court. (Wis.Stat. 48.34) Unless the judge does decide that the juvenile should be prosecuted as an adult, the juvenile has not committed a crime. (Wis.Stat. 48.34) The judge's decision to refer the case for adult criminal prosecution depends on whether he thinks the minor is suitable for rehabilitation and treatment and whether

Because demonstrators were blocking a freight elevator, police first asked them to move.

he thinks the public's safety might be endangered if the minor were treated as a juvenile. (Wis.Stat. 48.18)

THE ARREST

What are a minor's rights before he or she is arrested?

The U.S. Supreme Court has most often defined pre-arrest rights in terms of limits beyond which the police may not go. The setting of these limits, based on the interpretation of appropriate sections of the Bill of Rights in the United States constitution, is a whole body of law within the criminal law known as criminal procedure. Since the Supreme Court is the final interpreter of the constitution, state courts are bound by Supreme Court interpretation of the law.

Criminal procedure is a complex and ever-changing body of law whose safeguards were extended to minors by the Supreme Court in *In re Gault,* 387 U.S. 1 (1967). However, it is possible to make some general statements about adults' and minors' rights during the arrest process. (See figure 10.1 for a comparison of adult and juvenile arrest rates.)

An arrest can be made only in several prescribed ways: by warrant (a document signed by a judge ordering the authorities to arrest a named individual and stating the reasons); by the officer apprehending you after observing you commit a crime; or by an officer who did not

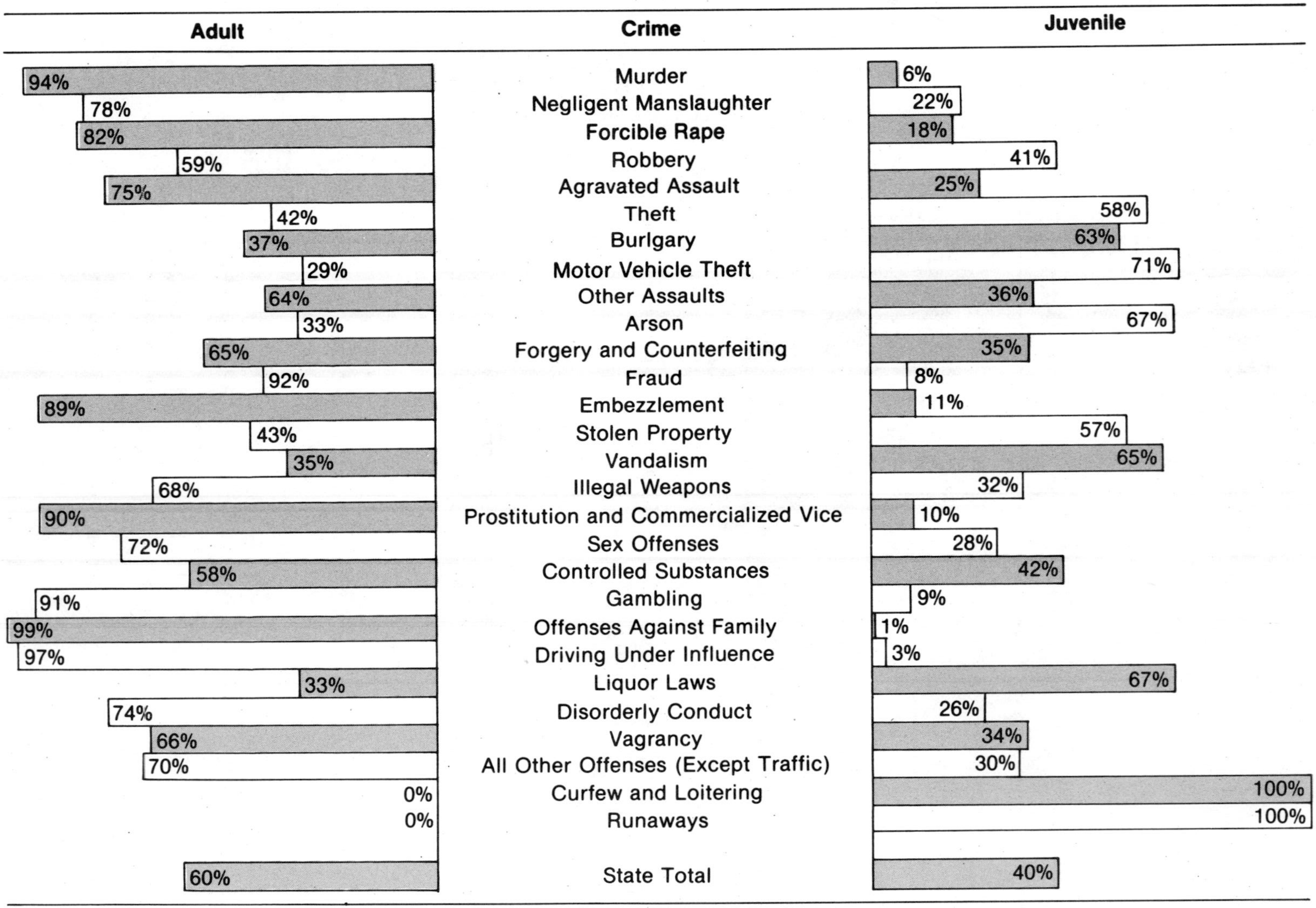

FIGURE 10.1. The proportion of juvenile arrests to adult arrests in Wisconsin in 1979. Source: *Wisconsin Criminal Justice Information; Crime and Arrests 1979.* Crime Information Bureau, Madison, WI. Reprinted by permission.

see you commit a felony, but who has probable cause to believe that you did. Probable cause is defined as "... a reasonable ground of suspicion supported by circumstances sufficiently strong in themselves to warrant a cautious man in believing the accused to be guilty." In other words, an officer at the scene of a bank robbery who sees an armed man running up the block with a bank sack would have probable cause to apprehend and arrest that man as the bank robber. Police may also make an arrest anywhere in the state without a warrant if they are in fresh pursuit of a suspect observed committing a crime or who they have probable cause to believe has committed a crime. (See figure 10.2 for a sample court citation.)

If the police accuse me of committing a crime, do I have to answer their questions?

No. The fifth amendment of the constitution says that no person can be forced to incriminate himself or herself. This means that you don't have to admit your guilt, or explain your actions or give the police an alibi unless you want to. In fact, if the police accuse you of a crime, they must warn you of your rights under the constitution. They must tell you:

that you have the right to remain silent—not to answer any of their questions at all;
that if you do answer anything, your answers can and will be used against you;
that you have a right to have a lawyer present during the questioning;
that if you can't afford a lawyer, one will be appointed for you without charge.

If they fail to tell you these things and you answer their questions, they cannot use your statements as evidence against you, although you could still be found guilty of a crime based on other evidence. (*Miranda* v. *Arizona,* 384 U.S. 436, 1966) Remember that if you do answer or volunteer information, you give up or waive your rights and your statements may be used against you.

Can I be arrested "on suspicion" or "for investigation?"

No. When a minor is taken into custody, it is not an arrest. (Wis.Stat. 48.19)

Under what conditions can the police search me or my property?

The court has defined limits beyond which the police may not go, depending on the circumstances. If you are stopped on the street by a police officer who does not arrest you, you can be searched only if your conduct and the officer's experience suggest that criminal activity may be going on and that you are armed and dangerous to the officer or to others. Even then he or she is limited to patting down your outer clothing for weapons and cannot go further unless he or she feels something that may be a weapon.

The U.S. Supreme Court recently ruled that as soon as you are legally arrested or taken into police custody, the police can conduct a full search of your person. This decision was reached in a case in which heroin was found on a man stopped and arrested for driving while his license was suspended. *(United States* v. *Robinson,* 414 U.S. 218, 1973)

Searches can also be initiated by the police through regular or **no-knock warrants.** A search warrant is a document signed by a judge allowing the authorities to search a specific place for specified (and sometimes related) items; a no-knock warrant allows the authorities to conduct the search without announcing themselves beforehand, because evidence can be easily removed or destroyed, because people would be endangered otherwise, or because suspects could escape. Searches without warrants, like arrests without warrants, must be based on probable cause. These searches must usually be limited to suspects and the immediate area around them. Police officers can also search an automobile without a warrant if they have probable cause to do so and the car can be driven away. Of course, the police can search you if you consent to the search or when you are to be confined in custody. They can seize any incriminating evidence that is in "plain view."

See Figure 10.2 Wisconsin Municipal Court Citation for an example of a court order an individual must obey.

If I break a law, can I be arrested?

The police can take you into custody, but it is not called an **arrest.** This means that you will not have an arrest record and that you can later truthfully say that you have never been arrested. (Wis.Stat. 48.396)

If I am taken into custody, can I be put in jail?

Minors cannot be kept in the same room in a jail as an adult offender, but they can be put in a separate room in a jail or police station. (Wis.Stat. 48.209)

TRIAL AND CONVICTION

If I am taken into custody for having committed a crime, will I go to adult court?

No. If you were under 18 years of age at the time you allegedly broke the law you must first be brought before the juvenile court. (Wis.Stat. 48.225) After a hearing based on all the circumstances, the judge would make a decision whether to refer your case for adult criminal prosecution or to retain your case in the juvenile criminal justice system. *(Kent* v. *United States,* 383 U.S. 541, 1966)

If the judge has to sentence a minor for the maximum number of years the law allows, does the minor have to stay in custody for

	Deposit	10% Assessment	Court Costs	Total
WISCONSIN UNIFORM MUNICIPAL COURT CITATION				

STATE OF WISCONSIN MUNICIPAL COURT ______ OF ______

The undersigned for and in behalf of the above municipality states on basis of personal knowledge (or upon information and belief) that said

defendant did on ______ 19 ___ at ______ A.M. P.M. violate Ord. No. (Res. or Bylaw) ______ TO WIT:

of ______ VS. Name-First ______ Middle Initial ______ Last ______

Designation of Offense:

Address (Residence) ______ Post Office ______ State ______ Zip ______

Birthdate ______ Other Identification ______

Describe Violation:

Description

Sex ______ Race ______ Eyes ______ Hair ______ Wt. ______ Ht ______

YOU ARE HEREBY NOTIFIED TO APPEAR IN THE ABOVE NAMED COURT

ON ______ 19 ___ AT ______ A.M. P.M.

Located at ______

AT

County ______ City/Village/Town ______

Officer's Signature ______ Date ______ Dept. ______

IMPORTANT: READ NOTICE ON BACK

Municipal Atty's Endorsement (if required)

Date of Issue

DEFENDANT'S COPY

FIGURE 10.2. Wisconsin Uniform Municipal Court Citation.

INSTRUCTIONS - READ CAREFULLY

STIPULATION AND DEPOSIT OPTIONS

A. You can obtain release from custody and satisfy this matter without being required to appear in court by making a STIPULATION AND DEPOSIT. To do this, you must prior to the court appearance date sign the stipulation below and mail or deliver this citation together with the total amount of the deposit to the municipal court. Remittance shall be made payable to the municipal court.

B. You can also obtain release from custody and may satisfy this matter without appearing in court by making a DEPOSIT ONLY. To do this, you must prior to the court appearance date mail or deliver the total amount of the deposit to the municipal court. Remittance shall be made payable to the municipal court. The court does not have to accept the deposit. If it does not accept it, you will be required to appear in court. In that event, a summons will be issued to you.

APPEARANCE OPTION

Even if you make a STIPULATION AND DEPOSIT or a DEPOSIT ONLY, you may appear in court at the time fixed in this citation and plead to the citation.

FAILURE TO APPEAR IN COURT

A. If you have not made a STIPULATION AND DEPOSIT or a DEPOSIT ONLY, the court may issue a summons or warrant for your arrest or may enter default judgment against you.

B. If you make a STIPULATION AND DEPOSIT, the court must accept it. The court will enter judgment against you for an amount not to exceed the total amount of the deposit.

C. If you make a DEPOSIT ONLY, the court may, but is not required to, accept the deposit. If it does accept it, it will enter a judgment against you for an amount not to exceed the total amount of the deposit. If the court does not accept your deposit, it will summon you to appear in court.

JURY TRIAL

Within 10 days of entry of a plea of not guilty, you may request in person or by mail a jury trial. Fees and deposit required by Section 300.04(1)(d), Wis. Stats., must accompany the request.

STIPULATION

I have read and understand the notice on the reverse side of the citation and the instructions above. I do hereby stipulate no contest to the offense charged on the reverse side and waive my right to a trial. I agree to pay the amount prescribed, which is enclosed.

Signature	Date of Signature	Total Amount of Deposit

FIGURE 10.2. (continued).

the whole time?

Not necessarily. Probation and parole are available.

SPECIFIC OFFENSES

Can I get into trouble for fighting?

Yes. It is a felony (called **battery**) to injure or try to injure other people or to purposely make them afraid that you will hurt them. (Wis.Stat. 940.19) If you fight in a public place where you know it will bother or disturb other people, you could be convicted of **disorderly conduct,** which is a misdemeanor. (Wis.Stat. 947.01)

Does this mean that if somebody hits me, I can't hit that person back?

You have the right to hit that person or use other "reasonable force" against the attacker if it is necessary to protect yourself or someone else from an attack. However, you can't use more force than is necessary to protect yourself and you can't really hurt the other person unless you are in danger, even if the other person does start the fight. (Wis.Stat. 939.48)

Is it illegal to demonstrate?

In general, peaceful demonstrations are legal, but there are some limits. It is a misdemeanor for more than three people to gather if they intend to do something illegal by force, if they intend to disturb the public peace, or if they are actually disorderly and disturb people. (Wis.Stat. 947.06) If a group like this uses violence, its members are guilty of a crime of unlawful assembly, and may be imprisoned for nine months or fined $10,000, or both.

What is the penalty for bombing?

If the bomb actually goes off and causes the death of anyone, the person setting the bomb is guilty of **arson** (causing a fire) and could be imprisoned for twenty years for arson and twenty years for second-degree murder. (Wis.Stat. 943.02, 940.02) If the bomb only damaged property, the bomber is guilty of arson and can be imprisoned for twenty years. If a persons sets a bomb or explosives with intent to damage something or blow it up and the bomb doesn't go off, he or she is still guilty of attempted arson. (Wis.Stat. 943.05)

Can I get in trouble if as a joke I call and tell someone there is a bomb planted in the building?

Yes. It is a felony punishable by two years in jail and/or a $10,000 fine to make bomb threats. (Wis.Stat. 947.015)

What is malicious mischief?

There is no offense called **malicious mischief** in Wisconsin, but the phrase is often used to mean intentionally damaging the property of another person. This is a felony if you cause more than $1,000 worth of damage. (Wis.Stat. 943.01)

Can I get in trouble for hiding a friend from the police?

Yes. If your friend has committed a felony and you hide the person from the police, you have committed a class E felony and could be jailed for not more than one year or fined $500, or both. (Wis.Stat. 946.47) This section does not apply if you are related to the offender as husband, wife, parent, or child at the time of hiding. (Wis.Stat. 947.47)

If I get angry and threaten somebody, am I guilty of a crime?

You might be. It is a felony to threaten people or their property or to threaten to tell another's secrets, if the threat is made to get that person to do something he or she doesn't want to do or to keep that person from doing something he or she does want to do. (Wis.Stat. 943.30, .31)

Is it illegal for me to have intercourse with my girlfriend?

It is illegal for anyone to have sexual intercourse with a person who is not one's husband or wife. (Wis.Stat. 944.15) This is a misdemeanor. It is a felony for any person to have sexual intercourse or sexual contact with any person under the age of twelve, or without consent between persons over twelve and under eighteen. A person under age fifteen is incapable of consent as a matter of law. (Wis.Stat. 940.225)

This temporary juvenile court in Madison contains all the essential participants (left to right) *of judge, alleged juvenile offender, bailiff, and court reporter.*

Is it illegal to go away with my girlfriend even if we are going to get married?

Yes. If she is under eighteen years of age and you take her away to get married without her parents' consent, you are guilty of abduction, which is a felony. (Wis.Stat. 940.32)

If my girlfriend gets pregnant, can I be arrested?

No, not for the pregnancy; however, remember that it is a misdemeanor to have intercourse with someone who is not your spouse. You might have to pay for her expenses, and the expenses of the child.

Is it a crime to write a bad check?

It isn't a crime if you really intended to pay your bill and just balanced your checkbook incorrectly or were temporarily short of money. It is a misdemeanor to write a bad check if you didn't intend to pay your debt. It is evidence that you never intended to pay if you fail to make up an overdraft within five days after getting notice of it. (Wis.Stat. 943.24)

What is the penalty for joyriding in a car?

If you take somebody's car for a drive without his consent, you are guilty of unauthorized use of a motor vehicle, which is punishable by imprisonment for two years or a fine of $10,000 or both. (Wis.Stat. 943.23) If you take somebody else's car and intend to keep it or sell it instead of returning it after a ride, you are guilty of theft and could be imprisoned for up to ten years, depending on the value of the car. (Wis.Stat. 943.20)

Is it illegal to buy something which I think is stolen?

Yes. It is theft to intentionally receive or buy stolen property. (Wis.Stat. 943.34)

If I find money or something else valuable, do I have to try to find the owner?

Yes. It is theft to keep lost property without making a reasonable effort to find the real owner and return it to him. (Wis.Stat. 943.20)

What can happen if I use somebody else's credit card without permission?

You would be guilty of misusing a credit card, which is a misdemeanor or felony, depending on the value of the illegally obtained monies, goods, services, or property. (Wis.Stat. 943.41)

Does theft include shoplifting?

YES! (Wis.Stat. 943.50)

Offense	Statute Section	Penalty (Maximum)
Murder		
First Degree (pre-planned)	940.01	Life imprisonment
Second Degree (intentional)	940.02	20 years
Manslaughter (intentional killing in heat of passion or non-intentional killing while committing a violent crime)	940.05	10 years/$10,000
Homicide by Reckless Conduct	940.06	10 years/$10,000
Criminal Negligence (negligent killing with a car, boat, or weapon)	940.08	2 years/$10,000
Aggravated Battery (causing great bodily harm to another)	940.19	10 years/$10,000
Assault with a Weapon	940.24	2 years/$10,000
Simple Robbery (taking property of another by force)	943.32	10 years/$10,000
Aggravated Robbery (robbery while armed or if great bodily harm is inflicted on the victim)	943.32	20 years
Kidnapping	940.31	20 years
If accompanied by demands for money	940.31	Life imprisonment
Aggravated Rape or Sodomy: Sexual Assault (forcing another to engage in sexual relations)	940.225	20 years
Bribery (giving or accepting bribes involving a public official)	946.10	5 years/$10,000
A witness to bribery	946.61	5 years/$10,000
Perjury (lying under oath	946.31	5 years/$10,000
Theft		
If property worth more than $2,500	943.20	10 years/$10,000
If $500-$2,500	943.20	2 years/$10,000
If under $500	943.20	9 months/$10,000
Arson		
To a building	943.02	20 years
Other than building	943.03	2 years/$10,000
Burglary		
Breaking and entering to commit a crime	943.10	10 years/$10,000
If done in a dwelling, or burglar possession weapon or tool, or burglar commits an assault in an occupied dwelling	943.10	20 years
Forgery	943.38	10 years/$10,000

TABLE 10.1. Adult criminal laws and their penalties. This list shows the felonies most commonly committed in the state of Wisconsin.

If I call somebody in the middle of the night and hang up, can I get in trouble even though it's only a joke?

Yes. It is a misdemeanor to call another person and hang up without giving your name if you intend to harass or annoy the person. (Wis.Stat. 947.01)

What other crimes should I know about?

It is a misdemeanor to:

1. Make a false report of a crime to the police. (Wis.Stat. 946.41)

2. Interfere with firemen who are trying to put out a fire. (Wis.Stat. 941.12, .13)

3. Remove the serial number or identification number from any property if you do so to keep people from trying to identify it. (Wis.Stat. 943.37)

4. Litter, whether on public or private land. (Wis.Stat. 396.94)

5. Refuse to leave someone's land when told to do so. (Wis.Stat. 943.13)

JUVENILE COURT

This institution of the juvenile justice system was specifically designed to meet the needs of the young. Once a determination is made that a young person be treated as a juvenile in the eyes of the law, he or she is afforded more individualized and protective care in the juvenile court system than an adult normally receives in the regular court system. You will find that it is an area of strict safeguards but wide flexibility within the law, which is exactly how and why it was written.

In the spring of 1978, the Wisconsin Legislature passed and the governor signed legislation resulting in a major revision of the laws relating to the operation of the juvenile court—known as "The Children's Code." The Code lists the following goals:

1. To provide judicial and other procedures through which children and other interested parties are assured fair hearings and their constitutional and other legal rights are recognized and enforced, while protecting the public safety.

2. To provide for the care, protection, and wholesome mental and physical development of children, preserving the unity of the family whenever possible.

3. Consistent with the protection of the public interest, to remove from children committing delinquent acts the consequences of criminal behavior and to substitute therefore a program.

4. To divert children from the juvenile justice system to the extent that this is consistent with protection of children and the public safety.

5. To respond to children's needs for care and protection through community-based programs and to keep children in their homes whenever possible.

6. To assure that children pending adoptive homes will be placed in the best homes available and protected from adoption by persons unfit to have responsibility for raising children. (Wis.Stat. 48.01)

7. To provide children in the state with permanent and stable family relationships. The courts and agencies responsible for child welfare should assist parents in changing any circumstances in the home which might harm the child or which may require the child to be placed outside the home.

Finally, the code indicates that "the best interests of the child should always be the paramount consideration."

What is juvenile court?

Juvenile court is not necessarily a separate court building. The Board of Supervisors of any county may authorize the circuit judge to appoint one or more juvenile court commissioners to serve at the discretion of the judge. The juvenile court commissioner must be an attorney and must have "demonstrated interest in the welfare of children." (Wis.Stat. 48.065) In a broader sense, the phrase juvenile court refers to a special set of rules and procedures that judges must use when a minor is accused of breaking the law or has family problems that come to court. In rural counties, the county courts have authority to handle juvenile cases. In larger counties, the juvenile court is typically a branch of the county court system, and handles only juveniles. In Milwaukee County, juvenile court commissioners hear all juvenile matters with the assistance of the staff of the Children's Court Center. (Wis.Stat. 48.06)

Why is there a special set of rules for juvenile court?

The juvenile court is set up to allow the problems of minors to be treated with informality and privacy so that a minor will not be labeled a criminal for a less serious offense. The law establishing the juvenile courts says that its purpose is to:

> . . . conserve human resources in Wisconsin; to provide a just and humane program of services to children in need of protection or services and children born out of wedlock; to prevent dependency, mental illness, developmental disability, mental infirmity, delinquency, crime, and other forms of social maladjustment by a continuous attack of causes; to provide effective aid and services to all persons in need thereof and to assist such persons to achieve or regain self-dependence at the earliest possible date; to provide a just, humane, and efficient program for the rehabilitation of juvenile delinquents and other offenders; to avoid duplication and waste of effort and money on the part of public and private agencies; and to coordinate and integrate a social welfare program. (Wis.Stat. 46.001)

Why does a person go to juvenile court?

A person may go to juvenile court if:

1. twelve years of age or older and it is claimed that he or she is delinquent because of a violation of federal or state criminal law. (Wis.Stat. 48.12)

2. it is claimed that the child violated a law punishable by forfeiture or a county, town, or municipal ordinance. (Wis.Stat. 48.125)

3. it is charged that the minor is in need of protection or services. (Wis.Stat. 48.13)

What rights do I have to legal counsel and due process in juvenile court proceedings?

The Children's Code details the requirements to assure fairness and efficiency. Specifically,

1. you may be taken into physical custody only by authorized persons for reasons stated in the law. (Wis.Stat. 48.19)

2. an intake worker or person having custody must attempt to notify your parents immediately. (Wis.Stat. 48.19)

3. being taken into custody is not an arrest. (Wis.Stat. 48.19)

4. a copy of the reasons for taking you into custody must be given to you. (Wis.Stat. 48.20)

5. when interviewed by the intake worker, you must be advised of your right to counsel and right against self-incrimination. (Wis.Stat. 48.20)

6. the intake worker must make every effort to release the child from custody. (Wis.Stat. 48.20)

7. you may be held in secure custody (confinement or supervision) only if you request it or where you meet certain limited criteria indicating that you will flee from a nonsecure custodial placement. (Wis.Stat. 48.205, .207)

8. you have a right to a hearing within twenty-four hours if in custody. Children in nonsecure custody may waive this right. (Wis.Stat. 48.21)

9. before a hearing, you must be informed by the judge of:

    a. the charges that have or may be made
    b. nature and possible consequences of the hearing
    c. the right to counsel regardless of ability to pay
    d. the right to remain silent
    e. the right to confront, cross-examine, and present witnesses.

10. any child alleged to be delinquent or held in secure detention

facilities must be represented by counsel at all stages of proceedings, unless willingly waived by a person fifteen years or older and the court accepts the waiver. If the child is thought to be in need of protection or services, the child may be represented by counsel at the discretion of the judge. If the child is not represented, the court cannot place the child outside his or her home in making a disposition or in approving a change of placement. (Wis.Stat. 48.23)

11. At the fact-finding hearing, motions can be made to attack illegally seized evidence, illegally obtained statements, defects in the proceedings, lack of probable cause, insufficiency or invalidity of the petition. (Wis.Stat. 48.297)

12. At the plea hearing, a record must be transcribed and you have the right to legal help or counsel. The general public must be excluded from the hearing. (Wis.Stat. 48.30)

13. You have a right to trial by jury if you request it.

14. Before disposition of cases, an agency must submit a report to the judge of a plan for rehabilitation and treatment which "employs the least restrictive means to accomplish the purpose." (Wis.Stat. 48.33)

15. At the dispositional hearing, anyone may present evidence relevant to the issue of the disposition. (Wis.Stat. 48.335)

16. When entering a judgment the judge must set forth his or her findings and disposition in the proceeding. A judgment in proceedings on a petition is not considered a crime, does not impose any civil disabilities ordinarily resulting from conviction of a crime, and cannot disqualify one from any civil service application or appointment. (Wis.Stat. 48.35)

17. You and your parents may petition for a revision of a dispositional order via a hearing with the child again entitled to counsel. (Wis.Stat. 48.363)

DELINQUENCY

What is a delinquent child?

A delinquent child is any person between the ages of twelve and eighteen years who has violated a federal law or state criminal law. (Wis.Stat. 48.12)

What happens if I am charged with delinquency?

There are several steps that must be followed before you can be found delinquent:

1. A juvenile case coming into the court system is first referred to an intake worker, who investigates and either recommends that a petition be filed, agrees to an informal disposition, or closes the case. (Wis.Stat. 48.20)

2. If a petition is filed about an **alleged** violation of a law, the court will issue a **summons** requiring the appearance of you and your parents unless you appear voluntarily. (Wis.Stat. 48.27)

3. The court may order you to be examined by a physician, psychologist, or psychiatrist if reasonable cause exists for such an examination. (Wis.Stat. 48.295)

4. A plea hearing will be held within thirty days of the filing of a petition or issuance of a citation for a child not held in secure custody or within ten days of the filing if you are held in secure detention. At the plea hearing, you may either accept or admit the facts in the petition or contest the petition. (Wis.Stat. 48.30)

5. If you contest the petition or citation (Wis.Stat. 778.25) the court must set a date for a **fact-finding** hearing within twenty to thirty days. (Wis.Stat. 48.30) The purpose of the fact-finding hearing is to determine if the allegations of the petition are supported "beyond reasonable doubt." At the conclusion of the hearing, the court or jury will make a determination of the facts. (Wis.Stat. 48.31)

6. A dispositional hearing will be conducted at which any party may present evidence to the issue of the disposition and make alternative dispositional recommendations. The judge may:
   a. counsel the child or parent.
   b. place child under supervision of a youth agency, Department of Health and Social Services, or an adult friend under rules of conduct prescribed by the judge.
   c. place the child in a foster home, residential treatment center, home of a relative, etc.
   d. transfer legal custody including sending the person to a secured correctional facility.
   e. order restitution for property damage or personal injury.
   f. order special treatment.
   g. restrict, suspend, or revoke the privilege of operating an automobile.
   h. impose a forfeiture of up to $50.00 and raise it $50.00 for subsequent adjudications of delinquency of the individual child.
   i. order participation in a supervised work program to promote rehabilitation of the child.
   j. order that a minor over seventeen be allowed to live independently under supervision. (Wis.Stat. 48.34)

VIOLATIONS OF CIVIL LAWS OR ORDINANCES

The juvenile court has **exclusive jurisdiction** over any child who violates a law punishable by forfeiture or a county, town, or municipal ordinance. In addition, regular courts of civil and criminal jurisdiction have concurrent jurisdiction with juvenile courts against minors sixteen years or older for violations punishable by forfeiture. (Wis.Stat. 48.125, .17)

In addition, for traffic violations, courts of criminal and civil jurisdiction have exclusive jurisdiction in proceedings against children sixteen years or older for violations of the motor vehicle code. Here you will be treated as an adult for sentencing purposes.

Is there any substantial difference between the treatment accorded minors aged 16 years or older for civil law and ordinance violations in juvenile court as compared to circuit-municipal courts?

No. For violations or ordinances both courts may:

1. impose a forfeiture,
2. counsel your parents,
3. suspend your driver's license.

However, in disposing of civil law or ordinance violations a juvenile court also has the options of ordering the minor to participate in a supervised work program and make restitution for personal injury or property damage done to others. (Wis.Stat. 48.17, .343)

CHILDREN IN NEED OF PROTECTION OR SERVICES

A child in need of protection or services is a person over whom the juvenile court has jurisdiction and includes a person who:

1. is without a parent or guardian.
2. has been abandoned or is a runaway.
3. has been the victim of sexual, emotional, or physical abuse.
4. needs special care or treatment that the parent is unable to provide.
5. is habitually truant from home or school.
6. is receiving inadequate care because the parent is missing, in prison, or hospitalized.
7. is the victim of parental neglect that endangers physical health.
8. committed a violation of federal or state criminal law (delinquent act) while under twelve years of age. (Wis.Stat. 48.13)

What happens to me if I need protection or services?

You could be taken into custody and an intake worker would immediately attempt to notify your parents. A petition may be filed with the court and hearing scheduled—although a hearing may be **waived** by the parent or—if over twelve years—by the child. If the judge determines that the best interests of the child and public are served, he or she may order a consent decree or order the petition dismissed and refer the matter to the intake worker for informal settlement. A hearing would be held if the petition is contested—that is, if all parties could not agree; if not contested, the court will set a date for disposition hearing. If the petition is contested, the court will set a date for a fact-finding hearing. (Wis.Stat. 48.30)

After the fact-finding hearing, the court will either dismiss the petition or find the child in need of protection or services. If found in need of protection or services, the judge may order a care and treatment plan like that available to delinquents except that the judge may not:

1. transfer custody to a correctional institution.
2. order restitution.
3. order payment of a forfeiture.
4. restrict, suspend, or revoke a driving privilege. (Wis.Stat. 48.345)

Can anyone see my juvenile record?

No. The law says that juvenile records must be kept separately from records of adults. Juvenile records remain absolutely confidential except:

1. in juvenile court proceedings or by court order.
2. for newspaper reporters who need to obtain information but who cannot reveal the identity of the child involved.
3. for confidential exchange of information between the police and school officials.
4. for law enforcement and social welfare agencies when the person is sixteen or older and the case is transferred to adult criminal courts. (Wis.Stat. 48.396)

Are the consequences of judgment and disposition in juvenile court limited compared to adult court?

Yes. A judgment in proceedings in juvenile court:

1. is not a conviction of a crime.
2. cannot impose any civil disabilities. (Wis.Stat. 48.35)

A disposition, and any record of evidence given in a hearing in juvenile court,

1. is not admissible as evidence in any other court after you reach eighteen except in sentencing proceedings after conviction of a felony.

2. bars any future proceedings on the same matter in criminal court when you reach age eighteen. (Wis.Stat. 48.35)

On the other hand, criminal conviction in an adult court may have the following consequences (among others). It may:

1. damage your reputation for a lifetime.
2. make you ineligible for a position of trust requiring bonding (truck driving, sales, banking, management).
3. make a military commission more difficult to secure.
4. make civilian or military security clearances very difficult to obtain.
5. make your entrance into certain professions (teaching, medicine, law, etc.) difficult or impossible.
6. result in loss of voting and other civil rights.
7. show your unfitness to adopt a child.
8. deny you a job since job application questionnaires often ask for arrest or conviction data.

CASE STUDY*
In re Gault

On June 7, 1964, an Arizona woman received an obscene phone call. The woman believed that 15-year-old Gerald Francis Gault, who lived nearby with his parents, was the culprit. Gerald had been in trouble before and was on probation at the time, so it didn't take juvenile authorities long to act. In fact, Gerald and a friend were taken into custody the next day by a deputy sheriff. Gerald's arrest, as it turned out, was the beginning of a three-year legal battle that ultimately ended up before the U.S. Supreme Court. At issue was whether a minor accused of a crime has the same constitutional protections, such as the right to an attorney, that an adult does.

The legal battle arose because of what happened to Gerald after his arrest. Following an overnight stay at the local children's detention home, Gerald was brought into juvenile court for a hearing. The hearing, which Gerald and his parents were notified of only a day in advance, was based on a petition filed by a juvenile probation officer named Flagg. In that petition, Flagg listed no specific charges against Gerald, stating only that he was "a delinquent minor." Moreover, a copy of the petition was never sent to Gerald's parents.

In line with Arizona juvenile court practices at that time, the hearing on Gerald's case was highly informal. No attorneys were present, no sworn testimony was taken (the woman who made the complaint was not at the hearing), and no record was kept of the proceedings. Lacking a record, later appeals courts received conflicting evidence about what was said at the hearing. But it did appear that Gerald had admitted to Flagg that he was involved in the phone call, although Gerald claimed a friend did most of the talking.

A second hearing was held June 15 before the same judge. At this hearing, Flagg's testimony was that Gerald had not admitted making any lewd remarks to the woman. And, once again, the woman herself was not called to testify about the phone call. Despite this, the judge concluded after the hearing that Gerald should be committed to the state Industrial School for up to six years on a charge of making an obscene phone call. (Had Gerald been an adult, the maximum sentence he could have received on the same charge would have been sixty days in jail.)

Gerald's parents then appealed the judge's ruling by filing a writ of habeas corpus for their son's release. They said Gerald's constitutional rights under the Fifth, Sixth, and Fourteenth Amendments had been violated during the juvenile court hearings. Among the rights denied to Gerald, his parents said, were: (1) the right to notice of charges; (2) the right to be represented by an attorney; (3) the right to confront and cross-examine witnesses; and (4) the right not to incriminate himself. The Arizona Supreme Court, however, refused to issue a writ of habeas corpus, ruling that Gerald's rights had not been violated during the hearings.

The case was finally appealed to the U.S. Supreme Court, which in May of 1967 issued a landmark ruling in Gerald's favor. Justice Abe Fortas, the author of the court's opinion, said in essence that juveniles accused of a crime are entitled to the same basic constitutional

---

*This is a summary of the case. For the court's complete opinion, see 387 U.S.1, 87 S.Ct. 1428, 18 L.Ed.2d 527 (1967).

rights and protections that adults in this country have always had.

The court's lengthy decision, from which two justices dissented in whole or in part, began by discussing the history of the juvenile court system since its inception in the early 1900s. The court noted that the system was designed to reform children rather than to determine their guilt or innocence. But the court said this supposedly benevolent system, with its emphasis on treatment rather than judgments arrived at through due process of law, actually worked to deny young people their basic constitutional rights. "Juvenile Court history," the court said, "has again demonstrated that unbridled discretion, however benevolently motivated, is frequently a poor substitute for principle and procedure."

In Gerald's case, the court said, this paternalistic system allowed him to be sent to prison while denying him the kind of constitutional safeguards an adult defendant would automatically receive. "The fact of the matter is that, however euphemistic the title, a 'receiving home' or an 'industrial school' for juveniles is an institution of confinement in which the child is incarcerated," the court said. "In view of this, it would be extraordinary if our Constitution did not require the procedural regularity and the exercise of care implied in the phrase 'due process.' Under our Constitution, the condition of being a boy does not justify a kangaroo court."

What follows is a look at how the Supreme Court ruled on four of the specific issues raised by Gerald and his parents in their appeal:

1. **Right to notice.** The court said Gerald and his parents were entitled to more than one day's advance notice that a juvenile court hearing would be held. One day, the court said, simply did not give them enough time to prepare their case. The court also said that the notice was inadequate because no specific allegations against Gerald were made in Flagg's petition.

2. **Right to be represented by an attorney.** In rejecting the request for a writ of habeas corpus, the Arizona appeals court had ruled that "the parent and probation officer may be relied upon to protect the infant's interest" at a juvenile court hearing. But the Supreme Court said this clearly was not the case during the proceedings against Gerald, when the probation officer—Flagg—was also the chief witness against the boy. The court concluded on this point that "in proceedings to determine delinquency which may result in commitment to an institution ... the child and his parents must be notified of the child's right to be represented by counsel."

3. **Right to confront and cross-examine witnesses.** The court could find no good reason for denying this right to juveniles. In Gerald's case, the court said, "confrontation and sworn testimony by witnesses available for cross-examination were essential for a finding of delinquency and an order committing Gerald to a state institution for a maximum of six years."

4. **Right to remain silent to avoid self-incrimination.** On this point, the court said that "it would indeed be surprising if the privilege against self-incrimination were available to hardened criminals but not to children. The language of the Fifth Amendment [which provides this right] ... is unequivocal and without exception." One reason why juveniles must have this right, the court said, is that they are sometimes tried as adults following juvenile court proceedings. For this and other reasons, the court thus concluded that Gerald's alleged confession to Flagg was unconstitutional because Gerald had not been notified beforehand of his right to remain silent.

QUESTIONS FOR DISCUSSION

1. Make a list of anything that happened to Gerald Gault that you consider unfair. Explain your reasoning for each item on the list.

2. How would you change any of the things you thought were unfair?

3. What rights that adults have were not granted in the *Gault* decision?

4. Do you agree with the *Gault* decision? Why or why not? Should adults and minors have the same legal rights? Why or why not?

5. Do you think Gerald Gault's hearing would have turned out differently if he had been given the rights the Supreme Court later ruled he was entitled to?

SUGGESTED ACTIVITIES

1. Role-Play

In Wisconsin, sixteen and seventeen year olds may be tried as adults if they are found unfit to be tried as juveniles. They face this prospect if they are charged with a crime. When the district attorney receives the case from the police and decides that the minor involved should be tried as an adult, he or she asks the juvenile judge to schedule a "fitness hearing" for the minor.

The judge may consider any one or a combination of the following criteria to determine whether or not the minor is fit to be tried as a juvenile:

1. the seriousness of the crime.
2. the minor's previous delinquent history.
3. the degree of criminal sophistication displayed by the minor.
4. whether or not the juvenile court has been successful in past attempts to rehabilitate the minor.
5. whether or not there is a chance the minor can be rehabilitated under the jurisdiction of the juvenile court.

If the minor is found fit he or she remains under the jurisdiction of the juvenile court, where there are fewer punishments. If found unfit, the minor is transferred to the adult court system and, if found guilty, may be sentenced to the state prison.

In the following role-play the class will decide whether Mark is fit to be tried as a juvenile. The purpose of this role-play is to provide you with a better understanding of the legal and human issues involved in a legal process—not necessarily to teach you court procedure.

Mark has been accused of intentional homicide (murder) because Tony died as a result of a head injury. Mark stated that he and Tony had been drinking and that they had a fight. Witnesses at the party said they saw both Mark and Tony fighting.

Role Play Procedure

Review the above five factors that a judge ponders when determining fitness. Next, review the probation report below. Seven students should volunteer or be selected to role-play the judge, district attorney, defense attorney, probation officer, Mark, his mother, his father. The role of observers will be played by the remaining students in class.

Role-play the fitness hearing according to the procedures summarized in the role description of the juvenile court judge below.

After the role-play, a debriefing can occur so that observers can comment on their impressions of the activity.

Probation Report

Name: Mark

Age: 17

Lives: With father and mother in a middle-class neighborhood

School: In grade 10 became involved in gang activity. For a short time, dropped out of school. His best friend had been killed in gang warfare. Eventually Mark returned to school and dropped gang activity. Has earned above average grades since returning to school.

Prior Record: Age 14, charged with being under the influence of alcohol: case dropped

Age 15, charged with taking car without owner's consent (joyriding): released to parents

Age 15½, charged with being under the influence of alcohol and vandalism to the school: placed on six months' formal probation.

Role Descriptions

Juvenile Court Judge. This hearing is held for the purpose of determining whether or not Mark is fit to be tried in the juvenile court. Your job as judge is to preside over the court, call the case, and follow these procedures:

1. Call upon the probation officer to present his or her report and recommendations on sentencing to the group.

2. Provide the defense attorney with an opportunity to respond to the report.

3. The defense attorney may want to examine and question the probation officer to get more information about the data contained in the report.

4. The district attorney may then cross-examine the probation officer, make pertinent comments, and present counter-arguments.

5. You as judge now call the parents to testify about and respond to all that has been presented in the court. Focus on questions that you think are necessary to help you better understand the relationship between Mark and his parents.

6. Next, you ask Mark to respond. Tell Mark that your goal is to decide what is in his best interest and question Mark as to his version of and attitudes about what has happened. Try to determine through questions his reaction to the testimony presented before him in court and the recommendations made by the probation officer, defense attorney, and district attorney.

7. Finally, you as judge must make a decision on what action you believe would be best after all parties have had an opportunity to present their positions.

Probation Officer. Drawing upon information obtained from such sources as police, school, parents, and social service agencies, you have prepared a probation report for the court. After summarizing your report, tell the courts why you think Mark is fit or unfit to be transferred (waived) to adult court for disposition. Remember that you will be questioned by both the district attorney and defense attorney—both of whom will ask for additional facts and information to support your recommendation. While you cannot alter the facts, you may provide information of a more detailed nature than that stated in the report you prepared for the court.

Defense Attorney. It is your function to argue that Mark—your client—is fit to be tried in juvenile court. Following the probation officer's report, you will have the chance to respond to that report and ask questions. The questions you ask the probation officer should be questions that will bring out positive factors in Mark's background, such as his satisfactory school record and his decision to give up his gang membership. These types of questions will reinforce your arguments that Mark should be found fit to be tried as a juvenile.

District Attorney. It is your job to speak for the people and to make sure that the community is protected from criminals. After you have listened to the probation report and the response of the defense attorney, tell the court why you feel that Mark should be found unfit for juvenile court and should be waived to adult court for trial. You should also cross-examine the probation officer and ask questions that will bring out answers which support your position on the matter. For example, you might want to focus on Mark's drinking problems and prior convictions.

Parents. The reason you are in court today is because the court requires you to appear with Mark. After hearing reports from the probation officer and both lawyers, Mark and you will be asked by the judge to respond to the recommendation that Mark be waived to adult court for trial. When called upon by the judge, you may respond in any manner you wish. For example, you may put the blame on Mark, accept responsibility yourself, indicate anger at the judge, the probation officer, etc. Act the way you believe a parent of Mark's might act under similar circumstances.

Mark. During the hearing, you will be given the chance to respond to and comment on the probation officer's report about you. While you cannot change the facts presented, you can and should give background information or explanations which might help your case and favorably influence the judge before the judge decides whether you are or are not fit to be tried in juvenile court. Prepare yourself to tell the judge what his or her decision should be . . . and why.

Observers. Your role is to evaluate what has occurred at the hearing. You will be expected to share your impressions with the class after the hearing has taken place. For example: (1) Do you think the players role-played their roles and behaved realistically? (2) Based on the testimony of the case, do you agree or disagree with the judge's decision? Explain.

Class Discussion. What things should be the most important factors in determining whether or not a person under 18 years of age should be tried as a juvenile rather than as an adult?

2. Interpretation Activity A

Table 10.2 provides data about crime in Wisconsin.

Number of Offenses, 1979	**207,089**
Percent change from 1978	+14%
Percent change from 1970	+72%
Rate Per 100,000 Population, 1976	**4,387.5**
Percent change from 1978	+13%
Percent change from 1970	+61%
Population, 1978	**4,720,000**
Percent change from 1978	+1%
Percent change from 1970	+7%

TABLE 10.2. Crime Index Offenses in Wisconsin, 1979. Source: *Wisconsin Criminal Justice Information: Crime and Arrests 1979.* Madison, WI: Crime Information Bureau, 1980. Reprinted by permission.

1. What general conclusions can be drawn from the data provided?

2. What do you think are the causes for the steady increases in crime in the state?

3. Interpretation Activity B

Figure 10.3 provides a breakdown of major crime in Wisconsin.

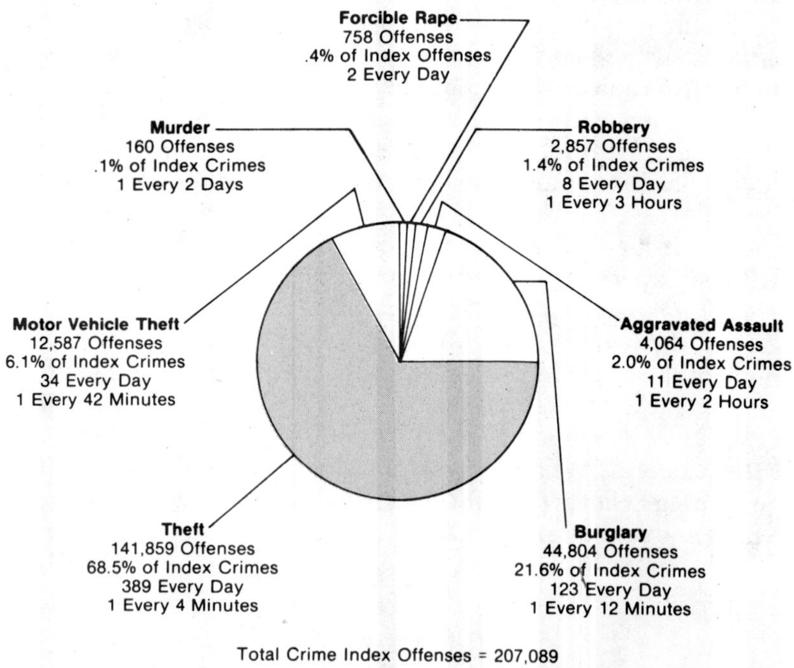

FIGURE 10.3. Crime index offenses in Wisconsin, 1979. Source: *Wisconsin Criminal Justice Information: Crime and Arrests 1979.* Madison, WI: Crime Information Bureau, 1980. Reprinted by permission.

1. Which crimes seem to be the most serious? Why do you think they are?

2. How does your community compare to the data and figures presented in the graph?

3. Why do you think we seem to have yearly increases in crime in Wisconsin?

4. Interpretation Activity C

Figure 10.4 provides information about theft in Wisconsin for 1979.

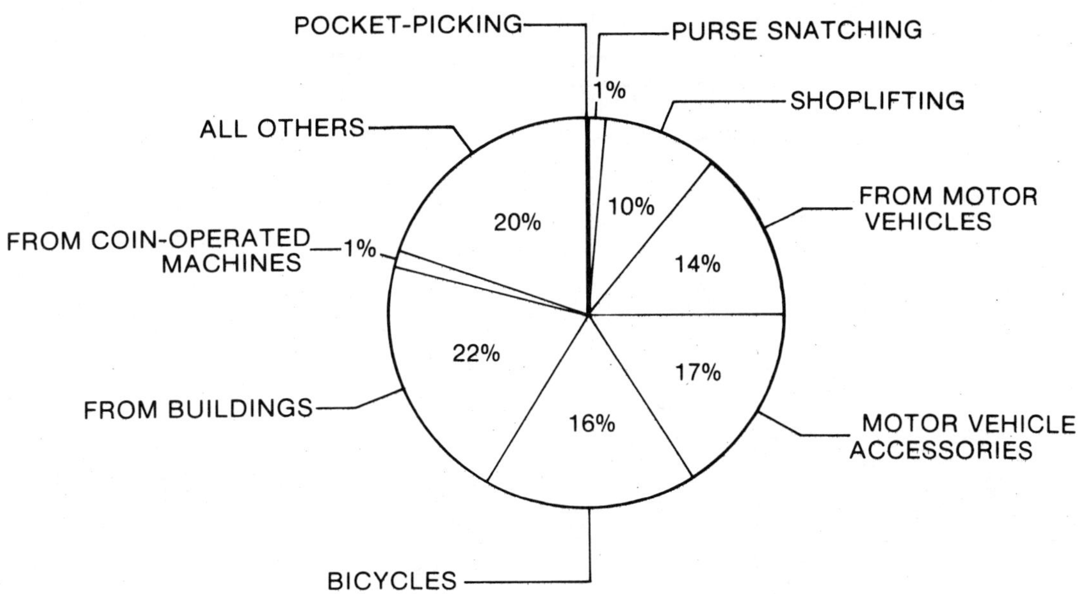

FIGURE 10.4. Breakdown of theft crimes in Wisconsin, 1979. Source: *Wisconsin Criminal Justice Information: Crime and Arrests 1979.* Madison, WI: Crime Information Bureau, 1980. Reprinted by permission.

1. Which types of theft seem to be the most:
   a. frequent?
   b. easy to accomplish? why?
   c. easy to prevent? why?

2. In the blank circle graph below compare 1979 to the same data for this school year. Your teacher may wish to provide a blank graph for you to use.

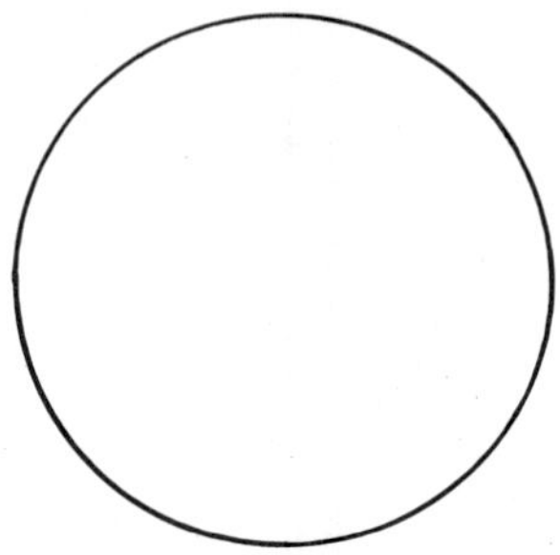

5. Interpretation Activity D

Table 10.3 provides additional information about theft in Wisconsin for 1979 including the percentage of change from last year, total value stolen, and average value stolen.

NUMBER OF THEFTS
PERCENT OF STATE TOTAL

	Number of Offenses			
	1979	Percent Change from 1978	Total Value Stolen	Average Value Stolen
Pocket-picking	384	+28%	$52,044	$136
Purse-snatching	1,542	-2%	$104,345	$68
Shoplifting	14,199	+3%	$480,378	$34
From motor vehicles	19,831	+17%	$4,042,587	$204
Motor vehicle accessories	23,920	+23%	$3,327,525	$139
Bicycles	22,384	+11%	$2,357,048	$105
From buildings	30,513	+14%	$7,728,223	$253
From coin operated machines	1,346	+10%	$85,771	$64
All Others	27,740	+12%	$6,177,512	$223
State Totals	141,859	+13%	$24,355,432	$172

TABLE 10.3. Theft in Wisconsin, 1979. Percentages are rounded off to nearest number. Source: *Wisconsin Criminal Justice Information: Crime and Arrests 1979.* Madison, WI: Crime Information Bureau, 1980. Reprinted by permission.

1. Which crime of theft was:
   a. the most frequent type of theft?
   b. the most costly type of theft?
   c. the theft that increased the most since 1978?
   d. the theft that showed the only decrease since 1978?
   e. the type of theft that averaged the most dollar value per theft?

2. Why do you think that theft is increasing in Wisconsin?

3. What can you do to assist law enforcement in helping decrease crimes of theft in your community?

6. Studying Crime Data

Obtain a copy of the current year publication, *Wisconsin Criminal Justice Information: Crime and Arrests 19 *, and compare the data presented to this year's new information and study the differences in the data.

Try to identify any reversals or new trends in crime in the State of Wisconsin.

To obtain a copy of the report contact:

Director
Division of Law Enforcement Services
Crime Information Bureau
Department of Justice
State Capitol
Madison, Wisconsin 53702.

7. Mock Trials

Mock Trials: Scripts for Wisconsin Lawyers and Teachers. Published by Wisconsin Department of Public Instruction in cooperation with the Wisconsin Bar Foundation. Bulletin No. 0166, 1980.

Mock Trials include Automobile Accident, Landlord-Tenant, Drunk Driving, Homicide, Burglary, and Child Abuse scripts.

VOCABULARY

Alleged
Arrest
Arson
Assault
Battery
Custody
Disorderly conduct
Exclusive jurisdiction
Fact-finding hearing
Forfeiture
Malicious mischief
Manslaughter
No-Knock warrant
Perjury
Plea
Prosecution
Rehabilitation
Restitution
Summons
Waive

RELATED LEGAL CASES

State Ex Rel Harris v. *Larson,* 64 Wis.2d 521, 219 N.W.2d 335 (pre-trial detention of minors)

State Ex Rel Hetget v. *Circuit Court for Waukesha County.* 84, Wis.2d 435, 267 N.W.2d 309 (1978) (juvenile records discoverable under certain circumstances)

State v. *Becker,* 74 Wis.2d 675 (1976), *Miller* v. *Quatsoe,* 348 Fed.Supp. 764 (1972), *D.H.* v. *State,* 76 Wis.2d 286, 251 N.W.2d 196. (waiver within sound discretion of court guidelines stated)

McKeiver v. *Pennsylvania,* 403 U.S.528 (1971) (no right to jury trial in juvenile court context)

State v. *Engler,* 80 Wis.2d 402, 259 N.W.2d 97 (1977) (court can place defendant on probation or commit him to custody of Department of Health and Social Services—Federal Youth Corrections Act)

Dorszynski v. *U.S.* 418 U.S. 424, 94 S.Ct. 3042, 41 L.Ed. 855. (court has power to sentence juvenile as adult)

SUGGESTED READINGS

"Simulation—The Best Interest of the Child," *Bill of Rights in Action,* April, 1979, vol. 13, no. 2, pp. 17-18.

"Juvenile Rights," *Crime and Criminals.* Minneapolis, MN: Greenhaven Press, Inc., 1976.

"How Can You Help Reduce Crime?", *Bill of Rights in Action,* February, 1979, vol. 11, no. 1, p. 2

SUGGESTED RESOURCES

Wisconsin Statutes

Youth Policy and Law Center Inc.
30 West Mifflin Street, Room 904
Madison, Wisconsin 53705

Local Juvenile Offices

Wisconsin Criminal Justice Information: Crime and Arrests 1980. Division of Law Enforcement Services: Crime Information Bureau, Department of Justice, State Capitol, Madison 53702.

SECTION V

THE CITIZEN-STUDENT AND CRITICAL PERSONAL ISSUES

CONTENTS

ESKY

11

The Citizen-Student and Alcohol

Young people of your age are more interested in participating in adult activities than ever before. Since Wisconsin lowered the age of majority to eighteen for most purposes, even young people under the age of eighteen have become very interested in drinking activities and some may already be experimenting with alcoholic beverages for themselves. A separate chapter on alcohol is included in this book to help you understand your rights and responsibilities with respect to alcoholic beverages.

It is an unfortunate fact that some people—young and old alike—become involved and dependent on alcohol. This fact affects all young people in some way, directly or indirectly. The purpose of this chapter is not to moralize or sermonize, but to present the legal facts about the use of alcohol. With all the present attention paid to the "drug problem," you may already realize the consequences of use and abuse. It is up to you to draw the conclusions which are right for your own life; this is the essence of adult responsibility.

What is an alcoholic beverage?

Generally, an alcoholic beverage is any drink which can make people drunk when taken in large quantities. Wisconsin law divides alcoholic beverages into two types and defines each exactly. The first type is fermented malt beverages (beer); beer contains less than 5% alcohol by weight. (Wis.Stat. 66.654) The second type of alcoholic beverages are called **intoxicating liquors;** these contain a minimum of .5% alcohol by weight. This group includes wine and "hard liquor."

May I buy or drink beer?

It is a misdemeanor for anyone under the age of eighteen to buy beer, or to drink it unless the minor is with his or her parents. (Wis.Stat. 66.20)

May I buy or drink hard liquor or wine?

It is illegal for a minor to consume, buy, attempt to buy, have another buy for him, or enter a liquor store to try to buy any beer, wine, or intoxicating liquors. All these acts are misdemeanors. (Wis.Stat. 176.30, 66.20)

Can the person who sells me liquor get into trouble?

Yes. Strict penalties make most bar and liquor store owners careful to check the age of their customers.

First, it is a misdemeanor to sell "intoxicating liquor" to a minor (Wis.Stat. 176.30) and a misdemeanor to sell beer to a minor. (Wis.Stat. 66.20)

Second, the seller could be found guilty of "contributing to the delinquency of a minor," a misdemeanor in Wisconsin. (Wis.Stat. 947.15)

Third, the owner's license could be taken away if he sells alcoholic beverages to a minor. (Wis.Stat. 66.054) This would mean that he would not be allowed to sell liquor any longer and would have to close up his business.

If an older friend gives me a drink or buys liquor for me, can he get in trouble?

Yes. The law treats this just as if it were a sale. It is a misdemeanor to give alcoholic beverages to a minor. (Wis.Stat. 176.30, 66.054) The friend could also be found guilty of contributing to the delinquency of a minor. (Wis.Stat. 947.15)

Can I drive a car while under the influence of an intoxicant or controlled substance?

No! The law says:

1. No person may drive or operate a motor vehicle while under the influence of an intoxicant or a controlled substance.

2. It is unlawful for any person to cause injury to another person by the negligent operation of a vehicle while under the influence of an intoxicant. No person shall be convicted under this subsection except on proof of causal negligence in addition to such operation while under the influence of an intoxicant.

3. In this section "drive" means the exercise of physical control over the speed and direction of a motor vehicle while it is in motion. "Operate" means the physical manipulation or activation of any of the controls of a motor vehicle necessary to put it in motion.

4. A person whose blood contains 0.1% or more by weight of alcohol

is under the influence of an intoxicant for purposes of this section. Notwithstanding s.885.235(1)(c), a chemical analysis of a person's blood, breath, or urine which has been admitted into evidence and which shows that there was 0.1% or more by weight of alcohol in the person's blood is sufficient evidence, on which to base a finding that the person's blood contained 0.1% or more by weight of alcohol.

Can I be prosecuted under other statutory provisions for use of a vehicle while intoxicated?

Yes. Chapter 940 of the Wisconsin Criminal Code under Crimes Against Life and Bodily Security says:

1. Whoever causes the death of another human being by a high degree of negligence in the operation or handling of a vehicle, firearm, airgun, knife, or bow and arrow is guilty of a Class E felony.

2. A high degree of negligence is conduct which demonstrates ordinary negligence to a high degree, consisting of an act which the person should realize creates a situation of unreasonable risk and high probability of death or great bodily harm to another.

3. Whoever by the negligent operation or handling of a vehicle, firearm, or airgun and while under the influence of an intoxicant causes the death of another is guilty of a Class D felony. No person may be convicted under this section except upon proof of casual negligence in addition to such operation or handling while under the influence of an intoxicant.

Do I need an identification card to buy alcoholic beverages?

Yes. Only a valid state identification card or certificate issued by the state is sufficient identification to purchase, possess, or consume alcoholic beverages. (Wis.Stat. 66.057)

What can happen if I borrow somebody's I.D. to buy liquor?

It is a misdemeanor to lie about your age to buy alcoholic beverages. (Wis.Stat. 176.31) Using someone else's identification is, in effect, a lie.

What can happen if I misrepresent my age?

> No person may falsely represent that he or she is at least eighteen years of age for the purpose of asking for or receiving fermented malt beverages from a keeper of any place for the sale of fermented malt beverages. A person who violates this subsection is subject to a forfeiture of not more than $25, except that disposition and proceedings against a person under eighteen years of age shall be as provided by (Wis.Stat. 48.344.)

To Procure Alcohol?

> **Wis.Stat. 176.31** Minors misrepresentation to procure intoxicating liquor; penalty. (1) No person may represent that he or she is of age for the purpose of asking for, or receiving, any liquor unless authorized by law.

A person who violates this subsection is subject to a forfeiture of not more than $25, except that disposition in proceedings against a person under eighteen years of age shall be as provided by s. 48.344.

(2) No person under the age of eighteen may procure, seek to procure, knowingly possess or consume in public intoxicating liquor. A person who violates this subsection is subject to a forfeiture of not more than $25, except that disposition in proceedings against a person under eighteen years of age shall be as provided by s. 48.344.

What happens if someone does sell alcohol to me and I am under 18?

The law plainly states that no one may:

1. sell, furnish, or give intoxicating liquor to a person under age eighteen.
2. procure intoxicating liquor for a person under age eighteen.
3. traffic or deal in intoxicating liquor with a person under age eighteen.

A person who violates this subsection is subject to prosecution under the law in Wisconsin.

Most Wisconsin educational institutions have their own alcohol policies to complement state and local ordinances.

CASE STUDY*
Olsen v. Copeland

It was the kind of tragic accident that seems to happen all too often on the highways. A man driving home from a tavern in the Milwaukee area collided with a car driven by DeAnna Olsen, the mother of five children. Mrs. Olsen was killed. Her husband then brought a lawsuit for wrongful death against the other driver, who allegedly was drunk at the time of the accident. But Mrs. Olsen's husband went one step further: he also sued the operator of the tavern where the man had allegedly become intoxicated. In many states, laws known as "dram shop" acts permit such suits against a tavernkeeper. However, Wisconsin has no "dram shop" law. Instead, Wisconsin goes by an old common law rule that says a tavernkeeper cannot be held liable for injuries to a third party caused by an intoxicated patron. As a result, when the lawsuit brought by Mrs. Olsen's husband came up for trial in 1977, a Milwaukee County Circuit Court judge ruled that there were no legal grounds for suing the tavernkeeper, John Q. Copeland.

The case didn't end there, however, because Mrs. Olsen's husband filed a motion asking the judge, George A. Burns, Jr., to reconsider his decision. Burns did just that and, in 1978, he reversed himself by ruling that Copeland could be sued in connection with Mrs. Olsen's death. "The time has come," Burns wrote in his decision, "to reject and lay to rest those social considerations which for many years past have exculpated negligent dispensers of liquor." Copeland immediately appealed Burns' ruling to the Wisconsin Supreme Court. Copeland argued that Burns' decision was clearly at odds with a 1970 ruling in which the Supreme Court had upheld the common law rule against suing tavernkeepers. The stage was thus set for the Supreme Court to reconsider its earlier ruling.

The Supreme Court published its decision on Copeland's appeal in June 1979. And once again, the court held that tavernkeepers cannot be held liable for the later behavior of intoxicated patrons. However, as was the case in 1970, the court was sharply divided on the issue, with three justices dissenting from the opinion of the court majority.

Writing for the majority, Justice Connor T. Hansen said the common law rule is sound public policy because it is based on the belief that "the responsibility for the act remains with the person whose voluntary intoxication resulted in the injury. The fact that today there may be more intoxicated persons behind the wheels of more autos is not a sufficient reason to change the rule." Hansen then went on to list three major reasons for maintaining the common law rule against suing tavernkeepers:

1. The act of serving liquor is a "remote cause" of any injuries later caused by the person who had the drinks. "The cause of an auto accident involving an intoxicated driver is the driver's inability to control his auto and this inability is the direct result of his voluntarily becoming intoxicated," Hansen said. "Assigning the blame to the one who provided that means for that intoxication carries the chain a link too far."

2. If tavernkeepers can be held liable for the subsequent behavior of intoxicated individuals, then so can anyone else who serves drinks to someone. Hansen said this would place an

*A summary of the case. For the court's complete opinion, see 90 Wis.2d 483, 280 N.W.2d 178 (1979).

"unreasonable burden" on bartenders, waiters and others—including social hosts—who regularly serve drinks. Even persons who serve alcohol at such functions as Fourth of July picnics and county fairs could be sued if the common law rule were abolished, Hansen said.

3. It is often difficult, if not impossible, to tell when someone has had too much to drink. "Each bartender, waiter and host will have ... different perceptions (about whether a person is intoxicated)," Hansen said. Moreover, he said that in some situations there simply would be no way of knowing how much alcohol a person has consumed. "To expect, for example, a hotel to be able to monitor the condition and behavior of guests who are free to circulate (from one part of the hotel to another) ... is to impose an unreasonable burden," Hansen said.

Hansen concluded by saying that the responsibility for controlling drinking and driving should rest with the state legislature and not the courts. Noting how widely laws vary from state to state in regard to "dram shop" lawsuits, Hansen said: "These differing positions illustrate the difficulty with a judicial resolution of the problem and reinforce our belief that the issue is one best dealt with by the legislature."

But Justice Roland B. Day, writing one of three dissents in the case, said the court majority had overlooked some key facts in making its decision. Among other things, Day said that "to call remote the link between a fatal automobile accident and the serving of alcohol to an intoxicated person is to ignore reality.... Of the 514 drivers who were killed in accidents (on Wisconsin highways in 1977), 422 were tested for blood alcohol content; 221 of those drivers were legally intoxicated."

Day went on to say that "we bear a tremendous social cost from the death and maiming that takes place on our highways because of drivers whose senses are dulled by alcohol. The tragedy of this family [the Olsens] ... is another example of the failure of a policy of placing sole responsibility on the consumer of alcohol. Until those who furnish alcohol to one who has obviously had more than he can handle are made to share responsibility, the scene will be repeated again and again and the list of innocent victims will continue to grow."

Can I get in trouble for just possessing liquor even if I'm not caught drinking?

It is a misdemeanor for anyone under the age of eighteen to possess alcoholic beverages unless accompanied by a parent, guardian, or **chaperone.** A chaperone is a "mature, responsible adult who is present to insure propriety at a gathering of young persons." (Wis.Stat. 176.31, 66.057) In addition, it is a violation of the "open bottle law" and a misdemeanor to have an open container of liquor in the passenger compartment of your car while it is on the road even though you have not been drinking any of the bottle's contents.

Also, minors who possess beer outside of a licensed premise when unaccompanied by a parent or chaperone shall have their motor vehicle license restricted or suspended. (Wis.Stat. 66.057, (24)b).

Can I go into a place that serves liquor if I only buy food?

It is illegal for the owner to permit a minor to **loiter** or to be in a room where alcoholic beverages are sold unless he or she is accompanied by parents. However, this part of the law does not apply to hotels, drugstores, grocery stores, bowling alleys, or restaurants where the principal business is serving food. (Wis.Stat. 66.054).

What can happen to an older person who is drunk in public?

Before 1973, public drunkenness was a crime. The state legislature changed that law and now persons who are publicly drunk are taken to detoxification centers where they may be confined for up to forty-eight hours. (Wis.Stat. 51.45) They are not confined for punishment, but so that they can be sobered up and given shelter, food, and counseling. However, if a person causes a disturbance or commits a crime while drunk he may still be arrested and put in jail as a result. Driving under the influence of alcohol remains a crime.

Can I get into trouble for possession of alcoholic beverages while at school?

> **Wis.Stat. 176.29** Possession of liquor on school grounds prohibited. (1) In this section:
>
> (a) "Motor vehicle" means a motor vehicle owned, rented or consigned to a school.
>
> (b) "School" means a public, parochial or private school which provides an educational program or one or more grades between grades 1 and 12 and which is commonly known as an elementary school, middle school, junior high school, senior high school or high school.
>
> (c) "School administrator" means the person designated by the governing body of a school as ultimately responsible for the ordinary operations of a school.
>
> (d) "School premises" means premises owned, rented or under the

control of a school.

(2) Except as provided by sub. (3) no person may possess or consume intoxicating liquor:

(a) On school premise;

(b) In a motor vehicle, if a pupil attending the school is in the motor vehicle; or

(c) While participating in a school-sponsored activity.

(3) Intoxicating liquor may be possessed or consumed on school premises, in motor vehicles or by participants in school-sponsored activities if specifically permitted in writing by the school administrator consistent with applicable laws and ordinances.

(4) A person who violates this section is subject to a forfeiture of not more than $200, except that disposition in proceedings against a person under 18 years of age shall be as provided by s.48.344.

QUESTIONS FOR DISCUSSION

1. What community agencies, both public and private, are available in your community to provide information, assistance, or referral services for individuals who have an alcohol abuse problem?

2. Where in your community can you receive emergency medical assistance if you, a friend, or a parent need help as a result of the use, abuse, or overindulgence of alcohol?

3. What can you do as an individual to show responsibility around alcoholic beverages at home, at a party, in a car, at school, and in the community?

VOCABULARY

Chaperone
Consume
Detoxification
Loiter
Sober

SUGGESTED ACTIVITY

Mock Trials: Scripts for Wisconsin Lawyers and Teachers. Published by Wisconsin Department of Public Instruction in cooperation with The Wisconsin Bar Foundation. Bulletin No. 0166, 1980.

Mock Trials include Automobile Accident, Landlord-Tenant, Drunk Driving, Homicide, Burglary, and Child Abuse scripts.

SUGGESTED READING

"Don't Go to Pot," in *You Can Change the Law* by Roy W. Seagraves, Henry B. McDaniel, and Betty A. Truce (Belmont, California: Fearon Publishers, 1973), pp. 17-24. Case discussion.

SUGGESTED RESOURCES

Let's Talk About Drug Abuse: Some Questions and Answers. Washington, D.C.: Department of Health and Human Services, 1980.

Bureau of Alcohol and Other Drug Abuse
Division of Mental Hygiene
One West Wilson Street
Madison 53702

12

The Citizen-Student and Controlled Substances

The state of Wisconsin is concerned for you about the use of controlled nonprescription drugs. You know from the literature, radio, television, and your peers that usage constitutes a dangerous threat to your health, to your family, and to your community. This chapter deals with some of the legal consequences of use of **controlled substances:** you will thus be well aware of the social and legal implications and potential adversary situations you can come face to face with in your community and state.

The Uniform Controlled Substance Act, Chapter 161 of the Wisconsin Criminal Code, begins with the Declaration of Intent:

The legislature finds that the abuse of controlled substances constitutes a serious problem for society. As a partial solution, these laws regulating controlled substances have been enacted with penalties. The legislature, recognizing a need for differentiation among those who would violate these laws makes this declaration of legislative intent.

(1) Persons who illicitly traffic commercially in controlled substances constitute a substantial menace to the public health and safety. The possibility of lengthy terms of imprisonment must exist as a deterrent to trafficking by such persons. Upon conviction for trafficking, such persons should be sentenced in a manner which will deter further trafficking by them, protect the public from their pernicious activities, and restore them to legitimate and socially useful endeavors.

(2) Persons who habitually or professionally engage in commercial trafficking in controlled substances and prescription drugs should, upon conviction, be sentenced to substantial terms of imprisonment to shield the public from their predatory acts. However, persons addicted to or dependent on controlled substances should, upon conviction, be sentenced in a manner most likely to produce rehabilitation.

(3) Upon conviction, persons who casually use or experiment with controlled substances should receive special treatment geared toward rehabilitation. The sentencing of casual users and experimenters should be such as

will best induce them to shun further contact with controlled substances and to develop acceptable alternatives to drug abuse.

Ch. 161, the uniform controlled substances act, precludes the enactment of municipal ordinances regulating the sale and possession of such controlled substances as marijuana. 63 Atty. Gen. 107.

You should be familiar with the following selected definitions used in the Uniform Controlled Substance Act.

(1) "Administer" means the direct application of a controlled substance, whether by injection, inhalation, ingestion or any other means, to the body of a patient or research subject by:

(3) "Bureau" means the bureau of narcotics and dangerous drugs, U.S. department of justice, or its successor agency.

(4) "Controlled substance" means a drug, substance or immediate precursor in schedules I to V of subch. II.

(5) "Counterfeit substance" means a controlled substance which, or the container or labeling of which, without authorization, bears the trademark, trade name or other identifying mark, imprint, number or device, or any likeness thereof, of a manufacturer, distributor or dispenser other than the person who in fact manufactured, distributed or dispensed the substance.

(6) "Deliver" or "delivery" means the actual, constructive or attempted transfer from one person to another of a controlled substance, whether or not there is any agency relationship.

(7) "Dispense" means to deliver a controlled substance to an ultimate user or research subject by or pursuant to the lawful order of a practitioner, including the prescribing, administering, packaging, labeling or compounding necessary to prepare the substance for that delivery.

(8) "Dispenser" means a practitioner who dispenses.

(9) "Distribute" means to deliver other than by administering or dispensing a controlled substance.

(10) "Distributor" means a person who distributes.

(11) "Drug" means a) substances recognized as drugs in the official United States Pharmacopoeia, official Homeopathic Pharmacopoeia of the United States or official National Formulary or any supplement to any of them; b) substances intended for use in the diagnosis, cure, mitigation, treatment or prevention of disease in man or animals; (c) substances, other than food, intended to affect the structure or any function or the body of man or animals; and d) substances intended for use as a component of any article specified in a), b) or c). It does not include devices or their components, parts or accessories.

(12) "Immediate precursor" means a substance which the controlled substances board has found to be and by rule designates as being the principal compound commonly used or produced primarily for use, and which is an immediate chemical intermediary used or likely to be used in the manufacture of a controlled substance, the control of which is necessary to prevent, curtail or limit manufacture.

(13) "Manufacture" means the production, preparation, propagation, compounding, conversion or processing of a controlled substance, either directly or indirectly by extraction from substances of natural origin, or independently by means of chemical synthesis, or by a combination of extraction and chemical synthesis, and includes any packaging or repackaging of the substance or labeling or relabeling of its container, except that this term does not include

the preparation or compounding of a controlled substance by an individual for his own use or the preparation, compounding, packaging or labeling of a controlled substance:

(a) By a practitioner as an incident to his administering or dispensing of a controlled substance in the course of his professional practice; or

(b) By a practitioner, or by his authorized agent under his supervision, for the purpose of, or as an incident to, research, teaching or chemical analysis and not for sale.

(14) "Marijuana" means all parts of the plant *Cannabis Sativa L.*, whether growing or not; the seeds thereof; the resin extracted from any part of the plant; and every compound, manufacture, salt, derivative, mixture or preparation of the plant, its seeds or resin. It does not include the mature stalks of the plant, fiber produced from the stalks, oil or cake made from the seeds of the plant, any other compound, manufacture, salt, derivative, mixture or preparation of the mature stalks (except the resin extracted therefrom), fiber, oil or cake or the sterilized seed of the plant which is incapable of germination.

(15) "Narcotic drug" means any of the following, whether produced directly or indirectly by extraction from substances of vegetable origin, or independently by means of chemical synthesis, or by a combination of extraction and chemical synthesis:

(a) Opium and opiate, and any salt, compound, derivative or preparation of opium or opiate.

(b) Any salt, compound, isomer, derivative or preparation thereof which is chemically equivalent or identical with any of the substances referred to in par. (a), but not including the isoquinoline alkaloids of opium.

(c) Opium poppy and poppy straw.

(16) "Opiate" means any substance having an addiction-forming or addiction-sustaining liability similar to morphine or being capable of conversion into a drug having addiction-forming or addiction-sustaining liability. It does not include, unless specifically designated as controlled under s. 161.11, the dextrorotatory isomer of 3-methoxy-n-methylmorphinan and its salts (dextromethorphan). It does include its racemic and levorotatory forms.

(17) "Opium poppy" means the plant of the species *Papaver Somniferum* except its seeds.

(18) "Poppy straw" means all parts, except the seeds, of the opium poppy, after mowing.

(19) "Practitioner" means:

(a) A physician, dentist, veterinarian, podiatrist, scientific investigator or other person licensed, registered or otherwise permitted to distribute, dispense, conduct research with respect to or administer a controlled substance in the course of professional practice or research in this state.

(b) A pharmacy, hospital or other institution licensed, registered or otherwise permitted to distribute, dispense, conduct research with respect to or administer a controlled substance in the course of professional practice or research in this state.

(20) "Production" includes the manufacture, planting, cultivation, growing or harvesting of a controlled substance.

(21) "Ultimate user" means a person who lawfully possesses a controlled substance for his own use or for the use of a member of his household or for administering to an animal owned by him or by a member of his household.

In addition to the definitions the Uniform Controlled Substance Act specifies in Subchapter II of the statutes the Controlled Substances Board has the following authority.

(1) The controlled substances board shall administer this subchapter and may add substances to or delte or reschedule all substances enumerated in the schedules in ss. 161.14, 161.16, 161.18, 161.20 and 161.22 pursuant to the rule-making procedures of ch. 227. In making a determination regarding a substance, the board shall consider the following:

(a) The actual or relative potential for abuse.

(b) The scientific evidence of its pharmacological effect, if known.

(c) The state of current scientific knowledge regarding the substance.

(d) The history and current pattern of abuse.

(e) The scope, duration and significance of abuse.

(f) The risk to the public health.

(g) The potential of the substance to produce psychic or physical dependence liability, and

(h) Whether the substance is an immediate precursor of a substance already controlled under this chapter.

(2) After considering the factors enumerated in sub. (1), the controlled substances board shall make findings with respect thereto and issue a rule controlling the substance if it finds the substance has a potential for abuse.

(3) If the controlled substances board designates a substance as an immediate precursor, substances which are precursors of the controlled precursor shall not be subject to control solely because they are precursors of the controlled precursor.

(4) If any substance is designated, rescheduled or deleted as a controlled substance under federal law and notice thereof is given to the controlled substances board, the board by affirmative action shall similarly control the substance under this chapter after the expiration of 30 days from publication in the federal register of a final order designating a substance as a controlled substance or rescheduling or deleting a substance, unless within that 30-day period, the board objects to inclusion, rescheduling or deletion. In that case, the board shall publish the reasons for objection and afford all interested parties an opportunity to be heard. At the conclusion of the hearing, the board shall publish its decision, which shall be final unless altered by statute. Upon publication of objection to inclusion, rescheduling or deletion under this chapter by the board, control under this chapter is stayed until the board publishes its decision.

(5) Authority to control under this section does not extend to intoxicating liquors, as defined in s. 139.01 (4), to fermented malt beverages as defined in s. 66.054 (1) (j), or to tobacco.

(6) (a) The controlled substances board shall not have authority to control a nonnarcotic substance if the substance may, under the federal food, drug and cosmetic act and the laws of this state, be lawfully sold over the counter without a prescription.

(b) If the board finds that any nonnarcotic substance barred from control under this chapter by par. (a) is dangerous to or is being so used as to endanger the public health and welfare, it may request the department of justice in the name of the state to seek a temporary restraining order or temporary injunction under ch. 813 to either ban or regulate the sale and possession of the substance. The order or injunction shall continue until the adjournment of the legislature convened next following its issuance. In making its findings as to nonnarcotic substances under this paragraph, the board shall consider the items specified in sub. (1).

161.115 Native American Church exemption. This chapter does not apply to the nondrug use of peyote and mescaline in the bona fide religious ceremonies of the Native American Church.

What is a narcotic or dangerous drug?

The law lists by name all the drugs, chemicals, or medicines which it considers to be **narcotics** or dangerous drugs. There are too many to list here, but in general any drug which cannot be taken without a doctor's prescription is included in these laws about narcotics and dangerous drugs. (Wis.Stat. 16101) Figure 12.1 lists the major narcotics and their effects.

What are the most common types of drugs?

The law divides drugs into five groups (see Figure 12.1):

1. Drugs which have no medical use and which are dangerous even if given by a doctor. Examples are heroin, LSD, and marijuana. These drugs are grouped together by the law, even though they have different effects on the person taking them, because they are all drugs that no doctor will ever prescribe to you. There is no state statute which permits doctors to prescribe these drugs.

2. Drugs which have a medical use in a few circumstances but which are very dangerous and may lead to severe physical or psychological dependance or addiction. Examples are methadone, a drug which doctors sometimes give to heroin addicts in place of their heroin, and morphine and other very strong painkillers, which doctors sometimes give to people in great pain.

3. Drugs which have medical uses and which are less dangerous than the drugs listed above, but which can cause some physical **addiction** and severe psychological dependence if abused. Examples are amphetamines and methamphetamines (uppers, speed, etc.) and strong barbiturates (downers).

4. Drugs which have medical use and are less likely to be abused than the drugs above but which may cause some physical or psychological dependance if abused. Examples are sedatives such as phenobarbital and paraldehyde.

5. Drugs which have medical use and are less likely to be abused than the drugs above. Examples are codeine cough syrups and very mild pain killers. (Wis.Stat. 161.14, .15, .16, .17, .18, .19, .20, .21, .22, .23, .24)

What does the law say about using these drugs?

It is legal to possess and use any of these drugs except the ones in the first group, if you have a written prescription for them from your doctor. It is illegal to:

1. sell these drugs or give them away to another person. (Wis.Stat. 161.41)
2. possess these drugs without a prescription. (Wis.Stat. 161.41)

Drug Used	Physical Symptoms	Dangers
Heroin **Morphine** **Codeine** *Classes I and II*	Stupor/drowsiness, needle marks, watery eyes, blood stains on shirt sleeve, running nose.	Death from overdose, mental deterioration, destruction of brain and liver.
Cough Medicine (containing codeine and opium) *Class V*	Drunk appearance, lack of coordination, confusion, excessive itching.	Causes addiction
Marijuana, Pot **Grass** *Class I*	Sleepiness, wandering mind, enlarged eye pupils, lack of coordination, craving for sweets, increased appetite.	Inducement to take stronger narcotics. Recent medical finding: Marijuana does injure organs.
LSD, DMT, **STP** *Class I*	Severe hallucinations, feeling of detachment, incoherent speech, cold hands and feet, vomiting, laughing and crying.	Suicidal tendencies, unpredictable behavior, chronic exposure causes brain damage.
Pep Pills **Uppers,** **Amphetamines** Class III	Aggressive behavior, giggling, silliness, rapid speech, confused thinking, no appetite, extreme fatigue, dry mouth, shakiness.	Death from overdose, hallucinations.
Goof Balls, **Downers,** **Barbituates** *Class III*	Drowsiness, stupor, dullness, slurred speech, drunk appearance, vomiting.	Death from overdose, unconsciousness and possible addiction.

FIGURE 12.1. The classes, physical symptoms, and dangers of some drugs.

3. get drugs or even try to get drugs by altering a prescription or by lying to get a prescription. (Wis.Stat. 161.43)
4. manufacture a drug like LSD or to grow marijuana. (Wis.Stat. 161.41)
5. drive under the influence of drugs. (Wis.Stat. 343.31)

Who can legally possess controlled substances?

Wis. Stat. 161.32 Possession authorization. (1) Persons registered under federal law to manufacture, distribute, dispense or conduct research with controlled substances may possess, manufacture, distribute, dispense or conduct research with those substances in this state to the extent authorized by their federal registration and in conformity with the other provisions of this chapter.

(2) The following persons need not be registered under federal law to lawfully possess controlled substances in this state:

(a) An agent or employee of any registered manufacturer, distributor or dispenser of any controlled substance if he is acting in the usual course of his business or employment;

(b) A common or contract carrier or warehouseman, or an employee thereof, whose possession of any controlled substance is in the usual

Offense	Wis. Stat.	First Narcotics Offense	One or More Prior Narcotic Offenses
Heroin, marijuana, mescaline, opiates, or coco derivative in **Class 1 or 2**			
Possession	161.41	15 yrs./$25,000	30 yrs./$50,000
Sale or possession with intent to sell	161.41	15 yrs./$25,000	1-30 yrs./$50,000
Obtaining by fraud	161.41	4 yrs./$30,000	8 yrs./$60,000
Barbiturics, stimulants, depressants **Class 3**			
Possession	161.41	1 yr./$250	same
Sale or possession with intent to sell	161.41	5 yrs./$15,000	1-10 yrs./$30,000
Obtaining by fraud	161.41	4 yrs./$30,000	8 yrs./$60,000
Any drug in **Class 4**			
Possession	161.41	1 yr./$250	same
Sale or possession with intent to sell	161.41	3 yrs./$10,000	6 yrs./$20,000
Obtaining by fraud	161.41	4 yrs./$30,000	8 yrs./$60,000
Any drug in **Class 5**			
Possession	161.41	1 yr./$250	same
Sale or possession with intent to sell	161.41	1 yr./$5,000	2 yrs./$2,000
Obtaining by fraud	161.41	4 yrs./$30,000	8 yrs./$60,000

TABLE 12.1. Offenses against the controlled substance laws and their penalties. Source: *Wisconsin Statutes.*

course of business or employment;

(c) An ultimate user or a person in possession of any controlled substance pursuant to a lawful possession of a schedule V substance.

(d) Any person exempted under federal law, or for whom federal registration requirements have been waived.

Does possession of a controlled substance require special authorization from a state agency?

Yes! This is specifically required by Wisconsin Statutes 161.335 sub (1) through (9).

Is it legal to possess a small amount of marijuana to use or give away?

It is a misdemeanor to possess or to give away any amount of marijuana. (Wis.Stat. 161.41)

What should I do if someone offers me a dangerous drug?

It is a very serious crime for an adult to give or sell drugs to a minor; the sentence the adult would serve had he or she sold the drugs to an adult instead of to a minor could be doubled. As a citizen you have a duty to report evidence of a serious crime to the proper authorities. (Wis.Stat. 161.46)

What can happen to me if I break the drug laws?

If you break these laws and are caught by the police you will have to go to juvenile court or to a municipal court if you are charged with **possession** under a municipal ordinance.

What is the state of Wisconsin doing about the problem of drug dependency beyond enforcing the laws?

Wis.Stat. 161.475 permits any person guilty of possession of a controlled substance to enter inpatient or outpatient programs for treatment and rehabilitation. At the end of treatment, the person may be released from sentence.

Also, a recently enacted law provides that those with a drug dependency problem may seek voluntary admission to get help from an approved treatment center. (Wis.Stat. 51.001)

What are the penalties for possession, manufacture or trafficking in narcotics and controlled substances?

Wis.Stat. 161.41 completely spells out the range of offenses and penalties. Table 12.1 gives a selected list of narcotics offenses and penalties.

If I am 18 years old and share, give, or force upon a person younger than 18 a controlled substance is the penalty severe?

> **Wis.Stat. 161.46.** Yes! Distribution to persons under age 18. Any person 18 years of age or over who violates s. 161.41 (1) by distributing a controlled substance listed in class I or I1 which is a narcotic drug to a person under 18 years of age who is at least 3 years his junior is punishable by the fine authorized by s. 161.41 (1) (a) or a term of imprisonment of up to twice that authorized by s. 161.41 (1) (a), or both. Any person 18 years of age or over who violates s. 161.41 (1) by distributing any other controlled substance listed in class I, II, III, IV, or V to a person under 18 years of age who is at least 3 years his junior is punishable by the fine authorized by s. 161.41 (1) (b), (c) or (d) or both.

Do I get any breaks under the law?

Yes. But you should not consider it a break. The court may exercise some options:

161.47. Conditional discharge for possession as first offense. (1) Whenever any person who has not previously been convicted of any offense under this chapter, or of any offense under any statute of the United States or of any state relating to narcotic drugs, marijuana or stimulant, depressant or hallucinogenic drugs, pleads guilty to or is found guilty of possession of a controlled substance under s. 161.41 (3), the court, without entering a judgment of guilt and with the consent of the accused may defer further proceedings and place him on probation upon terms and conditions. For violations of probation see statute 161.47.

If I am the one who has the abuse problem and this is my first offense, can the court provide me any other alternative?

Yes. At the court's option, you may go into treatment for your drug abuse problem. If the treatment is successful you do not have to serve your sentence. However if you fail to cooperate or the treatment is not successful, then you must return to serve your sentence. Statute 161.475.

What will happen if I am convicted a second time?

If you are convicted of a second (or subsequent) offense, you may be fined up to twice the amount otherwise authorized or imprisoned for a term up to twice the term otherwise authorized, or both.

A hashish smoker.

CASE STUDY*
Weatherall v. State of Wisconsin

Norman Weatherall of Milwaukee was not what you would call a big-time drug dealer. Even so, he attracted the attention of a police undercover agent, who in May 1973 allegedly bought $50 worth of heroin from Weatherall. Over the next few weeks, the same agent made two more purchases, in each case paying Weatherall $10 for a small amount of the drug. In February 1974 Weatherall finally was arrested and charged with three counts of selling heroin. But when the case came up for trial in June 1974, Weatherall's attorney offered an unusual defense on two of the counts. Ultimately, this defense strategy became the subject of an important ruling by the Wisconsin Supreme Court.

Weatherall's defense was that he had sold the two $10 bags of heroin to the agent only because the agent had claimed he was ill and needed drugs. (Weatherall simply denied making the first sale—for $50—to the agent.) Testifying on his own behalf, Weatherall told the jury that "on the last two occasions I obtained it [the heroin] ... to prevent him [the agent] from becoming sick and ill."

The jury, however, was not moved by Weatherall's claim that he had acted as a good Samaritan. As a result, Weatherall was convicted on all three counts. Milwaukee County Circuit Court Judge Christ T. Seraphim then sentenced Weatherall to a total of 24 years in prison (eight years on each count with the sentences to run consecutively). Judge Seraphim imposed the sentence after describing Weatherall as a "cancer in our society. Murderers many times kill in the heat of passion ... but this, a man like Weatherall killed many people, and we're going to remove him from the scene for a long, long, long time."

Weatherall's conviction was appealed by the Wisconsin Public Defender's office on the grounds that the defense offered at his trial was inadequate. In fact, the public defender contended that the good Samaritan defense advanced by Weatherall's attorney, Philip Murphy, was not even a legal defense to the charges. As a result, the public defender said, Weatherall had no chance of being acquitted. The public defender said Murphy should have based his defense on a claim that the undercover agent, by feigning illness, induced Weatherall into selling the heroin. Weatherall's case, the public defender concluded, "presented in its most classic form a setting for an entrapment defense." The public defender's office also claimed in its appeal that Judge Seraphim abused his discretion by sentencing Weatherall to 24 years in prison. Among other things, the public defender faulted the judge for failing to order a presentence report and for failing to give adequate reasons for imposing consecutive sentences.

But the Wisconsin Supreme Court, in a decision handed down in June 1976, upheld Weatherall's conviction and sentence. The court began by noting that "the standard for determining effective or adequate representation [by an attorney] is that it ... 'must be equal to that which the ordinarily prudent lawyer, skilled and versed in criminal law, would give to clients who had privately retained his services.'" In Weatherall's case, the court said,

---

*A summary of the case. For the court's complete opinion, see 73 Wis.2d 22, 242 N.W.2d 220 (1976).

the question was whether his attorney had a good reason for not attempting an entrapment defense. The court concluded that there was at least one such reason; namely, that an entrapment defense would not have worked. "With the defendant denying the first sale, he could hardly claim that he was entrapped into making the sale he claimed he did not make," the court said. "As to the second two sales, defendant's statement that he made the sales of heroin to help the agent ... falls far short of the degree of inducement required to be proved to establish entrapment. There is no evidence of the agent having to overcome refusals and reluctance to make the purchase."

Next, the court analyzed the good Samaritan defense offered on Weatherall's behalf. The court acknowledged that Weatherall's claim that he simply was trying to help the agent by selling him heroin "would not be a legal defense under the statute defining the crime charged." However, the court said that Murphy nonetheless had valid reasons for trying the good Samaritan strategy. "Counsel [Murphy] sought to increase the possibility of the jury accepting his client's denial as to the first sale by portraying his client as one who had sought to help someone in trouble and distress," the court said. In other words, the court said, Murphy was hoping that the jury—by hearing Weatherall's version of the heroin sales—might "temper justice with leniency." The court said Murphy, as an experienced trial lawyer, "was entitled to give weight to such extra-legal possibility. He is no more to be faulted for such exercise of professional judgment than is the defense counsel who, facing formidable adverse facts, advises his client to plead guilty, perhaps on a lesser charge, rather than to go to trial on a plea of not guilty. Later on, postconviction counsel may not agree with the advice given and followed, but that is always later on."

The court also rejected Weatherall's claim that he was sentenced improperly by Judge Seraphim. On the issue of a presentence report, the court noted that Wisconsin law says only that a report *may* be ordered. "While the use of a presentence investigation is to be encouraged, it is not required," the court said. As for the consecutive sentences imposed by Judge Seraphim, the court said the judge's reason that consecutive terms were needed "'to protect the public from further criminal conduct by the defendant'" was adequate. Judge Seraphim, the court said, clearly made such a finding when he called Weatherlal "a cancer in our society" and "the worst type of criminal" at the time of sentencing.

QUESTIONS FOR DISCUSSION

1. The severity of the law in the case of controlled substances seems to change as legislature and social concerns change. What are the major forces in our state that influence the legislation on controlled substances?

2. What agencies or professional people exist in your locality to help and assist you when you are concerned about drugs, controlled substances, and abuse?

3. What can you as an individual do to help prevent the abuse of controlled substances in your community?

SUGGESTED ACTIVITIES

1. Problems to Consider

Read each of the following incidents. Have the police authorities engaged in an unreasonable search and seizure? What would the penalties be if the person(s) were convicted?

To help you determine the answers, consult the state criminal statutes on drugs, crime, search and seizure, and evidence or consult with a local police officer, lawyer, district attorney, juvenile officer, judge, or local bar association representative.

Problem A. Pat accepts a ride with Alf, a classmate from school. The police stop the van for a taillight that is not working. When Alf steps out of the van, a small bag of marijuana falls on the ground. Both Alf and Pat are arrested on suspicion of possession. It is a first offense for Pat, a second offense for Alf.

Problem B. On a tip, the police go to Ellie's home. Her mother agrees to let them search for marijuana, and they find it in Ellie's closet. First offense for Ellie.

Problem C. Kurt is stopped by a policeman for violation of the local curfew. Kurt appears very nervous and refuses to identify himself. The officer notices Kurt's attempt to conceal his jacket pocket, conducts a search, and finds four marijuana cigarettes. Second offense for Kurt.

Problem D. Doug's neighbors report a disturbance of rowdy behavior and loud stereo playing. Police arrive but no one will answer the door. They knock, they enter the house, and find two small bags of marijuana, some pills, and some suspicious white powder in the sugar dish on the coffee table.

Problem E. The principal notices Russell—a suspected drug pusher—loitering across from the school and notifies the police. The police stop and search him and find a container with 75 amphetamines.

Problem F. After returning to the garage, the bus driver finds three marijuana cigarettes in the seat where Howie and Jackson were sitting and turns them over to the police.

Problem G. Ginger, a senior and 18 years old, asks Daria, a sophomore, to go home with her after school. They take a shortcut across the field near school. Ginger lights a marijuana cigarette and gives it to Daria for a drag. A sheriff's deputy sees the incident and stops both Ginger and Daria. After some discussion he decides to arrest and book both students.

2. Interpretation Activity

Study figure 12.2 which shows all the controlled-substances arrests in Wisconsin in 1979. Then answer the questions that follow.

		Opium Cocaine and Derivatives	Marijuana	Synthetic Narcotics	Other Dangerous Non-narcotic Drugs	Total
Adults	Sales/Manufacturing	282 (22%)	750 (59%)	96 (8%)	152 (12%)	1,280 (100%)
	Possession	220 (4%)	4,557 (88%)	193 (4%)	205 (4%)	5,175 (100%)
	Total	502 (8%)	5,307 (82%)	289 (4%)	357 (6%)	6,455 (100%)
Juveniles	Sales/Manufacturing	14 (3%)	335 (83%)	23 (6%)	30 (7%)	402 (100%)
	Possession	30 (1%)	4,060 (95%)	32 (1%)	148 (3%)	4,270 (100%)
	Total	44 (1%)	4,395 (94%)	55 (1%)	178 (4%)	4,672 (100%)
	State Totals	546 (5%)	9,702 (87%)	344 (3%)	535 (5%)	11,127 (100%)

FIGURE 12.2. Total controlled-substances arrests in Wisconsin in 1979. The figures in parentheses indicate a percentage of the total.

QUESTIONS FOR DISCUSSION

1. Which controlled substance seems to be the most frequently used?

2. Which controlled substance seems to be the most popular with juveniles and adults?

3. Adults seem to prefer stronger substances than juveniles. What kind of a warning should this be to you as a juvenile?

4. How can you help your school and community deal with the spread of controlled substances?

3. Drug Workshop

Invite to your class or school an interdisciplinary team from a police agency, social services, and medical profession from your community to conduct a workshop for the students in drug education and drug abuse problems.

VOCABULARY

Abuse
Addiction
Controlled Substance
Entrapment
Narcotic
Possession

SUGGESTED RESOURCES

Let's Talk About Drug Abuse: Some Questions and Answers. Washington, D.C.: Department of Health and Human Services, 1980.

Alternatives to Drug Abuse. Washington, D.C.: National Clearinghouse for Abuse Information, 1975.

SUGGESTED AGENCY

Bureau of Alcohol and Other Drug Abuse
Division of Mental Hygiene
One West Wilson Street
Madison 53702

13

The Citizen-Student and Sexual Behavior

This chapter is the most sensitive in the book. It requires you, the citizen-student, to face up to your personal sexual behavior and legal responsibility under the law in Wisconsin. To the state of Wisconsin, as to most states, your personal sexual behavior is of public interest. This chapter will present you with the law and thus set out for you what the state considers unacceptable sexual behavior or conduct.

In general, you can be prosecuted for your personal sexual behavior under the Wisconsin Criminal Code in Chapter 940: Crimes Against Sexual Morality of the Wisconsin Statutes. According to the section on bodily security in Chapter 940 you could, depending on circumstances and the facts of the incidents, be charged and convicted for battery:

> (1) Whoever causes bodily harm to another by an act done with intent to cause bodily harm to that person or another without the consent of the person so harmed is guilty of a Class A misdemeanor. (a Class A misdemeanor is punishable by nine months and/or $10,000 fine.
> (2) Whoever causes great bodily harm to another by an act done with intent to cause great bodily harm to that person or another with or without the consent of the person so harmed is guilty of a Class C felony. (A Class C felony is punishable by 10 years and/or a $10,000 fine.)

Depending on the circumstances you could also be charged with **child abuse:**

> Whoever tortures a child (anyone under 16 years of age) or subjects a child to cruel maltreatment, including, but not limited to, severe bruising, lacerations, fractured bones, burns, internal injuries or any injury constituting great bodily harm is guilty of a Class E felony. (A Class E felony is punishable by two years and/or $10,000 fine.)

The state of Wisconsin, the legislature, the courts, various state law enforcement, juvenile, social welfare, and community agencies are concerned with the **sexual exploitation** of citizens under the age of 18.

As a citizen-student you should be aware that the law is clear on the subject of sexual exploitation, and you should know what protections you have in Wisconsin.

> **940.203 Sexual exploitation of children.** (1) No person may knowingly employ, use, persuade, induce, entice or coerce any child to engage in sexually explicit conduct for the purpose of photographing, filming, videotaping, recording the sounds of or displaying in any way the conduct.
>
> (2) No person may photograph, film, videotape, record the sounds of or display in any way a child engaging in sexually explicit conduct.
>
> (3) No parent, legal guardian or other person exercising temporary or permanent control of a child may knowingly permit the child to engage in sexually explicit conduct which is filmed, photographed, videotaped, recorded for sound or displayed in any way.
>
> (4) No person may knowingly produce, perform in, profit from, promote, import, reproduce, advertise, sell distribute, or possess with intent to sell or distribute, any undeveloped film, photographic negative, photograph, motion picture, videotape, sound recording or other reproduction of a child engaging in sexually explicit conduct.
>
> (5) Whoever violates this section is guilty of a Class C felony.
>
> (6) In this section:
>
> (a) "Child" means any person under the age of 18 years.
>
> (b) "Sexually explicit conduct" means actual or simulated.

Class C felony = 10 years and/or $10,000

What would happen if a person was seriously or unusually injured?

The charge could be **mayhem:** Whoever, with intent to disable or disfigure another, cuts or mutilates the tongue, eye, ear, nose, lip, limb, or other bodily member of another is guilty of a Class B felony (punishable by up to 20 years).

Community standards often play a part in the determination of what is obscene.

What kinds of charges could be brought against me or what charges could I bring against another person for sexual assault?

The charges would depend on the nature of the incident and the type of sexual assault. The state code lists four kinds of **sexual assault.**

1. First Degree Sexual Assault. Whoever does any of the following is guilty of a Class B felony:

(a) Has sexual contact or sexual intercourse with another person without consent of that person and causes pregnancy or great bodily harm to that person.

(b) Has sexual contact or sexual intercourse with another person without consent of that person by use or threat of use of a dangerous weapon or any article used or fashioned in a manner to lead the victim reasonably to believe it to be a dangerous weapon.

(c) Is aided or abetted by one or more other persons and has sexual contact or sexual intercourse with another person without consent of that person by use or threat of force or violence.

(d) Has sexual contact or sexual intercourse with a person 12 years of age or younger.

2. Second Degree Sexual Assault. Whoever does any of the following is guilty of a Class C felony:

(a) Has sexual contact or sexual intercourse with another person without consent of that person by use or threat of force or violence.

(b) Has sexual contact or sexual intercourse with another person without consent of that person and causes injury, illness, disease or loss or impairment of a sexual or reproductive organ, or mental anguish requiring psychiatric care for the victim.

(c) Has sexual contact or sexual intercourse with a person who suffers from a mental illness or deficiency which renders that person temporarily or permanently incapable of appraising the person's conduct, and the defendant knows of such condition.

(d) Has sexual contact or sexual intercourse with a person who the defendant knows is unconscious.

(e) Has sexual contact or sexual intercourse with a person who is over the age of 12 years and under the age of 18 years without consent of that person, as consent is defined in sub. (4).

3. Third Degree Sexual Assault. Whoever has sexual intercourse with a person without the consent of that person is guilty of a Class D felony.

3m. Fourth Degree Sexual Assault. Whoever has sexual contact with a person without the consent of that person is guilty of a Class A misdemeanor.

4. Consent. "Consent", as used in this section, means words or overt actions by a person who is competent to give informed consent indicating a freely given agreement to have sexual intercourse or sexual contact. A person under 15 years of age is incapable of consent as a matter of law. The following persons are presumed incapable of consent but the presumption may be rebutted by competent evidence, subject to the provisions of s. 972.11 (2):

(a) A person who is 15 to 17 years of age.

(b) A person suffering from a mental illness or defect which impairs capacity to appraise personal conduct.

(c) A person who is unconscious or for any other reason is physically unable to communicate unwillingness to an act.

Could I be charged for sexual assault by my marriage partner?

No. You will not be prosecuted if the complaint is made by your legal spouse, unless you are living apart and one of you has filed for an annulment, legal separation, or divorce.

What other criminal charges might be related to sexual assault?

Two possibilities exist under current law: kidnapping and abduction. According to Wisc.Stat. 940.31 and 940.32:

Kidnapping. (1) Whoever does any of the following is guilty of a Class B felony:

(a) By force or threat of imminent force carries another from one place to another without his consent and with intent to cause him to be secretly confined or imprisoned or to be carried out of this state or to be held to service against his will; or

(b) By force or threat of imminent force seizes or confines another without his consent and with intent to cause him to be secretly confined or imprisoned or to be carried out of this state or to be held to service against his will; or

(c) By deceit induces another to go from one place to another with intent to cause him to be secretly confined or imprisoned or to be carried out of this state or to be held to service against his will.

(2) Whoever violates sub. (1) with intent to cause another to transfer property in order to obtain the release of the victim is guilty of a Class A felony punishable by life imprisonment; but if the victim is released without permanent physical injury prior to the time the first witness is sworn at the trial the defendant is guilty of a Class B felony (up to 20 years imprisonment).

Abduction. Whoever, for any unlawful or immoral purpose, does any of the following is guilty of a Class C felony (punishable by 10 years/ $10,000, or both):

(1) By force or threat of imminent force, takes any child under 18 years of age from his home or the custody of his parent or guardian; or

(2) Entices any child under 18 years of age from his home or the custody of his parent or guardian; or

(3) By force or threat of imminent force, detains any child under 18 years of age who is away from his home or the custody of his parent or guardian.

Sexual Crimes Which Involve Children

944.12 Enticing a child for immoral purposes. Any person 18 years of age or over, who, with intent to commit a crime against sexual morality, persuades or entices any child under 18 years of age into any vehicle, building, room, or secluded place is guilty of a Class C felony (10 years/ $10,000 or both).

Sexual Crimes Between Adults With Consent

944.15 Fornication. Whoever has sexual intercourse with a person not his or her spouse is guilty of a Class A misdemeanor.

History: 1977 c. 173.

Note: The defendant had no standing to challenge the fornication statute as an unconstitutional invasion of privacy of individuals when intercourse occurs between consenting adults because the act of intercourse was clearly not consensual. Byrd v. State, 65 W (2d) 415, 222 NW (2d) 696.

944.16 Adultery. Whoever does either of the following is guilty of a Class E felony (2 years/$10,00 or both):

(1) A married person who has sexual intercourse with a person not his spouse; or

(2) A person who has sexual intercourse with a person who is married to another.

Sexual Perversion

944.20 Lewd and lascivious behavior. Whoever does any of the following is guilty of a Class A misdemeanor (9 months/$10,000 or both):

(1) Commits an indecent act of sexual gratification with another with knowledge that they are in the presence of others; or

(2) Publicly and indecently exposes a sex organ; or

The protection of minors from lewd and obscene materials is a clear intent of sexual morality laws.

(3) Openly cohabits and associates with a person he knows is not his spouse under circumstances that imply sexual intercourse. (See *Marvin* v. *Marvin* case in chapter 8.)

In Chapter 944: Crimes Against Sexual Morality, the state spells out the sexual conduct, behavior, or relationships which the state considers socially, morally, and legally unacceptable.

Because sections of the statutes are explicitly stated, described, or defined we have made discretionary choices about the material covered in this section of chapter 13.

We realize your concern about this sensitive subject and recognize the interest of the school, your parents, and community when dealing with the area of sexual morality. Chapter 944 includes:

Sexual Crimes Which Affect the Family

944.05 Bigamy. (1) Whoever does any of the following is guilty of a Class E felony (2 years/$10,000 or both):

(a) Contracts a marriage in this state with knowledge that his prior marriage is not dissolved; or

(b) Contracts a marriage in this state with knowledge that the prior marriage of the person he marries is not dissolved; or

(d) Cohabits in this state with a person whom he married outside this state with knowledge that his own prior marriage had not been dissolved or with knowledge that the prior marriage of the person he married had not been dissolved.

(2) In this section "cohabit" means to live together under the representation or appearance of being married.

944.06 Incest. Whoever marries or has nonmarital sexual intercourse with a person he or she knows is a blood relative and such relative is in fact related in a degree within which the marriage of the parties is prohibited by the law of this state is guilty of a Class C felony (10 years/$10,000 or both).

944.21 Lewd, obscene or Indecent matter, pictures and performances. (1) Whoever intentionally does any of the following is guilty of a Class D felony (5 years/$10,000 or both):

(a) Imports, prints, advertises, sells, has in his possession for sale, or publishes, exhibits, or transfers commercially any lewd, obscene or indecent written matter, picture, sound recording, or film; or

(b) Advertises, produces or performs in any lewd, obscene or indecent performance; or

(c) Has in his possession, with intent to transfer or exhibit to a person under the age of 18 years, any matter prohibited by this section.

(2) Whoever requires, as a condition to the purchase of periodicals, that a retailer accept material known by the distributor to be lewd, obscene or indecent is guilty of a Class D felony.

944.23 Making lewd, obscene or indecent drawings. Whoever makes any lewd, obscene or indecent drawing or writing in public or in a public place is guilty of a Class C misdemeanor (30 days/$500.00 or both).

Hypothetical Case
Exploitation

A sixteen-year-old female high school student has filed sexual exploitation and abuse charges against two of her male classmates—one fifteen and one eighteen years of age.

The citations against the two boys, filed in circuit court, charge that on Saturday of last week her two classmates forced her to pose for indecent photographs in the home of the eighteen-year-old's parents.

Paul Smith, of the district attorney's office, stated that this series of events insulted basic human decency and that he felt the situation called for speedy justice.

The sequence of events has resulted in the arrest and charging of the two young men involved in the incident.

Authorities said that the two suspects enticed Nancy Doe (not her real name) into the eighteen-year-old's home on the pretext that he wanted her to listen to his new stereo. Later in the afternoon the eighteen-year-old made suggestions about her posing for photographs with his instant color camera under the pretext that he would use the photos for his high school sketching class.

When she stated that she wished to leave, the eighteen-year-old with cooperation from the other juvenile forced her to pose for indecent and explicit photographs.

Nancy's parents brought the charges after the two boys were found passing the photos of Nancy around the high school locker room after physical education class Monday.

The boys deny the charges and the circumstances but admit to taking the pictures in cooperation with Nancy. Case will be heard next week in circuit court. The boys were released on $2,000.00 bond.

QUESTIONS FOR DISCUSSION:

Based on the information presented in the hypothetical case:

1. What could the fifteen- and eighteen-year-olds be charged with under the laws of the State of Wisconsin?

2. What might the charges be if Nancy was indeed found to have cooperated with the boys in taking the photographs?

3. Discuss the pros and cons. In this kind of case do you think the names of the individuals involved should be published in the paper?

QUESTIONS FOR DISCUSSION

1. Of the laws affecting sexual crimes described in this chapter which one, if any, do you think should be changed and why?

2. Of the laws affecting sexual morality described in this chapter which ones, if any, do you think should be changed? Why? How would you go about changing them under the legislative process in Wisconsin?

3. Under what authority does the state derive its power to regulate sexual behavior between consenting adults in public? In private?

4. From your experience, do you find that the range of the laws covered in this chapter also reflect social mores, customs, and religious codes of behavior?

5. Do you think the present state statutes on morality favor the male or the female? The perpetrator or the victim?

SUGGESTED ACTIVITY

Interview local law enforcement, juvenile, probation, social services, and court personnel about the severity of the problems described in this chapter in your own community.

VOCABULARY

Child abuse
Mayhem
Sexual assault
Sexual harassment

RELATED LEGAL CASES

State v. *Driscoll,* 53 Wis.2d 699, 193 N.W.2d 851 (1972). Indecent liberty statute 944.11 (2) and (3) not vague or over broad. *Wheeler* v. *State,* 87 Wis.2d 626, 275 N.W.2d 651 (1979).

SUGGESTED READINGS

"The Rape Victim," *Bill of Rights in Action,* April, 1978, pp. 13-14.

"Victimless Crime," *Bill of Rights in Action,* April, 1978, p. 23.

SUGGESTED RESOURCES

*Cry Rape.** Audio tapes dealing with a rape case available from:
Correctional Services of Minnesota
1427 Washington Avenue South
Minneapolis, Minnesota 55454

*Materials should be previewed prior to class use.

SECTION VI

THE CITIZEN-STUDENT AND CIVIL LAWS

CONTENTS

14

The Citizen-Student and Civil Law Protection

While criminal laws seek to regulate the conduct of an individual and to provide a punishment if his or her conduct does not conform to the rules, the civil law deals with relationships among individuals. If you violate a criminal law you may be arrested and tried and punished by the state. If you violate a civil law that injures your neighbor, you may or may not have broken a criminal law but whether you have or not the neighbor may sue you and perhaps recover money damages because of the wrong that you have done.

The injury you caused may have been an intentional or an unintentional act. If, for example, you tell lies about people and they are injured as a result they may sue you. If you cause someone to receive personal injuries, whether intentionally (as in a fight) or unintentionally (you carelessly leave your rake on the sidewalk and he or she trips over it) he or she may sue you and recover. These kinds of acts are called **torts.**

Similarly, if you make a binding legal promise and then fail to keep your promise, the person to whom the promise was made may sue you and recover because you have broken your **contract.** The law governing the making and keeping of contracts is complex but in simple terms we can say that the law establishes formal rules that must be complied with to create a binding contract and that if a binding contract is created both parties are expected to live up to it. If one of them does not fulfill his or her obligations the law provides a remedy to the other party which, as nearly as possible, puts him or her in the same position he or she would have been in had the contract been performed.

This chapter tells you something about the rules of tort and the rules of contract as they apply to young people. You will see that in some cases young people are treated just like anyone else and in other cases they are given certain advantages. The chapter will also touch on property rights of minors and wills. To round out this brief study of civil law, special problem areas that could affect you will be discussed.

What is the civil law?

Civil law is the opposite of criminal law in that it deals with private rights. Under the criminal law the state takes a person to court and asks that he be punished by fine or imprisonment for an act harmful to society. Civil law involves one person taking another to court to settle a dispute between them. Usually the person who sues asks for **damages** (the payment of money) from the other. Sometimes one person will ask the court to forbid the other person from doing something—this is called an **injunction.** The person asking for relief is called the plaintiff; the person sued is called the defendant. (Wis.Stat., Ch. 260)

Are there different procedures used in civil cases compared to criminal cases?

Yes. Table 14.1 compares the general steps that characterize the criminal and civil processes:

TORTS

What is a tort?

A tort is an injury to a person or damage to someone's property that is caused by another person's acts. There are four main kinds of torts: intentional torts (injury done on purpose); negligent torts (caused by carelessness); strict **liability** (torts arising out of defects in certain products); and liability without fault (torts arising from conduct which, by its very nature, creates a high degree of risk). A person who commits a tort can be sued and may have to pay for the damage he caused.

Can a minor be sued for a tort?

Yes. Even children over age seven can be sued for their torts. (Wis.Stat. 891.44) Being under age does not allow one to hurt other people. The person you hurt could get a judgment against you and wait until you are older and have some money and property to collect. A judgment is an official court paper that says that you have lost a lawsuit and that the person who won is entitled to receive a certain amount of money from you.

What kinds of things might be torts?

Liability without fault is uncommon and it is unlikely that you would do anything which would result in this although it might apply if you were using dynamite or some other explosive. If you do that, you could be liable for damages to anyone who was hurt even though you were

Criminal Procedures	Civil Procedures
1. Begins with an arrest when police take person into custody. Booking and fingerprinting the person. A complaint is issued by the district attorney stating the facts in the alleged crime.	1. Complaint is filed by the plaintiff. The plaintiff files papers claiming a civil wrong has been done by the defendant.
2. The defendant makes his or her initial appearance. The judge reads the complaint:	2. Answer by defendant. The defendant files papers denying plaintiff's claim and stating the defense in the case.
A. In felony matters, the judge sets bail, and sets the date for a preliminary hearing.	
B. In misdemeanor cases, if judge finds probable cause that a crime was committed, sets bail, takes defendant's plea of guilty or not guilty, and sets a trial date.	
3. Preliminary Hearing. In felony cases, the judge finds probable cause to believe a crime was committed. If the judge believes the state has enough evidence the case is "bound over" for trial.	3. Pretrial proceedings and motions (requests by the parties to the court) are filed requesting discovery (an exchange of information between the parties).
4. Trial. Presentation of evidence by the prosecution and defense.	4. Trial. Presentation of evidence by plaintiff and defendant.
5. Verdict. A decision is made by trier of fact (judge or jury).	5. Judgment. A pronouncement by judge in favor of plaintiff or defendant.
6. Sentence. Judge imposes penalty, which may be in the form of a prison term, probation, fine, or other punishment.	6. Enforcement of judgement. Court orders the person against whom the judgment was pronounced to say or to do something.

TABLE 14.1. Comparison of criminal and civil procedures.

very careful and could not have avoided hurting them.

Strict liability is also uncommon and arises in the case of the production of goods for use by the general public. Liability arises if damages are incurred as a result of a defect in a product which would be dangerous if defective.

You are not likely to commit an intentional tort either. The most common of these are assault (hurting somebody in a fight or deliberately injuring them in some other way); fraud (deliberately lying to someone to cheat them); and libel or slander (telling lies about someone and hurting that person's reputation).

Negligent torts are more common. There are many ways to hurt someone by carelessness, but the one most familiar to most of us is the automobile accident. If you drive a car or other motor vehicle carelessly and cause an accident you may be liable. It is obviously negligence to drive while you are intoxicated, to speed, to drive on the wrong side of the road, or to run a red light. In other cases, whether you were careless depends on the specific facts; if you are sued, a jury would decide whether you were careless.

Are minors treated differently than adults?

There are two major differences when a minor is sued for a tort. First, no minor can go to court without a **guardian ad litem**—that is, an adult appointed by the court to represent you at the time of the trial. The guardian works with your lawyer to protect your interests and usually has the power to make decisions about how the lawsuit is to be handled. The guardian is often one of your parents, although it can be any other adult; if you need a guardian, you can go to court and ask the court to appoint one for you. (Wis.Sat. 88.15) Second, in deciding whether a minor has been negligent, the law compares his or her acts with those of a reasonably careful adult. The minor's more limited experience is taken into account and he or she is not required to act as quickly or as well as an older person who has more experience. However, when minors operate an automobile, airplane, or boat, they lose this special protection. The law says that when they use these dangerous machines they must act as reasonably careful adults would in the same circumstances. (Wis.Stat. 895.048)

Can a minor sue another person for a tort?

Yes. However, again you must have a guardian, and if you have medical bills, your parents must sue to collect the bills since they are liable to pay them. Your parents or guardian ad litem may settle the suit for you if the other side offers to pay you some money without going to court.

Do my parents have to pay for damages caused by my torts?

Usually no person has to pay for the torts of another person, but there are some exceptions. Your parents can be required to pay for any malicious damage you do to a person or property, if you are living at home and under eighteen, but the total amount that they will have to pay is $1,000. (Wis.Stat. 895.035) You could still be sued to pay for the rest of the bills if the damage was greater than $1,000. If you cause an accident with your parents' car they will be liable for the damage you cause. This is not because they are your parents, but because they are responsible for the acts of anyone who borrows their car with their permission. (Wis.Stat. 895.048) You will still be liable too, and both you and your parents could be sued.

Does this mean that if I borrow a friend's car he or she is liable for what I do?

Yes. The rule also applies if you use your employer's car while on the job. It also means that you should be careful about lending your own car to other people, because you can be forced to pay for the damage they cause.

Is it true that being sued for a tort can ruin me and my family for life?

It is possible but not very likely. However, if you injure somebody badly or cause the death of a breadwinner, the loss of this person to his or her family can be very large. Since most people cannot afford to pay the damages arising from such injuries, they protect themselves with liability insurance. This kind of insurance pays the person you injured whenever you would be responsible to pay. Nearly everyone has automobile accident liability insurance, and most people have homeowner's insurance to protect the members of the family from other kinds of negligent torts. If, for example, you carelessly hit a baseball into the pitcher's head, your parents' homeowner's insurance might pay for the damages. There is no insurance you can buy which will insure you against your liability for an intentional tort, so if you deliberately hurt somebody you might have to pay a great deal of money from your pocket.

CONTRACTS

What is a contract?

A contract is an agreement which a court will enforce in a lawsuit. It does not have to be written in most cases, but if it is verbal it will be harder to prove the contract was made. Each person must give something of value to the other person or promise to give something of value before a contract exists. If a person breaks his or her agreement, he or she can be sued and might have to pay damages to the other person so that the other person will be as well off as he would have been if the agreement had been carried out. Courts may refuse to enforce contracts secured by force or fraud or entered into by incompetent persons.

In rural Wisconsin, raising livestock is one way for young people to earn money.

Is it true that minors can't make contracts?

This is not exactly true. Minors can make contracts, but the contract of a minor is voidable at the minor's option. This means that the minor can refuse to go through with his or her agreement and cannot be forced to pay damages. Even if the contract has been carried out a minor may decide while still a minor or within a reasonable time after becoming of age to undo the contract and get his or her money back in the case of a purchase.

Can a minor ever be forced to go through with his contract?

Yes. A minor can be required to pay a reasonable price under a contract to purchase necessities (the things which he or she needs to live in a normal and moderate manner). However, most courts that have heard such cases have decided that a car is not a necessity!

Does this mean I can buy a car, keep it and get my money back by voiding the contract?

No. In order to recover your money you must return the property if you still have it. Even if the car has been wrecked you probably will still be able to void the contract but in Wisconsin you will probably have to account to the seller for such benefit as you may have received from having the car in your possession.

What happens if I lie about my age so that someone will make a contract with me?

This makes no difference; the contract is still voidable. This is due to the inexperience of minors in understanding the nature and propriety of contracts they may make.

Can an adult who contracts with me refuse to go through with the contract?

No. A minor's contracts are voidable at the minor's election. This means that they bind any adult who agrees to them. It is only the minor who can choose to break the contract.

PROPERTY RIGHTS

Can a minor own property?

Yes. However, if the property he or she owns is substantial or valuable, the minor normally cannot use it or decide how it will be used. Normally property owned by a minor is "in trust." This means that the money is managed by a **trustee**—a person or bank which is required to protect the property and use it for the minor's best interests. A trust will sometimes have very specific rules about how the property is to be used and usually the minor will get complete control of the property on his eighteenth birthday.

Why can't a minor manage his or her own money?

Usually any property a minor owns has been left to him or her by relatives at their death or by a family member. Normally minors do have control, at least as a practical matter, over the money they earn or personal items they own. However, the law believes that minors do not have the experience to manage large sums of money or valuable property. Wills of parents or other relatives often are written to put the property in trust. If there is no will, a court will appoint a guardian of the minor's property.

WILLS

A will is really nothing more than a letter from you to the probate judge, legally binding on him, telling him what to do with your property upon your death. It must, however, comply with certain formalities if it is to be accepted by the court as your will. This is to ensure its authenticity. (There are situations in which no formality is required, but this is beyond this discussion.) These formalities are: a) It must be in writing; b) It must be signed by the **testator** (the person whose will it is) or some appropriate proxy; c) It must be signed by two or more witnesses at the request of the testator, in the presence of the testator, and in the presence of each other. It is also helpful if the witnesses declare in the will that, to their knowledge, the testator was of sound mind, over 18 years old, and under no undue influence at the time of signing the will.

Any person of sound mind, 18 years of age or older, may make a will. The disadvantages of old age—forgetfulness, delusions, senility—do not necessarily disqualify a person from making a will. Neither does mental incompetency or even guardianship, as long as the testator, at the time of making and signing the will, understood and intended what he was doing. Sometimes a person is unable to sign a will because of some physical problem. In those cases, he may be assisted in signing or someone else may even sign for him if the proper formalities are observed. No one should be a witness to a will if he is a beneficiary under the will. If he is, he will lose what has been given to him by the will over and above the amount he would have received if the testator had died without a will.

What if my father dies without a will?

The process by which property is distributed when there is no will is called intestate succession. If your father dies without a will, you are entitled to a share of all his property. The size of the share depends on whether your mother is still alive and how many brothers and sisters you have. In general, your mother would get at least one-third and you and your brothers and sisters would divide up the rest. Property would be distributed in the same way if your mother died. (Wis.Stat. 852.01) A parent can disinherit a child, however, because the law does not forbid it.

Can a minor make a will?

No. (Wis.Stat. 853.01)

Who gets a minor's property when he or she dies?

Any property which you inherited from one of your parents would go to any other children that parent had or grandchildren or other descendants of that parent. Other property, in the case of an unmarried minor, goes to the minor's brothers and sisters or, if there are none, to some other more distant relative. (Wis.Stat. 852.01)

CONSUMER PROTECTION

Home Solicitation Selling

Wisconsin law defines "home solicitation sales" as the offering of consumer goods or services for sale or lease away from the sellers' place of business. This could be at your home, your job, or any place other than what the seller calls his "regular" place of business. The law covers sales made in hotel or motel rooms, at county fairs, or at other "temporary" sales locations. Personal solicitations made over the phone, person-to-person, or through promotional mailing are also included under this law.

How are door-to-door sales regulated in Wisconsin?

Some misleading come-ons have been used by some door-to-door sellers to persuade consumers to purchase their goods or services. Examples: "I am working my way through college." "We'll give you half-price on this product if you let us use your name as one of our satisfied customers." "This is a 'special offer' to a limited number of people." Such time-worn gimmicks and deceptive sales offers put consumers at a serious disadvantage. State law protects consumers against fraudulent practices used by some door-to-door sellers.

Are door-to-door sellers required to identify themselves?

Before a door-to-door seller says anything other than a short greeting, state law requires that the seller must give you his or her name, the name of the company, and the type of product or service that is being offered.

In addition, many localities require sellers to apply for a permit from the local officials. If your locality has such an ordinance, ask to see the seller's permit; otherwise demand a business identification card.

Are free goods offered by door-to-door sellers "free?"

There may be hidden costs. Most free gifts depend on the purchase of another product or a package deal involving a lengthy sales presentation and a costly commitment. The seller should tell you what your exact obligation is in order to qualify for something presented as "free."

What is referral selling?

Some sellers even offer to pay you a certain amount of cash or promise a discount on your purchase if you supply them with names of consumers who will later buy their merchandise. In most cases, you will rarely benefit from these referrals even if a purchase is made by one of the people you suggested. This offer, called referral selling, is illegal if it is made before you purchase. Referral selling often occurs among sellers of food plans, appliances, sewing machines, fire alarms, and books.

What factors should I consider before deciding to purchase something from door-to-door sellers?

Some door-to-door sellers are expert in persuading you to buy products or services you do not really need. Ask yourself these questions:

1. Do I really need the product or service?

Reading fabric composition tags and proper care instructions will often help you to decide about a clothing purchase.

2. If so, will it serve my needs?
3. What can I afford to spend?
4. Is the price in line with goods of the same quality available elsewhere?

Don't be afraid to say NO! Again, state law requires that a sales person leave your home when asked to do so.

If I agree to buy or sign a contract to purchase from a door-to-door seller, what must the seller tell me?

The seller must tell you,

1. Total price, including tax, any credit or finance charge and installation fees.

2. Special conditions of the sale, such as trade-in allowances and payment schedules.

Be sure to read the entire contract. Remember any paper you sign can be a legally binding contract. Make sure all spoken statements promised by the sales person are stated in the contract in writing. If the salesman tells you something that's not in the contract, make him write it in. If there are any terms you do not understand, DON'T SIGN! Check first with a lawyer, or your legal aid office.

Before any money is paid, you must be given a copy of the contract. If a foreign language is used in the sales talk, all contracts and papers must be written in both English and the language spoken during the sale.

What information is required by law to be in the contract?

The contract must show:

1. date of sale,
2. the seller's name,
3. the address and telephone number of the company involved,
4. Notice of Cancellation Form and statement explaining the "three-day cooling-off period" if applicable.

What other deceptive practices should I be alert to in door-to-door sellers?

It is against the law for the seller to misrepresent:

1. His or her identify as the sales person—such as falsely claiming to be the vice-president of a firm or a government inspector.
2. Identity of the company—including attempts to associate an unfamiliar product with a well established business, government organization or some charitable cause.
3. The length of the sales pitch—such as fast-talking sales people who say they want 10 minutes of your time. Don't let a seller corner you! The law requires a seller to leave upon your request.
4. Amount of savings in price—such as quoting only part of the total price.
5. Delivery dates or length of service promised.

Do I have a right to cancel a contract for purchases made from door-to-door sellers?

Under Wisconsin law, a "cooling-off period" allows you three business days to think about the sale and cancel if you wish. This applies to most credit transactions and cash sales of $25 or more which were solicited and completed away from the seller's regular place of business. To cancel the sale, sign, date and return the notice of cancellation by midnight of the third business day. To avoid problems, keep a copy of the cancellation for your records by photo-copying the notice and sending it by registered or certified mail so you will have written proof that your cancellation notice was sent on time.

All money paid to the seller must be returned within 10 days. The customer must hold the goods for 20 days after they have been received. If the seller does not pick up the merchandise after 20 days, the goods may be kept by the consumer.

What about goods I receive in the mail?

If a company sends you goods you did not order, either orally or in writing, you are not required to pay for them or return the goods. The law states unsolicited merchandise is considered a gift and may be kept without any obligation to the sender. Don't be pressured to pay by companies who make a practice of mailing unordered merchandise on a "trial basis."

But remember, when you order items like books or records under what's called a "negative option sales plan," the merchandise will be sent to you automatically under obligation to pay unless you notify the seller in advance that you do not want it.

What should I do if I have a consumer problem?

Should you have reason to believe a seller has violated any part of the Wisconsin law which regulates home solicitation selling, file a complaint with the Office of Consumer Protection in the Wisconsin Justice Department. Write to the Madison Office at 114 East, State Capitol, Madison, Wisconsin 53702 or the Milwaukee Office at 819 N. 6th St., Rm. 520, Milwaukee, Wisconsin 53203.

Wisconsin law provides you with a private remedy of twice the amount of any money lost, plus court costs and attorney's fee. Contact your personal attorney to discuss the application of these private remedies in your situation.

Home Improvement and Repairs

Each year fraudulent home repair schemes take thousands of dollars from Wisconsin consumers. Wisconsin's Home Improvement Trade Practices Code is designed to protect home owners from such unscrupulous operations.

What does the Wisconsin home improvement code cover?

The code covers routine repairs to the house itself, as well as the installation of wall-to-wall carpeting, heating and air-conditioning equipment, furnaces, water softeners, and fire protection devices. Improvements to residential property such as the addition of garages, swimming pools, sidewalks, driveways, patios, porches, and landscaping also come under the provisions of this code.

What are some common ploys practiced by fraudulent operators?

Some tactics found in unscrupulous businesses are:

1. the phony building code inspector or health official who tries to gain entry into your house to conduct an investigation. All government personnel and utility workers carry business credentials. Insist upon seeing a form of proper identification.

2. the person soliciting home repairs who offers you a discount after

telling you your home will be used as a demonstrator model. This "model home" pitch is used frequently and generally provides no real savings in price.

3. the representative that uses scare tactics to pressure you into buying services you do not really need. He or she may falsely claim that your furnace is a serious safety hazard or that you need a fire detection device in your home.

4. any person who uses "bait and switch" tactics and attempts to bait you with cheaply priced repairs or materials in order to switch you to a more expensive job later. Be suspicious when the main thrust of the sales pitch moves away to a different product than the one advertised.

Are there any guidelines I can use in selecting a reliable contractor for home improvements?

When selecting a contractor, you should:

1. deal only with reputable firms.

2. get estimates from different contractors. Make sure all costs are covered in the estimate including the down payment, finance charges, building permit fees, installation costs, and all materials and supplies to be used in the job.

3. request names of past customers and contact them to find out if they were satisfied.

4. never select a contractor who has not come to your home to assess the job.

5. Ask questions: What methods or materials will be used? When will work begin? How long before the job is completed? What method of payment is required? What guarantees are provided?

6. Don't let a persuasive seller push you into signing a contract on the spot until you have received several estimates and are completely sure of the contract terms.

7. You may be asked to sign documents other than the contract. Read these papers thoroughly so you know exactly what you are signing.

What should I do if I have second thoughts about dealing with a contractor?

Wisconsin law allows you three business days to cancel the contract if it was solicited and signed away from the seller's regular place of business and if it involved a cost of over $25. "Away from the seller's regular place of business" means that you may have been contacted at your home, at your place of employment or at the seller's transient headquarters. In such transactions, the seller is required to provide you with cancellation forms. To cancel the sale, sign and date the notice of cancellation, and send it to the contractor before midnight of the third business day. Be sure to send the cancellation notice by registered or certified mail.

When all the work has been finished you may be asked to sign a paper certifying that the work has been completed. Carefully inspect the work for quality workmanship and materials as specified in the contract.

How does a "lien waiver" protect me from unscrupulous contractors?

A **lien waiver** is a form of receipt which prevents a contractor from collecting money from you twice for the same job. Often when you contract to remodel a part of your home, the job may be sub-contracted to another firm or may require special laborers to do the plumbing, the cabinetmaking, or the electrical wiring. As you pay the contractor for the job, he in turn is supposed to pay these laborers. If he fails to pay them, each laborer or materials supplier is entitled to collect payment from you.

Also beware of the contractor who asks you for advance payments for materials. Require him to provide you with a lien waiver from the place where he gets the materials. The lien waiver is proof that al materials and labor used in sub-contracting arrangements have been paid for. Wisconsin law requires that you receive a lien waiver whenever you make partial or final payments.

What if I have been defrauded by home improvement contractors?

If you have reason to believe a seller has violated any of the Wisconsin laws regulating home improvements or basement waterproofing you have a remedy. In Wisconsin, you are entitled to a private recovery of twice the amount of any money lost plus court costs and attorney's fee. Contact your personal attorney to discuss the application of these private remedies in your situation.

Landlord-tenant Relationships

Many landlord-tenant problems result from confusion as to the rights and responsibilities of each. If you, as a potential tenant, know your rights and obligations, misunderstandings can often be avoided.

What are property-owners' rights in renting?

A property owner has the right to:

1. determine the amount of rent.
2. set rules and conditions for the tenant.
3. collect payment for damage to the property.

Finding the right apartment is often frustrating and time consuming because it involves weighing so many factors.

4. sell the rental unit—if there is a written lease it continues to its expiration date.

5. refuse to rent to families with children or pets. However, a property owner cannot refuse to rent to anyone based on their race, religion or national origin.

What are the tenants' rights in renting?

A tenant has the right to:

1. use the rental unit in agreement with the rules.
2. occupy the rental unit without unjust interference by the landlord.
3. expect that the property be kept in reasonably good repair.

Is it important to check out the property before I rent it? What should I look for?

1. Be sure to see the actual unit you plan to rent—not a model.
2. Note if it needs painting, cleaning, or repairing.
3. Be sure the unit is what you want before you sign any papers. Should you change your mind, you may lose the security deposit.
4. If you rent the unit "as is" and without a promise for repairs, the landlord is not responsible for defects unless they violate health or building codes.

If the landlord requires a security deposit, what can I do to help get it back before I leave?

Before you move into and when you leave the unit:

1. list the damaged or unusually torn items.
2. list the necessary repairs.
3. note the cleanliness.
4. have this memo signed and dated by the landlord, and give him a photocopy. Be sure to keep the original.
5. When you move from the unit, repair any damages you have caused, clean the unit, and show your list to the owner.

These steps will be a great help in getting your security deposit back.

What is a lease? What should it state?

The **lease** is an agreement between you and the landlord; it may be written or spoken. If there is no written lease, the property is usually being rented from month-to-month, and you must give at least 28 days written notice before you leave.

A written lease is good protection because it prevents any change in rental conditions (an increase in rent, for example) for the term of the lease.

1. Before you sign the lease, read everything carefully. Be sure all blank spaces are filled, in the terms you have agreed to.
2. If you do not understand everything it says, be sure to get legal assistance.
3. Make sure that all promises are included in the lease; you may do this by attaching a list of promises made by the landlord and signed by him.
4. The lease should state whether the landlord or tenant must pay for utilities such as gas, electricity, and water. Be sure to check carefully to determine your responsibilities.
5. Keep your copy of the lease signed by you and the owner.

Are there any restrictions on the landlord evicting me from the place I am renting?

The law allows the landlord to collect rent when it is due, and, if there is no written lease, requires him to give notice if he wishes you to move. He may give a "Five-Day Quit or Pay Rent Notice" when rent is overdue. When he does, you must pay all rent due within the five days or move.

Any other violations of the rental agreement usually require a 14-day notice to you to move from the property. If the landlord wants you

The reason for strange noises coming from the apartment upstairs.

to move when no violation of the lease exists, he has to give you 28 days notice on a month-to-month lease.

Eviction is a lawsuit against you in small claims court. If successful, the court will order the sheriff to remove you from the premises. If someone gives you a summons to sue you for eviction, you should seek help from an attorney or legal services office. Otherwise, if you agree with your landlord and you want to leave the premises, you should inform him when you will move.

Do I have to give advance notice to the landlord if I intend to move?

If there is no written lease, it is very important to give proper notice if you do not want to lose your security deposit or be made to pay additional rent when you move. This notice must be in writing, and must be delivered to the landlord or his agent 28 days or more before your next rental period.

If you have a written lease, be sure to read it to find out what moving notice is required.

What should I do if my landlord has violated my legal rights?

If you believe your legal rights have been violated, contact your attorney, legal services office, or the Department of Justice Office of Consumer Protection.

Automobile Purchase and Repairs

There is more to purchasing and maintaining a car than kicking the tires, looking under the hood, and adding fuel. Too often, prospective buyers are mislead by the appearance of a car and fail to get satisfactory repairs. In purchasing a car, you should ask yourself, "What do I need and what can I afford?" Then begin to shop around to find out what is available in your price range. It is smart to shop with reputable dealers who will stand behind their sales. The following is a guide to common sense and state law to assist you in making intelligent choices in purchasing a motor vehicle.

1. *Manufacturer's List Price.* The manufacturer's suggested list price is usually displayed on new cars and is just that, a suggested price. It generally represents a starting point for bargaining between you and the seller. A car dealer expects you to bargain with him.

2. *Window Sticker and Odometer Statement.* The window sticker on a used car must provide information about how the car was used—whether as a demonstrator, taxi or rental. Be sure to check for this information. For a used car, you should also check the prior owner's odometer statement which lists the approximate mileage at the time of the trade-in or car's transferral to the dealer. This statement also gives you the name of the previous owner whom you might want to contact for more information about the car.

3. *Mechanical Condition.* If you have any questions about the mechanical condition of the car, have a mechanic check it for an objective opinion.

Under Wisconsin law, licensed car dealers must inform you in writing of significant existing mechanical and structural defects in their used cars. Be sure to speak up and ask the salesman for this disclosure checklist before you begin to inspect a car.

Items which must be included in the check are the frame and body, the engine, the transmission and drive shaft, as well as the

The large investment made in the purchase of a car suggests the importance of making a careful choice.

electrical, cooling and fuel systems. Certain accessories must also be checked to determine whether or not they work. If any malfunctions or defects are found, you must be given an explanation of the probable cause. In this way, you should have a fairly good idea of exactly what you are getting for your money and how much it will cost for any needed repairs.

4. *Safety Check.* Safety equipment must also be checked and you must be informed of any malfunctions. All safety equipment must be operating correctly before the vehicle may be driven legally on Wisconsin roads. If equipment does not function correctly, a warning must be posted on the contract and you must tow the car from the lot. You cannot get a license for the car until the defects are corrected and the car passes an inspection.

5. *Warranty.* Be sure to find out exactly what the warranty provides. The warranty should tell you what is covered, how long it is covered, who will honor it and what you have to do to keep the warranty in effect.

6. *Protect Yourself.* Don't be swayed by pressure selling and don't be rushed. You don't have to finance a car where you buy it. If you do decide to finance a car, you could save money by financing it from another source. Check with a local bank or credit union to compare rates.

Always make certain you know what you are signing. A salesman might ask you to sign a paper in order to hold a car for you. Be careful.

This is called an offer to purchase and becomes a binding sales contract if it is accepted by the dealer within two business hours.

7. *If You Have a Complaint.* After you have your car, speak up if the dealer doesn't keep his promise. Talk to the salesman, the sales manager, and the head of the business, if necessary. If you think you have been defrauded, call the Motor Vehicle Division of the Wisconsin Department of Transportation, the Wisconsin Department of Justice Office of Consumer Protection, your district attorney, or legal aid agency.

The Wisconsin Department of Justice rules also regulate automobile repair shops in Wisconsin. It provides that where the price to the customer of a repair may exceed $25.00 and where the customer brings the vehicle to the shop in a face-to-face contact with a shop representative, the customer must be given a written repair order describing the work to be done and a written price quotation or a choice of estimated alternatives. In addition, this rule prohibits the following practices by repair shops:

1. misrepresenting the cost of repairs, the terms of any warranty, that repairs are necessary, or that repairs have been made.

2. attempting to collect for unauthorized or unnecessary repairs, or for repairs which have not been made.

3. refusing to return a customer's vehicle because she refuses to pay for unauthorized repairs or for changes in excess of the price authorized for the repairs requested.

Small Claims Court

Does someone owe you money? Has your landlord unjustifiably failed to return your security deposit? Did you order merchandise that the retailer has failed to deliver? Has a merchant failed to comply with the terms of his guarantee? Have you tried to get an adjustment from the business without success? If so, you should consider the possibility of bringing a lawsuit in small claims court. You may not need a lawyer and the rules are more simple than in most court proceedings.

Who may sue in small claims court?

Any person can bring a small claims court action. However, the court may require the appointment of a guardian for those under eighteen years of age.

Whom can I sue in small claims court?

You may sue any individual or corporation doing business in the state of Wisconsin.

When can I sue in small claims court?

CASE STUDY*
Halbman v. Lemke

Like most young people, James Halbman, Jr., wanted to own a car. In July of 1973 he got his chance. Halbman, of Greenfield, Wisconsin, was working then at a gas station owned by a man named Michael Lemke, who had a 1968 Oldsmobile for sale. Halbman, who was not yet eighteen years old, liked the car and agreed to buy it for $1,250. He gave Lemke $1,000 in cash, arranged to pay the rest of the purchase price in $25 weekly installments, and took possession of the Oldsmobile. But just five weeks later the car broke down, setting off a chain of events that ultimately led to an important ruling by the Wisconsin Supreme Court on the rights of minors who sign contracts with adults.

The case got into court because Halbman, faced with a large bill to fix the disabled Oldsmobile, repudiated his contract with Lemke and demanded a refund of the $1,100 he had thus far paid toward the purchase price. Halbman based his action on a longstanding legal principle known as "the infancy doctrine." It says that a minor has an absolute right to repudiate (or, in legal language, "disaffirm") any contract with an adult to purchase an item that is not considered a necessity. The doctrine, as the Wisconsin Supreme Court noted in Halbman's case, is designed to protect minors "from foolishly squandering their wealth through improvident contracts with crafty adults who would take advantage of them in the marketplace."

But Halbman's case was complicated by the fact that he did not attempt to disaffirm his contract until October of 1973, which was a month after he had taken the car into a mechanic and had it repaired at a cost of $637. Moreover, Halbman never paid the repair bill, so the mechanic put a lien on the car. (A lien gives a person the legal right to hold property until a claim—in this case, the repair bill—is paid.) The mechanic kept the car until the spring of 1974, but the bill remained unpaid. The mechanic finally decided to satisfy the lien by removing the Oldsmobile's engine and transmission. The car was then towed to Halbman's house, where it sat for a time on blocks. However, vandals soon got into the car and did so much damage that it became an unsalvageable wreck.

In the meantime, Lemke had been taking some legal steps of his own. In October of 1973 he signed the car's title over to Halbman in hopes of avoiding any liability for the cost of repairing or maintaining the Oldsmobile. And when Halbman sued to get back his $1,100, Lemke quickly filed a counterclaim in which he asked to be paid the remaining $150 of the agreed-upon purchase price.

When the case came to trial before a judge in Milwaukee, there was no dispute about Halbman's right to disaffirm his contract with Lemke and return the car or, at least, what was left of it. But Lemke argued that he was also entitled to recover some money for the damage done to the car up until the time Halbman disaffirmed his purchase contract. Lemke said the amount Halbman should pay him was $637—the cost of repairing the car. Halbman, of course, argued that under the infancy doctrine his only obligation was to return the car

*A summary of the case. For the court's complete opinion, see 99 Wis.2d 241, 298 N.W.2d 562 (1980).

in exchange for his money back. As for the damage, Halbman said that was not his fault and so he could not be held responsible for it.

The judge eventually ruled in favor of Halbman, saying that the law did not require him to pay for any unintentional damage done to the car. Lemke then took his case to an intermediate appeals court, but the ruling was the same. In 1980 Lemke went the next step up the legal ladder, to the Wisconsin Supreme Court, in hopes of getting back at least some of the $1,100 he had lost in his deal with Halbman.

The case was argued before the Supreme Court in October of 1980. Lemke took the position that since Halbman was unable to return the car in exchange for his money back, he should at least be required to make some restitution for the damage that had been done. To back up his argument, Lemke cited an earlier ruling by the court in a somewhat similar case. In that ruling, Lemke contended, the court had suggested that a minor might be required to make restitution if he were able to do so. And Halbman, Lemke said, was clearly able to make restitution because he had paid $1,100 for the car before disaffirming the contract. Halbman, meanwhile, stuck by his earlier position that all Lemke was entitled to was the car, regardless of its condition.

In a decision handed down in November of 1980, the Supreme Court upheld the lower court rulings in Halbman's favor. The court said its decision had been made difficult by the fact that the law regarding disaffirmed contracts "is characterized by confusion, inconsistency, and a general lack of uniformity." But in Halbman's case, the court said, the law clearly did not permit Lemke to make any recovery for the damage done to the Oldsmobile. "Such a recovery," the court said, "would require Halbman to return more than that remaining in his possession. It seeks compensatory value for that which he cannot return." The court said that had Halbman deliberately damaged or destroyed the car, Lemke might then have been able to recover damage through a civil court action. "But absent these factors, as in the present case, we believe that to require a disaffirming minor to make restitution for diminished value is, in effect, to bind the minor to a part of the obligation which by law he is privileged to avoid."

QUESTION FOR DISCUSSION

The recent *Halbman* v. *Lemke* case sets relationships between the vendor (seller) and the purchaser, in this case a minor.

Study the facts of the case, the arguments on each side and determine if you feel this decision was fair. Why?

If you made an agreement with an individual or corporation and that party has breached the terms of the agreement, you can sue.

If you were injured or your property was damaged by someone who was more at fault than you, you can sue.

Although your claim may exceed $1,000.00, the small claims court cannot award you more than that amount.

Where can I sue in small claims court?

For claims based upon a contract or agreement between you and the other party which you feel hasn't been lived up to, you can generally bring the lawsuit in the county court of the county where the defendant resides or can be found. If the other party is a Wisconsin corporation, its residence is its main office in the state. If the other party is an out-of-state corporation, you can sue in any county where the corporation does a substantial amount of business. For information about a corporation's main office and its agents, contact the Secretary of State's Corporation Division. If there are several defendants, you can sue in the county where any one of them resides.

For personal injury or property damage claims, you can sue in the county where the injury took place or where the other party resides.

How do I start the suit in small claims court?

Go to the courthouse and the small claims court clerk will supply you with the necessary forms to commence your action and give you the date of your first court appearance. If forms are not available at the courthouse, the clerk should be able to advise you where they may be obtained. After completing the forms, you may have to take them to the Sheriff's Office in order to have them served on the other party for you. An average filing and service fee of $7 to $10 must be paid before the suit is processed; this fee is returned if you win the case.

How should I go about preparing my case for small claims court?

First think about how you are going to prove that the defendant owes you money. Collect and preserve any receipts you may have received in dealing with the other party. Cancelled checks are very useful. Make a detailed chronological history of the transaction so the facts are clear in your mind. Remember your testimony may be the most important information you have. Talk to people who may have witnessed important aspects of the dispute. For example, if you are suing your landlord for the return of your security deposit, get together a copy of your lease, the cancelled check you gave the landlord for the security deposit, and any disinterested persons who can testify concerning the condition of the rental unit when you started renting and when you left it.

If you are suing on the basis of defective merchandise or faulty repairs, it may be very helpful to get an 'expert' witness to testify on your behalf. A written statement concerning the nature of the defect and the decrease in value due to the defect is often helpful. If it is necessary to go to trial, it will be necessary to get the witness to testify in person. Full-time mechanics and repairmen with several years of experience will often qualify as experts.

After your claim is filed, the court will probably set an informal conference at your first court appearance to review the facts in your case. Many small claims court cases are settled at these informal conferences. If your case is not settled at that time, you may wish to hire a lawyer to help present your case to the judge. In preparing your own case, plan to get your proof together so that it is more convincing than the other side's evidence. Arrange to have your witnesses, contracts, and receipts in court at the designated time.

If you win the case, a judgment will be entered in court stating what the opposing party owes you. In many cases, the opposing party will pay the judgment immediately. In other instances, you may find it necessary to take further informal action or consult an attorney who can proceed with more formal legal steps to collect the money to which you are entitled.

QUESTIONS FOR DISCUSSION

1. Why have consumer protection laws become increasingly important in the United States?

2. What do you think is meant by consumer self-protection? What are some of the things consumers need protection from?

3. What might happen if no contracts were enforceable in a court of law?

4. Do you agree or disagree that buyers are at a disadvantage when receiving salespeople in their homes? Why?

SUGGESTED ACTIVITY

Mock Trials: Scripts for Wisconsin Lawyers and Teachers. Published by Wisconsin Department of Public Instruction in cooperation with The Wisconsin Bar Foundation. Bulletin No. 0166, 1980.

Mock Trials include automobile accidents, landlord-tenant, drunk driving, homicide, burglary, and child abuse scripts.

VOCABULARY

Consumer
Contract
Damages
Defraud
Disaffirm
Eviction
Guardian ad litem
Injunction
Intentional tort
Lease
Liability
Lien waiver
Small claims court
Testator
Trustee
Vendor

RELATED LEGAL CASES

Berg v. *United States Leather Company,* 125 Wis. 264, 265 (1905). (once a minor backs out of a contract, he or she must usually return any items that were obtained, but the minor cannot be forced to continue making payments; the primary exception to this is that a minor can be required to pay for "necessities")

Zurn v. *Whatley,* 213 Wis. 365, 370 (1933) and *Grosset* v. *Goelzer,* 177 Wis. 455, 468 (1922). (a parent is responsible for the child's negligence if the child was an "agent" for the parent—doing something which the parent requested or from which the parent received an advantage)

Gerlat v. *Christianson,* 13 Wis.2d 31, 35 (1961). (a parent may be liable for damages caused by the child's negligence if the parent failed to exercise reasonable control over the child in a situation which the parent could control and knew or should have known that there was a need to control the child)

Goller v. *White,* 20 Wis.2d 402, 413 (1963). (while children may sue parents over contracts and property rights, the exceptions include the parent's act involving an exercise of parental authority or parental discretion regarding food, clothing, housing, medical, and dental care or similar items)

Whithers v. *Tucker,* 32 Wis.2d 496, 145 N.W.2d 665 (1966). (minor has no capacity to contract)

Kiefer v. *Fred Howe Motors, Inc.,* 39 Wis.2d 20, 23 (1968). (minors can enforce contracts against adults but adults cannot usually enforce contracts against minors. This is true even if the minor lies about his or her age when making the contract. A minor can still back out of the contract but might be held responsible for any damages caused to the other person if there was fraudulent misrepresentation)

Metcalf v. *Consolidated Badger Coop,* 28 Wis.2d 552 (once a child is seven years old, he is capable of negligence)

Christy v. *Schwartz,* 49 Wis.2d 760, 183 N.W.2d 81 (1971), Wisconsin Statute 260.22. (minor has right to sue in tort; action can be commenced by guardian ad litem)

SUGGESTED READINGS

"Emotional Distress: A Mock Civil Trial," *Bill of Rights in Action,* April, 1980, vol. 14, no. 2, pp. 3-4.

"Hypos on Minor and Contracts, " *Update,* Spring, 1979, pp. 47-49.

SUGGESTED RESOURCES

Wisconsin Department of Justice
Office of Consumer Protection
114 E. State Capitol
Madison, Wisconsin 53702
(608) 266-1852

819 N. 6th Street
Room 520
Milwaukee, Wisconsin 53203
(414) 224-1867

Wisconsin Statutes

Legal Assistance:
Wisconsin Judicare
403 Third Street
Wausau, Wisconsin
1-(800) 472-1638

Limited legal assistance to qualified residents in selected Wisconsin counties.

Appendix A

THE CONSTITUTION OF THE UNITED STATES

PREAMBLE

We the People of the United States, in Order to form a more perfect Union, establish Justice, insure domestic Tranquility, provide for the common defence, promote the general Welfare, and secure the Blessings of Liberty to ourselves and our Posterity, do ordain and establish this Constitution for the United States of America.

ARTICLE I

Section 1. All legislative Powers herein granted shall be vested in a Congress of the United States, which shall consist of a Senate and House of Representatives.

Section 2. [1] The House of Representatives shall be composed of Members chosen every second Year by the People of the several States, and the Electors in each State shall have the Qualifications requisite for Electors of the most numerous Branch of the State Legislature.

[2] No Person shall be a Representative who shall not have attained to the Age of twenty five Years, and been seven Years a Citizen of the United States, and who shall not, when elected, be an Inhabitant of that State in which he shall be chosen.

[3] Representatives and direct Taxes shall be apportioned among the several States which may be included within this Union, according to their respective Numbers, which shall be determined by adding to the whole Number of free Persons, including those bound to Service for a Term of Years, and excluding Indians not taxed, three fifths of all other Persons. The actual Enumeration shall be made within three Years after the first Meeting of the Congress of the United States, and within every subsequent Term of ten Years, in such Manner as they shall by Law direct. The Number of Representatives shall not exceed one for every thirty Thousand, but each State shall have at Least one Representative; and until such enumeration shall be made, the State of New Hampshire shall be entitled to chuse three, Massachusetts eight, Rhode Island and Providence Plantations one, Connecticut five, New York six, New Jersey four, Pennsylvania eight, Delaware one, Maryland six, Virginia ten, North Carolina five, South Carolina five, and Georgia three.

[4] When vacancies happen in the Representation from any State, the Executive Authority thereof shall issue Writs of Election to fill such Vacancies.

[5] The House of Representation shall chuse their Speaker and other Officers; and shall have the sole Power of Impeachment.

Section 3. [1] The Senate of the United States shall be composed of two

Senators from each State, chosen by the Legislature thereof, for six Years; and each Senator shall have one Vote.

[2] Immediately after they shall be assembled in Consequence of the first Election, they shall be divided as equally as may be into three Classes. The Seats of the Senators of the first Class shall be vacated at the Expiration of the Second Year, of the second Class at the Expiration of the fourth Year, and of the third Class at the Expiration of the sixth Year, so that one third may be chosen every second Year; and if Vacancies happen by Resignation, or otherwise, during the Recess of the Legislature of any State, the Executive thereof may make temporary Appointments until the next Meeting of the Legislature, which shall then fill such Vacancies.

[3] No Person shall be a Senator who shall not have attained to the Age of thirty Years, and been nine Years a Citizen of the United States, and who shall not, when elected, be an Inhabitant of that State for which he shall be chosen.

[4] The Vice President of the United States shall be President of the Senate, but shall have no Vote, unless they be equally divided.

[5] The Senate shall chuse their other Officers, and also a President pro tempore, in the Absence of the Vice President, or when he shall exercise the Office of President of the United States.

[6] The Senate shall have the sole Power to try all Impeachments. When sitting for that Purpose, they shall be on Oath or Affirmation. When the President of the United States is tried, the Chief Justice shall preside: And no Person shall be convicted without the Concurrence of two thirds of the Members present.

[7] Judgment in Cases of Impeachment shall not extend further than to removal from Office, and disqualification to hold and enjoy any Office of honor, Trust, or Profit under the United States: but the Party convicted shall nevertheless be liable and subject to Indictment, Trial, Judgment, and Punishment, according to Law.

Section 4. [1] The Times, Places and Manner of holding Elections for Senators and Representatives, shall be prescribed in each State by the Legislature thereof; but the Congress may at any time by Law make or alter such Regulations, except as to the Places of chusing Senators.

[2] The Congress shall assemble at least once in every Year, and such Meeting shall be on the first Monday in December, unless they shall by Law appoint a different Day.

Section 5. [1] Each House shall be the Judge of the Elections, Returns, and Qualifications of its own Members, and a Majority of each shall constitute a Quorum to do Business; but a smaller Number may adjourn from day to day, and may be authorized to compel the Attendance of absent Members, in such Manner, and under such Penalties as each House may provide.

[2] Each House may determine the Rules of its Proceedings, punish its Members for disorderly Behavior, and, with the Concurrence of two thirds, expel a Member.

[3] Each House shall keep a Journal of its Proceedings, and from time to time publish the same, excepting such Parts as may in their Judgment require Secrecy; and the Yeas and Nays of the Members of either House on any question shall, at the Desire of one fifth of those Present, be entered on the Journal.

[4] Neither House, during the Session of Congress, shall, without the Consent of the other, adjourn for more than three days, nor to any other Place than that in which the two Houses shall be sitting.

Section 6. [1] The Senators and Representatives shall receive a Compensation for their Services, to be ascertained by Law, and paid out of the Treasury of the United States. They shall in all Cases, except Treason, Felony and Breach of the Peace, be privileged from Arrest during their Attendance at the Session of their respective Houses, and in going to and returning from the the same; and for any Speech or Debate in either House, they shall not be questioned in any other Place.

[2] No Senator or Representative shall, during the Time for which he was elected, be appointed to any civil Office under the Authority of the United States, which shall have been created, or the Emoluments whereof shall have been increased during such time; and no Person holding any Office under the United States, shall be a Member of either House during his Continuance in Office.

Section 7. [1] All Bills for raising Revenue shall originate in the House of Representatives; but the Senate may propose or concur with Amendments as on other Bills.

[2] Every Bill which shall have passed the House of Representatives and the Senate, shall, before it become a Law, be presented to the President of the United States; If he approve he shall sign it, but if not he shall return it, with his Objections to the House in which it shall have originated, who shall enter the Objections at large on their Journal, and proceed to reconsider it. If after such Reconsideration two thirds of that House shall agree to pass the Bill, it shall be sent together with the Objections, to the other House, by which it shall likewise be reconsidered, and if approved by two thirds of that House, it shall become a Law. But in all such Cases the Votes of both Houses shall be determined by yeas and Nays, and the Names of the Persons voting for and against the Bill shall be entered on the Journal of each House respectively. If any Bill shall not be returned by the President within ten Days (Sundays excepted) after it shall have been presented to him, the Same shall be a Law, in like Manner as if he had signed it, unless the Congress by their Adjournment prevent its Return in which Case it shall not be a Law.

[3] Every Order, Resolution, or Vote, to Which the Concurrence of the Senate and House of Representatives may be necessary (except on a question of Adjournment) shall be presented to the President of the United States; and before the Same shall take Effect, shall be approved by him, or being disapproved by him, shall be repassed by two thirds of the Senate and House of Representatives, according to the Rules and Limitations prescribed in the Case of a Bill.

Section 8. [1] The Congress shall have Power To lay and collect Taxes, Duties, Imposts and Excises, to pay the Debts and provide for the common Defence and general Welfare of the United States; but all Duties, Imposts and Excises shall be uniform throughout the United States;

[2] To borrow money on the credit of the United States;

[3] To regulate Commerce with foreign Nations, and among the several States, and with the Indian Tribes;

[4] To establish a uniform Rule of Naturalization, and uniform Laws on the subject of Bankruptcies throughout the United States;

[5] To coin Money, regulate the Value thereof, and of foreign Coin, and fix the Standard of Weights and Measures;

[6] To provide for the Punishment of counterfeiting the Securities and current Coin of the United States;

[7] To Establish Post Offices and Post Roads;

[8] To promote the Progress of Science and useful Arts, by securing for limited Times to Authors and Inventors the exclusive Right to their respective Writings and Discoveries;

[9] To constitute Tribunals inferior to the supreme Court;

[10] To define and punish Piracies and Felonies committed on the high Seas, and Offenses against the Law of Nations;

[11] To declare War, grant Letters of Marque and Reprisal, and make Rules concerning Captures on Land and Water;

[12] To raise and support Armies, but no Appropriation of Money to that Use shall be for a longer Term than two Years;

[13] To provide and maintain a Navy;

[14] To make Rules for the Government and Regulation of the land and naval Forces;

[15] To provide for calling forth the Militia to execute the Laws of the Union, suppress Insurrections and repel Invasions;

[16] To provide for organizing, arming, and disciplining, the Militia, and for governing such Part of them as may be employed in the Service of the United States, reserving to the States respectively, the Appointment of the Officers, and the Authority of training the Militia according to the discipline prescribed by Congress;

[17] To exercise exclusive Legislation in all Cases whatsoever, over such District (not exceeding ten Miles square) as may, by Cession of particular States, and the Acceptance of Congress, become the Seat of the Government of the United States, and to exercise like Authority over all Places purchased by the Consent of the Legislature of the State in which the Same shall be, for the Erection of Forts, Magazines, Arsenals, dock-Yards, and other needful Buildings;—And

[18] To make all Laws which shall be necessary and proper for carrying into Execution the foregoing Powers, and all other Powers vested by this Constitution in the Government of the United States, or in any Department or Officer thereof.

Section 9. [1] The Migration or Importation of Such Persons as any of the States now existing shall think proper to admit, shall not be prohibited by the Congress prior to the Year one thousand eight hundred and eight, but a Tax or duty may be imposed on such Importation, not exceeding ten dollars for each Person.

[2] The privilege of the Writ of Habeas Corpus shall not be suspended, unless when in Cases of Rebellion or Invasion the public Safety may require it.

[3] No Bill of Attainder or ex post facto Law shall be passed.

[4] No Capitation, or other direct, Tax shall be laid, unless in Proportion to the Census or Enumeration herein before directed to be taken.

[5] No Tax or Duty shall be laid on Articles exported from any State.

[6] No Preference shall be given by any Regulation of Commerce or Revenue to the Ports of one State over those of another: nor shall Vessels bound to, or from, one State be obliged to enter, clear, or pay Duties in another.

[7] No money shall be drawn from the Treasury, but in Consequence of Appropriations made by Law; and a regular Statement and Account of the Receipts and Expenditures of all public Money shall be published from time to time.

[8] No Title of Nobility shall be granted by the United States: And no Person holding any Office of Profit or Trust under them, shall, without the Consent of the Congress, accept of any present, Emolument, Office, or Title, of any kind whatever, from any King, Prince, or foreign State.

Section 10. [1] No State shall enter into any Treaty, Alliance, or Confederation; grant Letters of Marque and Reprisal; coin Money; emit Bills of Credit; make any Thing but gold and silver Coin a Tender in Payment of Debts;

pass any Bill of Attainder, ex post facto Law, or Law impairing the Obligation of Contracts, or grant any Title of Nobility.

[2] No State shall, without the Consent of the Congress, lay any Imposts or Duties on Imports or Exports, except what may be absolutely necessary for executing its inspection Laws: and the net Produce of all Duties and Imposts; laid by any State on Imports or Exports, shall be for the Use of the Treasury of the United States; and all such Laws shall be subject to the Revision and Controul of the Congress.

[3] No State shall, without the Consent of Congress, lay any Duty of Tonnage, keep Troops, or Ships of War in time of Peace, enter into any Agreement or Compact with another State, or with a foreign Power, or engage in War, unless actually invaded, or in such imminent Danger as will not admit of delay.

ARTICLE II

Section 1. [1] The executive Power shall be vested in a President of the United States of America. He shall hold his Office during the Term of four Years, and, together with the Vice President, chosen for the same Term, be elected, as follows:

[2] Each State shall appoint, in such Manner as the Legislature thereof may direct, a Number of Electors, equal to the whole Number of Senators and Representatives to which the State may be entitled in the Congress; but no Senator or Representative, or Person holding an Office of Trust or Profit under the United States, shall be appointed an Elector.

[3] The Electors shall meet in their respective States, and vote by Ballot for two Persons, of whom one at least shall not be an Inhabitant of the same State with themselves. And they shall make a List of all the Persons voted for, and of the Number of Votes for each; which List they shall sign and certify, and transmit sealed to the Seat of the Government of the United States, directed to the President of the Senate. The President of the Senate shall, in the Presence of the Senate and House of Representatives, open all the Certificates, and the Votes shall then be counted. The Person having the greatest Number of Votes shall be the President, if such Number be a Majority of the whole Number of Electors appointed; and if there be more than one who have such Majority, and have an equal Number of Votes, then the House of Representatives shall immediately chuse by Ballot one of them for President; and if no Person have a Majority; then from the five highest on the List the said House shall in like Manner chuse the President. But in chusing the President, the Votes shall be taken by States the Representation from each State having one Vote; A quorum for this Purpose shall consist of a Member or Members from two thirds of the States, and a Majority of all the States shall be necessary to a Choice. In every Case, after the Choice of the President, the Person having the greater Number of Votes of the Electors shall be the Vice President. But if there should remain two or more who have equal Votes, the Senate shall chuse from them by Ballot the Vice President.

[4] The Congress may determine the Time of chusing the Electors, and the Day on which they shall give their Votes; which Day shall be the same throughout the United States.

[5] No person except a natural born Citizen, or a Citizen of the United States, at the time of the Adoption of this Constitution, shall be eligible to the Office of President; neither shall any Person be eligible to that Office who shall not have attained to the Age of thirty five Years, and been fourteen Years a Resident within the United States.

[6] In case of the removal of the President from Office, or of his Death,

Resignation or Inability to discharge the Powers and Duties of the said Office, the Same shall devolve on the Vice President, and the Congress may by Law provide for the Case of Removal, Death, Resignation or Inability, both of the President and Vice President, declaring what Officer shall then act as President, and such Officer shall act accordingly, until the Disability be removed, or a President shall be elected.

[7] The President shall, at stated Times, receive for his Services, a Compensation, which shall neither be increased nor diminished during the Period for which he shall have been elected, and he shall not receive within that Period any other Emolument from the United States, or any of them.

[8] Before he enter on the Execution of his Office, he shall take the following Oath or Affirmation: "I do solemnly swear (or affirm) that I will faithfully execute the Office of President of the United States, and will to the best of my Ability, preserve, protect and defend the Constitution of the United States."

Section 2. [1] The President shall be Commander in Chief of the Army and Navy of the United States, and of the militia of the several States, when called into the actual Service of the United States; he may require the Opinion, in writing, of the principal Officer in each of the Executive Departments, upon any Subject relating to the Duties of their respective Offices, and he shall have Power to grant Reprieves and Pardons for Offenses against the United States, except in Cases of Impeachment.

[2] He shall have Power, by and with the Advice and Consent of the Senate to make Treaties, provide two thirds of the Senators present concur; and he shall nominate, and by and with the Advice and Consent of the Senate, shall appoint Ambassadors, other public Ministers and Consuls, Judges of the supreme Court, and all other Officers of the United States, whose Appointments are not herein otherwise provided for, and which shall be established by Law; but the Congress may by Law vest the Appointment of such inferior Officers, as they think proper, in the President alone, in the Courts of Law, or in the Heads of Departments.

[3] The President shall have Power to fill up all Vacancies that may happen during the Recess of the Senate, by granting Commissions which shall expire at the End of their next Session.

Section 3. He shall from time to time give to the Congress Information of the State of the Union, and recommend to their Consideration such Measures as he shall judge necessary and expedient; he may, on extraordinary Occasions, convene both Houses, or either of them, and in Case of Disagreement between them, with Respect to the Time of Adjournment, he may adjourn them to such Time as he shall think proper; he shall receive Ambassadors and other public Ministers; he shall take Care that the Laws be faithfully executed, and shall Commission all the Officers of the United States.

Section 4. The President, Vice President and all civil Officers of the United States, shall be removed from Office on Impeachment for, and Conviction of, Treason, Bribery, or other high Crimes and Misdemeanors.

ARTICLE III

Section 1. The judicial Power of the United States, shall be vested in one supreme Court, and in such inferior Courts as the Congress may from time to time ordain and establish. The Judges, both of the supreme and inferior Courts, shall hold their Offices during good Behaviour, and shall, at stated Times, receive for their Services a Compensation, which shall not be diminished during their Continuance in Office.

Section 2. [1] The judicial Power shall extend to all Cases, in Law and Equity, arising under this Constitution, the Laws of the United States, and Treaties made, or which shall be made, under their Authority;—to all Cases affecting Ambassadors, other public Ministers and Consuls;—to all Cases of admiralty and maritime Jurisdiction;—to Controversies to which the United States shall be a Party;—to Controversies between two or more States;—between a State and Citizens of another State;—between Citizens of different States;—between Citizens of the same State claiming Lands under the Grants of different States, and between a State, or the Citizens thereof, and foreign States, Citizens or Subjects.

[2] In all Cases affecting Ambassadors, other public Ministers and Consuls, and those in which a State shall be a Party, the supreme Court shall have original Jurisdiction. In all the other Cases before mentioned, the supreme Court shall have appellate Jurisdiction, both as to Law and Fact, with such Exceptions, and under such Regulations as the Congress shall make.

[3] The trial of all Crimes, except in Cases of Impeachment, shall be by Jury; and such Trial shall be held in the State where the said Crimes shall have been committed; but when not committed within any State, the Trial shall be at such Place or Places as the Congress may by Law have directed.

Section 3. [1] Treason against the United States, shall consist only in levying War against them, or, in adhering to their Enemies, giving them Aid and Comfort. No Person shall be convicted of Treason unless on the Testimony of two Witnesses to the same overt Act, or on Confession in open Court.

[2] The Congress shall have Power to declare the Punishment of Treason, but no Attainder of Treason shall work Corruption of Blood, or Forfeiture except during the Life of the Person attainted.

ARTICLE IV

Section 1. Full Faith and Credit shall be given in each State to the public Acts, Records, and judicial Proceedings of every other State. And the Congress may by general Laws prescribe the Manner in which such Acts, Records and Proceedings shall be proved, and the Effect thereof.

Section 2. [1] The Citizens of each State shall be entitled to all Privileges and Immunities of Citizens in the several States.

[2] A Person charged in any State with Treason, Felony, or other Crime, who shall flee from Justice, and be found in another State, shall on demand of the executive Authority of the State from which he fled, be delivered up, to be removed to the State having Jurisdiction of the Crime.

[3] No Person held to Service or Labour in one State, under the Laws thereof, escaping into another, shall, in Consequence of any Law or Regulation therein, be discharged from such Service or Labor, but shall be delivered up on Claim of the Party to whom such Service or Labour may be due.

Section 3. [1] New States may be admitted by the Congress into this Union; but no new State shall be formed or erected within the Jurisdiction of any other State; nor any State be formed by the Junction of two or more States, or Parts of States, without the Consent of the Legislatures of the States concerned as well as of the Congress.

[2] The Congress shall have Power to dispose of and make all needful Rules and Regulations respecting the Territory or other Property belonging to the United States; and nothing in this Constitution shall be so construed as to Prejudice any Claims of the United States, or of any particular State.

Section 4. The United States shall guarantee to every State in this Union a Republican Form of Government, and shall protect each of them against

Invasion; and on Application of the Legislature, or of the Executive (when the Legislature cannot be convened) against domestic Violence.

ARTICLE V

The Congress, whenever two thirds of both Houses shall deem it necessary, shall propose Amendments to this Constitution, or, on the Application of the Legislatures of two thirds of the several States, shall call a Convention for proposing Amendments, which, in either Case, shall be valid to all Intents and Purposes, as part of this Constitution, when ratified by the Legislatures of three fourths of the several States, or by Conventions in three fourths thereof, as the one or the other Mode of Ratification may be proposed by the Congress; Provided that no Amendment which may be made prior to the Year One thousand eight hundred and eight shall in any Manner affect the first and fourth Clauses in the Ninth Section of the first Article; and that no State, without its Consent, shall be deprived of its equal Suffrage in the Senate.

ARTICLE VI

[1] All Debts contracted and Engagements entered into, before the Adoption of this Constitution shall be as valid against the United States under this Constitution, as under the Confederation.

[2] This Constitution, and the Laws of the United States which shall be made in Pursuance thereof; and all Treaties made, or which shall be made, under the Authority of the United States, shall be the supreme Law of the Land; and the Judges in every State shall be bound thereby, any Thing in the Constitution or Laws of any State to the Contrary notwithstanding.

[3] The Senators and Representatives before mentioned, and the Members of the several State Legislatures, and all executive and judicial Officers, both of the United States and of the several States, shall be bound by Oath or Affirmation, to support this Constitution; but no religious Test shall ever be required as a Qualification to any Office or public Trust under the United States.

ARTICLE VII

The Ratification of the Conventions of nine States shall be sufficient for the Establishment of this Constitution between the States so ratifying the Same.

ARTICLES IN ADDITION TO, AND AMENDMENT OF, THE CONSTITUTION OF THE UNITED STATES OF AMERICA, PROPOSED BY CONGRESS, AND RATIFIED BY THE LEGISLATURES OF THE SEVERAL STATES PURSUANT TO THE FIFTH ARTICLE OF THE ORIGINAL CONSTITUTION.

AMENDMENT I (1791)

Congress shall make no law respecting an establishment of religion, or prohibiting the free exercise thereof; or abridging the freedom of speech, or of the press; or the right of the people peaceably to assemble, and to petition the Government for a redress of grievances.

AMENDMENT II (1791)

A well regulated Militia, being necessary to the security of a free State, the right of the people to keep and bear Arms, shall not be infringed.

AMENDMENT III (1791)

No Soldier shall, in time of peace be quartered in any house, without the consent of the Owner, nor in time of war, but in a manner to be prescribed by law.

AMENDMENT IV (1791)

The right of the people to be secure in their persons, houses, papers, and effects, against unreasonable searches and seizures, shall not be violated, and no Warrants shall issue, but upon probable cause, supported by Oath or affirmation, and particularly describing the place to be searched, and the persons or things to be seized.

AMENDMENT V (1791)

No person shall be held to answer for a capital, or otherwise infamous crime, unless on a presentment or indictment of a Grand Jury, except in cases arising in the land or naval forces, or in the Militia, when in actual service in time of War or public danger; nor shall any person be subject for the same offence to be twice put in jeopardy of life or limb; nor shall be compelled in any criminal case to be a witness against himself, nor be deprived of life, liberty, or property, without due process of law; nor shall private property be taken for public use, without just compensation.

AMENDMENT VI (1791)

In all criminal prosecutions, the accused shall enjoy the right to a speedy and public trial, by an impartial jury of the State and district wherein the crime shall have been committed, which district shall have been previously ascertained by law, and to be informed of the nature and cause of the accusation; to be confronted with the witnesses against him; to have compulsory process for obtaining witnesses in his favor, and to have the Assistance of Counsel for his defence.

AMENDMENT VII (1791)

In Suits at common law, where the value in controversy shall exceed twenty dollars, the right of trial by jury shall be preserved, and no fact tried by jury, shall be otherwise re-examined in any Court of the United States, than according to the rules of the common law.

AMENDMENT VIII (1791)

Excessive bail shall not be required, nor excessive fines imposed, nor cruel and unusual punishments inflicted.

AMENDMENT IX (1791)

The enumeration in the Constitution, of certain rights, shall not be construed to deny or disparage others retained by the people.

AMENDMENT X (1791)

The powers not delegated to the United States by the Constitution, nor prohibited by it to the States, are reserved to the States respectively, or to the people.

AMENDMENT XI (1798)

The Judicial power of the United States shall not be construed to extend to any suit in law or equity, commenced or prosecuted against one of the United States by Citizens of another State, or by Citizens or Subjects of any Foreign State.

AMENDMENT XII (1804)

The Electors shall meet in their respective states and vote by ballot for President and Vice President, one of whom, at least, shall not be an inhabitant of the same state with themselves; they shall name in their ballots the person voted for as President, and in distinct ballots the person voted for as Vice President, and they shall make distinct lists of all persons voted for as President, and of all persons voted for as Vice President, and of the number of votes for each, which lists they shall sign and certify, and transmit sealed to the seat of the government of the United States, directed to the President of the Senate; — The President of the Senate shall, in the presence of the Senate and House of Representatives, open all the certificates and the votes shall then be counted; — The person having the greatest number of votes for President, shall be the President, if such number be a majority of the whole number of Electors appointed; and if no person have such majority, then from the persons having the highest numbers not exceeding three on the list of those voted for as President, the House of Representatives shall choose immediately, by ballot, the President. But in choosing the President, the votes shall be taken by states, the representation from each state having one vote; a quorum for this purpose shall consist of a member or members from two-thirds of the states, and a majority of all the states shall be necessary to a choice. And if the House of Representatives shall not choose a President whenever the right of choice shall devolve upon them before the fourth day of March next following, then the Vice President shall act as President, as in the case of the death or other constitutional disability of the President. — The person having the greatest number of votes as Vice-President, shall be the Vice-President, if such number be a majority of the whole number of Electors appointed, and if no person have a majority, then from the two highest numbers on the list, the Senate shall choose the Vice President; a quorum for the purpose shall consist of two-thirds of the whole number of Senators, and a majority of the whole number shall be necessary to a choice. But no person constitutionally ineligible to the office of President shall be eligible to that of Vice President of the United States.

AMENDMENT XIII (1865)

Section 1. Neither slavery nor involuntary servitude, except as a punishment for crime whereof the party shall have been duly convicted, shall exist within the United States, or any place subject to their jurisdiction.

Section 2. Congress shall have power to enforce this article by appropriate legislation.

AMENDMENT XIV (1868)

Section 1. All persons born or naturalized in the United States, and subject to the jurisdiction thereof, are citizens of the United States and of the State wherein they reside. No State shall make or enforce any law which shall abridge the privileges or immunities of citizens of the United States; nor shall any State deprive any person of life, liberty, or property, without due process of law; nor deny to any person within its jurisdiction the equal protection of the laws.

Section 2. Representatives shall be apportioned among the several States according to their respective numbers, counting the whole number of persons in each State, excluding Indians not taxed. But when the right to vote at any election for the choice of electors for President and Vice President of the United States, Representatives in Congress, the Executive and Judicial officers of a State, or the members of the Legislature thereof, is denied to any of the male inhabitants of such State, being twenty-one years of age, and citizens of the United States, or in any way abridged, except for participation in rebellion, or other crime, the basis of representation therein shall be reduced in the proportion which the number of such male citizens shall bear to the whole number of male citizens twenty-one years of age in such State.

Section 3. No person shall be a Senator or Representative in Congress, or elector of President and Vice President, or hold any office, civil or military, under the United States, or under any State, who having previously taken an oath, as a member of Congress, or as an officer of the United States, or as a member of any State legislature, or as an executive or judicial officer of any State, to support the Constitution of the United States, shall have engaged in insurrection or rebellion against the same, or given aid or comfort to the enemies thereof. But Congress may by a vote of two-thirds of each House, remove such disability.

Section 4. The validity of the public debt of the United States, authorized by law, including debts incurred for payment of pensions and bounties for services in suppressing insurrection or rebellion, shall not be questioned. But neither the United States nor any State shall assume or pay any debt or obligation incurred in aid of insurrection or rebellion against the United States, or any claim for the loss or emancipation of any slave; but all such debts, obligations and claims shall be held illegal and void.

Section 5. The Congress shall have power to enforce, by appropriate legislation, the provisions of this article.

AMENDMENT XV (1870)

Section 1. The right of citizens of the United States to vote shall not be denied or abridged by the United States or by any State on account of race, color, or previous condition of servitude.

Section 2. The Congress shall have power to enforce this article by appropriate legislation.

AMENDMENT XVI (1913)

The Congress shall have power to lay and collect taxes on incomes, from whatever source derived, without apportionment among the several States, and without regard to any census or enumeration.

AMENDMENT XVII (1913)

[1] The Senate of the United States shall be composed of two Senators from each State, elected by the people thereof, for six years; and each Senator shall have one vote. The electors in each State shall have the qualifications requisite for electors of the most numerous branch of the State legislatures.

[2] When vacancies happen in the representation of any State in the Senate, the executive authority of such State shall issue writs of election to fill such vacancies: *Provided,* That the legislature of any State may empower the executive thereof to make temporary appointments until the people fill the

vacancies by election as the legislature may direct.

[3] This amendment shall not be so construed as to affect the election or term of any Senator chosen before it becomes valid as part of the Constitution.

AMENDMENT XVIII (1919)

Section 1. After one year from the ratification of this article the manufacture, sale, or transportation of intoxicating liquors within, the importation thereof into, or the exportation thereof from the United States and all territory subject to the jurisdiction thereof for beverage purposes is hereby prohibited.

Section 2. The Congress and the several States shall have concurrent power to enforce this article by appropriate legislation.

Section 3. This article shall be inoperative unless it shall have been ratified as an amendment to the Constitution by the legislatures of the several States, as provided in the Constitution, within seven years from the date of the submission hereof to the States by the Congress.

AMENDMENT XIX (1920)

[1] The right of citizens of the United States to vote shall not be denied or abridged by the United States or by any State on account of sex.

[2] Congress shall have power to enforce this article by appropriate legislation.

AMENDMENT XX (1933)

Section 1. The terms of the President and Vice President shall end at noon on the 20th day of January, and the terms of Senators and Representatives at noon on the 3d day of January, of the years in which such terms would have ended if this article had not been ratified; and the terms of their successors shall then begin.

Section 2. The Congress shall assemble at least once in every year, and such meeting shall begin at noon on the 3d day of January, unless they shall by law appoint a different day.

Section 3. If, at the time fixed for the beginning of the term of the President, the President elect shall have died, the Vice President elect shall become President. If the President shall not have been chosen before the time fixed for the beginning of his term, or if the President elect shall have failed to qualify, then the Vice President elect shall act as President until a President shall have qualified; and the Congress may by law provide for the case wherein neither a President elect nor a Vice President elect shall have qualified, declaring who shall then act as President, or the manner in which one who is to act shall be selected, and such person shall act accordingly until a President or Vice President shall have qualified.

Section 4. The Congress may by law provide for the case of the death of any of the persons from whom the House of Representatives may choose a President whenever the right of choice shall have devolved upon them, and for the case of the death of any of the persons from whom the Senate may choose a Vice President whenever the right of choice shall have devolved upon them.

Section 5. Sections 1 and 2 shall take effect on the 15th day of October following the ratification of this article.

Section 6. This article shall be inoperative unless it shall have been ratified as an amendment to the Constitution by the legislatures of three-fourths of the several States within seven years from the date of its submission.

AMENDMENT XXI (1933)

Section 1. The eighteenth article of amendment to the Constitution of the United States is hereby repealed.

Section 2. The transportation or importation into any State, Territory, or possession of the United States for delivery or use therein of intoxicating liquors, in violation of the laws thereof, is hereby prohibited.

Section 3. This article shall be inoperative unless it shall have been ratified as an amendment to the Constitution by conventions in the several States, as provided in the Constitution, within seven years from the date of the submission hereof to the States by the Congress.

AMENDMENT XXII (1951)

Section 1. No person shall be elected to the office of the President more than twice, and no person who has held the office of President, or acted as President, for more than two years of a term to which some other person was elected President shall be elected to the office of President more than once. But this Article shall not apply to any person holding the office of President when this Article was proposed by the Congress, and shall not prevent any person who may be holding the office of President, or acting as President, during the term within which this Article becomes operative from holding the office of President or acting as President during the remainder of such term.

Section 2. This article shall be inoperative unless it shall have been ratified as an amendment to the Constitution by the legislatures of three-fourths of the several States within seven years from the date of its submission to the States by the Congress.

AMENDMENT XXIII (1961)

Section 1. The District constituting the seat of Government of the United States shall appoint in such manner as the Congress may direct:

A number of electors of President and Vice President equal to the whole number of Senators and Representatives in Congress to which the District would be entitled if it were a State, but in no event more than the least populous state; they shall be in addition to those appointed by the states, but they shall be considered, for the purposes of the election of President and Vice President, to be electors appointed by a state; and they shall meet in the District and perform such duties as provided by the twelfth article of amendment.

Section 2. The Congress shall have power to enforce this article by appropriate legislation.

AMENDMENT XXIV (1964)

Section 1. The right of citizens of the United States to vote in any primary or other election for President or Vice President, for electors for President or Vice President, or for Senator or Representative in Congress, shall not be denied or abridged by the United States or any State by reason of failure to pay any poll tax or other tax.

Section 2. The Congress shall have power to enforce this article by appropriate legislation.

AMENDMENT XXV (1967)

Section 1. In case of the removal of the President from office or of his death or resignation, the Vice President shall become President.

Section 2. Whenever there is a vacancy in the office of the Vice President, the President shall nominate a Vice President who shall take office upon confirmation by a majority vote of both Houses of Congress.

Section 3. Whenever the President transmits to the President pro tempore of the Senate and the Speaker of the House of Representatives his written declaration that he is unable to discharge the powers and duties of his office, and until he transmits to them a written declaration to the contrary, such powers and duties shall be discharged by the Vice President as Acting President.

Section 4. Whenever the Vice President and a majority of either the principal officers of the executive departments or of such other body as Congress may by law provide, transmit to the President pro tempore of the Senate and the Speaker of the House of Representatives their written declaration that the President is unable to discharge the powers and duties of his office, the Vice President shall immediately assume the powers and duties of the office as Acting President.

Thereafter, when the President transmits to the President pro tempore of the Senate and the Speaker of the House of Representatives his written declaration that no inability exists, he shall resume the powers and duties of his office unless the Vice President and a majority of either the principal officers of the executive department or of such other body as Congress may by law provide, transmit within four days to the President pro tempore of the Senate and the Speaker of the House of Representatives their written declaration that the President is unable to discharge the powers and duties of his office. Thereupon Congress shall decide the issue, assembling within forty-eight hours for that purpose if not in session. If the Congress, within twenty-one days after receipt of the latter written declaration, or, if Congress is not in session, within twenty-one days after Congress is required to assemble, determines by two-thirds vote of both Houses that the President is unable to discharge the powers and duties of his office, the Vice President shall continue to discharge the same as Acting President; otherwise, the President shall resume the powers and duties of his office.

Appendix B

HOW A BILL BECOMES LAW IN WISCONSIN

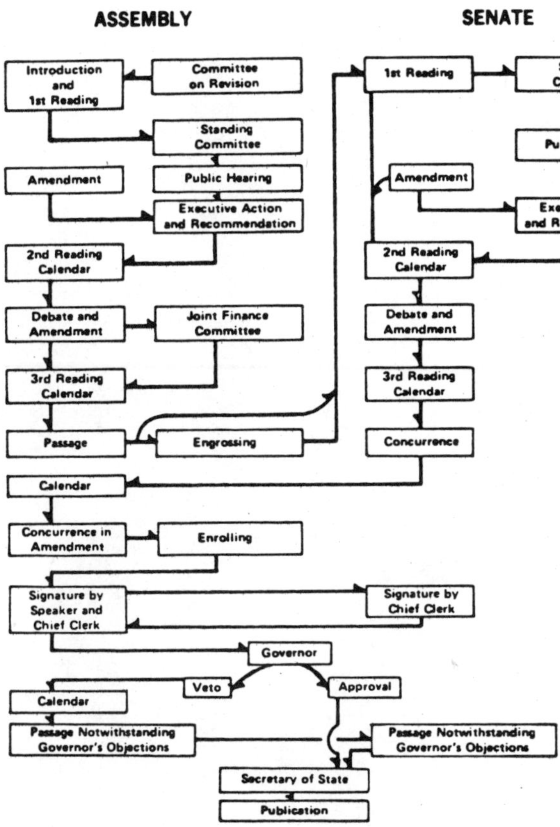

The chart traces through the legislative process the normal course of a bill introduced in the assembly, amended in the senate and approved by the governor, or passed over his veto.

The course of a senate bill would be much the same, except for minor differences in the rules of the two houses.

Glossary of Terms

Allegation. A statement made in a legal proceeding that sets out a fact someone intends to prove

Annotation. A remark, note, or commentary on some passage of a book, intended to illustrate its meaning

Appeal. An application by an appellant to a higher court to rectify the order of the court below

Appellant. One who appeals from a judicial decision

Appellate court. A higher court which hears a case from a lower court on appeal

Appellee. The person against whom an appeal is taken; the respondent to an appeal

Arbitrary. In an arbitrary manner—fixed or done capriciously or at pleasure, without an adequate determining principle; not founded in the nature of things; nonrational; not done or acting according to reason or judgment; depending on the will alone; absolutely in power; capriciously; tyrannical; despotic

Arbitration. The settlement of a civil dispute by a third party or parties agreed upon by both the plaintiff and the defendant

Assault. Threatening to strike or harm

Battery. Beating and wounding, including every touching or laying hold, however trifling, of another's person or clothes in an angry, insolent, or hostile manner

Bill. A formal declaration, complaint, or statement of particular things in writing

Breach. A breaking; either the invasion of a right, or the violation of a duty

Breach of Contract. Breaking or failing to perform the terms of a contract

Certiorari. An original writ or action whereby a case is removed from a lower to a higher court for trial. The record of proceedings is then transmitted to the higher court. The term is most commonly used when requesting the U.S. Supreme Court to hear a case from a lower court

Citation. A writ issued out of a court of competent jurisdiction, commanding a person therein named to appear on a day named and do something therein mentioned, or show cause why he should not

Civil Action. An action which has for its object the recovery of private or civil rights, or compensation for their infraction

Class Action. Usually a large group of people joining together to sue someone; class actions often involve hundreds of persons who claim they have been injured by the same wrong-doing of some company or individual

Code. A compilation of statutes, scientifically analyzed into chapters, subheadings, and sections with a table of contents and an index; a collection or system of laws

Common law. Legal principles derived from usage and custom, or from court decisions affirming such usages and custom, or from the acts of Parliament in force at the time of the American Revolution, as distinguished from law created by enactment of American legislatures

Compensatory damages. The sum of money a civil jury may award the plaintiff in a civil suit for his or her suffering or injuries

Complaint. The formal papers filed by a plaintiff in a lawsuit stating the reasons or cause of action on which the suit is based

Contingency fee arrangement. An agreement by which a lawyer charges a client nothing for his legal services in a lawsuit unless he or she wins the case; then the lawyer takes a percentage of the damages as his or her fee

Contract. A promissory agreement between two or more persons that creates, modifies, or destroys a legal relationship

Contributory negligence. Negligence of the plaintiff which, combined with the negligence of the defendant, was the proximate cause of the injury complained of

Court of record. A court which keeps a permanent record of its proceedings; appellate courts are frequently called courts of records since their proceedings are published

Damages. A pecuniary compensation or indemnity, which may be recovered in the courts by any person who has suffered loss, detriment, or injury, whether to his person, property, or rights through the unlawful act or omission or negligence of another

Decree. The judgment of a court

De facto. In fact: A de facto officer is in actual possession of an office without lawful title; A de facto corporation may be reorganized as legally effective even though defective in some particular

Defamation. Scandalous words written or spoken about another, tending to the injury of the person's reputation

Defendant. One required to make answer in a suit, the one against whom the suit is brought

De jure. By right: A de jure officer has just claim and rightful title to an office, though not necessarily in actual possession thereof; A legal or true corporation or officer as opposed to one that is De facto

Deposition. Oral testimony of a witness recorded out of court and under oath to be used when the case comes to trial

Discovery. The procedure of allowing the attorneys in a civil case to secure and examine each other's evidence before trial; discovery is more limited in criminal cases

Discretionary power. Involves the exercise of judgment in reaching a decision

Dissenting opinion. An opinion disagreeing with that of the majority, handed down by one or more members of the court

Due process. Law in the regular course of administration through courts of justice, according to those rules and forms which have been established for the protection of private rights

Eminent domain. The power to take private property for public use

Enjoin. To require, command, positively direct; to require a person by writ of injunction from a court of equity, to perform, or to abstain or desist from some act

Ex officio. By virtue of his office

Ex post facto. After the fact: Act passed after another act which retroactively changes the legal consequences of that act; federal constitution prohibits passage of ex post facto criminal law

Ex rel. ex relatione: at the instance of; on behalf of; on relation of information

Executory contract. Contracts where some future act is to be done, as where an agreement is made to build a house in six months, or to do an act on or before some future day, or to lend money upon a certain interest, payable at a future time

Guardian ad litem. An individual appointed by the court to insure the rights of a juvenile during court proceedings.

Governmental function. One imposed or required of a municipal corporation for the protection of the general public; a function relating to the corporation's purpose for existing

Hearsay evidence. Evidence not proceeding from the personal knowledge of the witness, but from the mere repetition of what he has heard others say

Immunity. Not capable of being held legally responsible or liable

In loco parentis. In place of the parent; charged with some of the parents' rights, duties, and responsibilities

In re. In the affair, in the matter of, concerning; this is the usual method of entitling a judicial proceeding in which there are no adversary parties

Injunction. A prohibitive writ issued by a court of equity forbidding the defendant to do some act he is threatening, or forbidding him to continue doing some act which is injurious to the plaintiff and cannot be adequately redressed by an action at law

Interrogatories. Written questions sent by the lawyer on one side of a civil case to a witness on the other side; part of the discovery process

Legacy. Any gift by will.

Lawsuit. A civil action in which one person or party sues another in civil court

Liability. The word is a broad legal term meaning legal responsibility for some act

Litigant. One side or person in a civil suit

Litigation. The process of bringing a lawsuit or defending against a lawsuit

Libel. Defamation by printed or written communication

Liquidated. Fixed, ascertained, e.g., damages, the exact amount of which must be paid, or may be collected, upon a default or breach of contract

Malfeasance. The commission of an unlawful act

Malice. Hatred, ill will; a formed design of doing an unlawful act

Malpractice. Neglectful and unprofessional treatment which causes injury or suffering

Mandamus. A writ of mandamus is a command from a court of law directed to an inferior court, officer, corporate body, or person regarding him or them to do some particular thing

Mandatory. Required; something someone must do

Misfeasance. A wrongful act, negligence, or the improper performance of some lawful act

Municipal corporation. A body politic created by the incorporation of the inhabitants as an agency of the state to regulate and administer the local affairs

Negligence. Want of care

Nonfeasance. Nonperformance of some act which ought to be performed, omission to perform a required duty, or total neglect of duty

Nuisance. Anything that unlawfully results in harm, inconvenience, or damage

Original jurisdiction. The jurisdiction of a court to hear a case from the beginning, as contrasted with the appellate jurisdiction

Out of court settlement. An agreement over differences acceptable to both the plaintiff and defendant arrived at outside of trial

Parol. By word of mouth

Per se. By itself, alone

Petition. Written application or prayer to the court for the redress of a wrong or the grant of privilege or license

Plaintiff. Person who brings an action, a lawsuit against another party—the defendant

Police power. Inherent or full legislative power to enact laws for comfort, health, and prosperity of the state; the right to modify for the common good—in short, the right of the sovereign to govern

Prayer. The request contained in a bill in equity that the court will grant the process, aid, or relief which the complaint desires

Precedent. A decision considered as furnishing an example or authority for an identical or similar case afterward arising on a similar question of law

Privies of parties. Persons connected with mutual interest in the same action

Product liability. The responsibility of manufacturers for injuries caused by their products

Punitive damages. Damages which sometimes can be assessed over and above compensatory damages in a civil suit in order to punish the losing defendant or to set an example for others who may commit the same wrongful act in the future

Quasi. As if; almost; quasi-legal

Quasi-municipal corporation (or quasi corporation). A political or civil subdivision of the state, created by law, to assist the state in administering the state's affairs—an involuntary corporation, for example, a school district

Ratification. In a broad sense, the confirmation of a previous act done either by the party himself or by another; confirmation of a voidable act

Remand a case. An action by an appellate court to send the case back to the court from which it came for futher proceedings there

Respondeat superior. The responsibility of a master for the acts of his servants

Respondent. The one making an answer—the defendant

Restrain. To prohibit from action; to enjoin

Restraining order. An injunction

Slander. Defamation by spoken word

Specific performance. A requirement by a court of equity that both parties go through with a contract

Stare decisis. Adherence to precedent; when the court has made a declaration of legal principle it is the law until changed by a competent authority

Statute. Law enacted by the legislative power of a country or state

Substantive law. The positive law of rights and duties

Tenure. Right to perform duties and receive emoluments thereof

Title to property. Title is the means whereby the owner of lands has the just possession of his property

Tort. Legal injury or wrong committed upon the person or property of another independent of contract

Trespass. The unauthorized entry upon, taking, or interfering with the property of another

Void. Null, ineffectual, nugatory; having no legal force or binding effect; unable, in law, to support the purpose for which it was intended

Voidable. That may be avoided, or declared void; not absolutely void, or void in itself

Whereas. A word which introduces a recital of a fact

Index

†